www.wadsworth.com

www.wadsworth.com is the World Wide Web site for
Thomson Wadsworth and is your direct source to dozens
of online resources.

At www.*wadsworth.com* you can find out about
supplements, demonstration software, and student
resources. You can also send e-mail to many of our
authors and preview new publications and exciting new
technologies.

www.wadsworth.com
Changing the way the world learns®

The Sambia

Ritual, Sexuality, and Change in Papua New Guinea

Second Edition

Gilbert Herdt
San Francisco State University

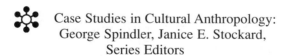

Case Studies in Cultural Anthropology:
George Spindler, Janice E. Stockard,
Series Editors

Australia • Brazil • Canada • Mexico • Singapore
Spain • United Kingdom • United States

THOMSON
WADSWORTH

The Sambia: Ritual, Sexuality, and Change in Papua New Guinea, Second Edition
Gilbert Herdt

Senior Acquisitions Editor: *Lin Marshall*
Assistant Editor: *Leata Holloway*
Technology Project Manager: *Dee Dee Zobian*
Marketing Manager: *Lori Grebe Cook*
Marketing Assistant: *Teresa Jessen*
Marketing Communications Manager: *Linda Yip*
Project Manager, Editorial Production: *Christine Sosa*
Creative Director: *Rob Hugel*
Executive Art Director: *Maria Epes*
Print Buyer: *Nora Massuda*
Permissions Editor: *Roberta Broyer*

Production Service: *Sara Dovre Wudali,*
    Buuji, Inc.
Copy Editor: *Kristina Rose McComas*
Cover Designer: *Rob Hugel*
Cover Image: *Gilbert Herdt*
Cover Printer: *Courier*
    Corporation/Stoughton
Compositor: *Interactive Composition*
    Corporation
Printer: *Courier Corporation/Stoughton*

The logo for the Cultural Anthropology series is based on an ancient symbol representing the family: man, woman, and children.

All photos are reprinted with the permission of the author except where noted.

Printed in the United States of America
1 2 3 4 5 6 7 09 08 07 06 05

For more information about our products, contact us at:
Thomson Learning Academic Resource Center
1-800-423-0563

For permission to use material from this text or product, submit a request online at
http://www.thomsonrights.com
Any additional questions about permissions can be submitted by e-mail to
thomsonrights@thomson.com

Thomson Higher Education
10 Davis Drive
Belmont, CA 94002-3098
USA

Asia
Thomson Learning
5 Shenton Way #01-01
UIC Building
Singapore 068808

Australia/New Zealand
Thomson Learning
102 Dodds Street
Southbank, Victoria 3006
Australia

Canada
Nelson
1120 Birchmount Road
Toronto, Ontario M1K 5G4
Canada

Europe/Middle East/Africa
Thomson Learning
High Holborn House
50/51 Bedford Row
London WC1R 4LR
United Kingdom

Library of Congress Control Number: 2005935133

ISBN 0-534-64383-3

*This book is dedicated to my father and mother,
Gilbert and Delores Herdt.*

Contents

Foreword

ABOUT THE SERIES

These case studies in cultural anthropology are designed for students in beginning and intermediate courses in the social sciences, to bring them insights into the richness and complexity of human life as it is lived in different ways, in different places. The authors are men and women who have lived in the societies they write about and who are professionally trained as observers and interpreters of human behavior. Also, the authors are teachers; in their writing, the needs of the student reader remain foremost. It is our belief that when an understanding of ways of life very different from one's own is gained, abstractions and generalizations about the human condition become meaningful.

The scope and character of the series has changed constantly since we published the first case studies in 1960, in keeping with our intention to represent anthropology as it is. We are concerned with the ways in which human groups and communities are coping with the massive changes wrought in their physical and sociopolitical environments in recent decades. We are also concerned with the ways in which established cultures have solved life's problems. And we want to include representation of the various modes of communication and emphasis that are being formed and reformed as anthropology itself changes.

We think of this series as an instructional series, intended for use in the classroom. We, the editors, have always used case studies in our teaching, whether for beginning students or advanced graduate students. We start with case studies, whether from our own series or from elsewhere, and weave our way into theory, and then turn again to cases. For us, they are the grounding of our discipline.

ABOUT THE AUTHOR

Gilbert Herdt was born the eldest of four children in Oakley, Kansas, in a small farm town his grandparents, first-generation German immigrants from Russia, helped homestead. His early schooling was near Wichita, where his father was a research engineer for the Boeing Company. He finished high school in California and began undergraduate studies in geology, history, and psychology, but after his first course, he knew he wanted to be an anthropologist. His first fieldwork as an undergraduate was with Japanese-Americans in the San Francisco Bay Area. His master's thesis in medical anthropology (1972) was based on a year of fieldwork in a large psychiatric ward, studying rituals of psychotherapy. The same year he began two years' graduate study in cultural anthropology and New Guinea studies at the University of Washington, where he was mentored by the late K. E. Read, and received a Ph.C. (1973). He was awarded the 1974 Fulbright predoctoral fellowship to Australia and became a graduate student in the Department of Anthropology of the Research School of

Pacific Studies, in The Australian National University. He spent two years studying the Sambia tribe of the Eastern Highlands in Papua New Guinea, after which he received his Ph.D. from the ANU in 1978. Following this he was awarded an Individual Postdoctoral fellowship of the National Institute of Mental Health, which he used in cross-training into psychiatry and gender research at the University of California, Los Angeles (1978–1979) under the mentoring of the late Robert J. Stoller, MD. From 1979 to 1985 he taught at Stanford University. From 1985–1997 he was Professor of the Committee on Human Development at The University of Chicago, where he was Chair (1990–1992) and founder of the Center for Culture and Mental Health. In 1991 he was visiting Professor at the University of Amsterdam, where he created and directed the Summer Institute on Sexuality, Society, and Culture (1996–2000). He was a Guggenheim Fellow and visiting professor at Vanderbilt University in 1997 and visiting professor at the University of Washington in 2001. Since 1998, Herdt has been the Director and Professor of Human Sexuality Studies at San Francisco State University, where he founded the Summer Institute on Sexuality, Society, and Health, and in 2002 he became Director of the National Sexuality Resource Center, a long-term project of the Ford Foundation. Herdt conducted 13 field trips to the Sambia, culminating in the creation of the BBC film *"Guardians of the Flutes"* (1994). Herdt has written or co-written eight books and edited or co-edited 26 books and monographs, and has published approximately 100 referred journal articles and chapters on the Sambia; American sexuality and gender development; and the clinical ethnography of sexuality and sexual narratives, including gay and lesbian adolescent development and the studies of the parents and families of these youth. Currently Herdt is studying sexual literacy in the United States and why American social and health policy have fallen behind other developments of our civilization.

Preface

This year (2005) marks the 30th anniversary of my first field observations of ritual initiation among the Sambia, a people who have come to be known the world over for their remarkable sexual culture in a world of war. Over these past three decades not only have the Sambia radically changed and experienced a sexual revolution but their country (Papua New Guinea) achieved independence. In addition, the concepts of sexuality and gender have undergone dramatic transformation. That is, the meanings by which anthropologists, sociologists, psychologists, and other scientists understand Sambia sexuality have actually changed. We will study these changes in this book.

The Sambia inhabit the fringe of the Southeastern Highlands of Papua New Guinea. They number about 2,000 people spread thinly over a vast rain forest. Their hamlets are tiny and from the air appear dotted like small clusters of mushrooms popping up on the ridges of high river valleys. On all sides, tribes belonging to the cognate Anga language family surround the Sambia. These other tribal groups number from a few hundred to several thousand and extend from the Eastern Highlands to the far south, near the coast of the Papuan Gulf of New Guinea. In pre-colonial times they typically acted as enemies because warfare was chronic and was believed to reach back into ancient times. To adapt to these conditions, Sambia created a sexual culture and gender roles through initiation rituals that fit a harsh and unpredictable world.

You will find the Sambia fascinating and exotic, but do not be distracted by this appearance. Sambia sexual rituals have become associated with the question of whether homosexuality is universal, whether sexuality can be learned, and what role gender plays in its expression. I will explore these questions and some of the potential answers to these questions with you. We will also consider the question of whether there is a universal milestone at age 10 for the development of sexual attraction and desire. You will discover how historical warfare made the Sambia behavioral environment dangerous for individual and group survival. So challenging was it that males were brought up to be fierce and aggressive warriors who, if necessary, were able to kill on demand. The great fear of the Sambia was that boys would fail to achieve this masculinity and hence, the culture would die. This fierce manhood accompanied traditional sexual antagonism between men and women. And yet this masculinity was created, not natural, a conditional masculinity that depended upon the rituals and secrecy for its existence. All males were initiated into a secret society that practiced boy-insemination between younger and older boys as the normal pathway to adulthood. Boys grow up in one world, that of the women, but were forced into a new world, that of the men, when they acquired a new secret identity and warrior status. Secrecy made a utopian world that survived through control of everything and created social inequalities for women and children in the process. The Sambia case study thus opens a unique window on understanding how culture, sexuality, and power structure masculinity and femininity, desire, and sexual development, through ritual.

This second edition of *The Sambia* appears 18 years after the original text, and it has been substantially rewritten to reflect the huge changes that have overtaken the Sambia—including their place in Melanesia. I have also reflected upon the many changes that have occurred, not only in the cultural experience of undergraduates but in the larger place that we all share—a global society in which sexuality and gender play a very different role than in my time as an undergraduate.

My world as an undergraduate was the late 1960s in Northern California. You could hardly imagine a cultural context more ripe for the lessons of learning cultural anthropology as an undergraduate major than that faraway time of counterculture, Hippies, sexual revolution, and the peace and freedom movement protesting the Vietnam war. I was an eyewitness to dramatic change in my own society, and I can truly say that cultural period is gone. At the time, a whole new set of social movements was in the making. The rise of black power and second-wave feminism in the 1960s were part and parcel of how sex and gender were being modernized and packaged for a new age of media. Women expected equal rights and respect in all areas of their lives, not the least of which was their reproductive rights and health. The birth control pill, introduced in the early 1960s, radically disrupted the traditional relationship between women, reproduction, gender roles, and sexual pleasure. Women could expect to have professional careers and egalitarian relationships with men. Masters and Johnson (1966), in their famous studies of sexual response, encouraged women to explore their bodies and appreciate the role of pleasure, including masturbation. Meanwhile, gay men and lesbians were becoming visible for the first time, their rising power giving voice to demands for social and sexual rights, as a new social movement began to challenge the fear, shame, and silence of homosexuality common since the Cold War period of the 1950s, when to be accused of being a homosexual was to be a communist (Herman 1997), and vice versa! By 1969 and the famous Stonewall Tavern riots in New York, now commemorated around the United States by Pride Day Parades, gays, lesbians, and their allies began to lobby for the normalization of homosexuality. By the end of 1973, homosexuality had been officially declassified as a disease by the American Psychiatric Association. Also in 1973, a true watershed year in the American history of reproductive and sexual rights, the Supreme Court upheld *Rowe vs. Wade,* giving women the right to chose a legal abortion in the United States. These changes were highly contested but have held through time, providing expanded citzenship for women and gay and lesbian people. Many challenges to these reforms have occurred since that time, and indeed, as social critic Lisa Duggin (2003) has argued, the United States may well be in the "twilight" of the liberal democracy phase of sexual and gender rights.

In fact, by 2004, the United States was embroiled in an historic debate over the legal right of gays and lesbians to marry. In my own city, San Francisco, the mayor permitted thousands of same-sex couples to tie the knot, only to have it undone a few months later by the court. What a long way from those early days of sexual liberation! And yet it is only three decades, the blink of an eye to anthropology!

I journeyed to Papua New Guinea (1974) and began long-term fieldwork during these tumultuous times. I had learned through correspondence with linguists, missionaries, and the French anthropologist Maurice Godelier, who was working among the neighboring Baruya people, that the Sambia people continued to practice traditional male initiation. Like others of my generation, I was not prepared to study their sexuality and gender, or their intricate secret society. None of us were in those days; the anthropology of sexuality had not yet been born. And as sociologist John Gagnon (2004) has summed it up, every one of our generation who dared to study sexuality did so as an accident, incidental to something else such as HIV, and we risked careers by crossing into this tabooed arena of science sexuality.[1]

Of course, we were not the first anthropologists to risk this journey, as we have followed the great ethnographers Bronislaw Malinowski and Margaret Mead, the founders of sexual and gender study in Melanesia. They showed in myriad studies that it is the relationship between men and women, including power, economics, and religion, which influences gender roles and beliefs connected with sexuality in ways distinctive of this culture area (Knauft 1999; Herdt and Leavitt 1998). Like others of my generation, I had little choice but to improvise and learn "on the job," to figure out what the meanings and practices—the core of culture—were for the Sambia. But as you will see in this book, the incredible secret society of the men, the institution responsible for warfare, marriage exchange, and the initiation of young boys into manhood made the investigation of gender and sexuality among the Sambia a terribly difficult and tenuous process. In fact, my access to women was extremely limited by the men, who were threatened by my being a single man but also jealous to keep me as a resource to themselves. Only time and patience—the great tools of the anthropologist in the field who would seek to know another social world—enabled me to some extent to unlock the secrets of the Sambia and go beyond their taboos and restrictions placed upon me.

A generation later my student, Dr Birgitta Stolpe (2003) returned to the same area of the Sambia to look more closely at women and their bodies, and the meaning of sexual and reproductive practices to them. Now we were able to learn new things about the lives and experiences of Sambia women. Her invaluable insights have greatly increased our understanding of Sambia society, including the changing role of masculinity and femininity (Herdt and Stolpe 2006), and they are reflected in the final chapter of this new edition.

Since the original publication of this case study I have been able to make a total of 12 field trips back to the Sambia and to complete the film *"Guardians of the Flutes"* with a crew from the British Broadcasting Corporation. These subsequent studies and the change that has ensued have been incorporated into this new edition, including a CD-ROM that accompanies this case study, along with

---

[1]See Vance (1991) and Lewin and Leap (1996) for seminal reviews of the issues. On a personal note, it was precisely this lack of professional training in sexuality that has been addressed in the founding of our Program in Human Sexuality Studies at San Francisco State University, providing the training of a whole new generation of young scholars to take on the challenges of sexuality and gender study around the world.

additional photographs of the Sambia, traditional and contemporary. I am proud to be able to offer this unique case study to a new generation of readers.

ACKNOWLEDGMENTS

Field research among the Sambia from 1974 to 1976 was mainly supported by the Australian-American Education Foundation and the Department of Anthropology, Research School of Pacific Studies, the Australian National University, and I wish to kindly thank these institutions. Subsequent research trips in 1979, 1981, 1983, 1985, and 1988 were funded by the National Institute of Mental Health, the Department of Psychiatry at UCLA, the Wenner-Gren Foundation for Anthropological Research, Stanford University, the Spencer Foundation, and the University of Chicago, and I gratefully acknowledge their assistance. Field trips in 1990 and 1993 to complete the documentary film, *Guardians of the Flutes,* were supported by the British Broadcasting Commission. Sincere thanks to members of the New Tribes Mission of Papua New Guinea, whose help and kindness were invaluable. Several scholars and mentors read the first edition of this book, some of whom are now gone—Derek Freeman, Theodore and Ruth Lidz, Fitz J. Poole, Kenneth E. Read, Robert J. Stoller, and the late George Devereux. In addition, Gregory Guldin, James L. Gibbs, Jr., Donald F. Tuzin, and George Westermark were important readers. For assistance with the revised edition, I am grateful to Birgitta Stolpe for her insights on Sambia women and cultural change; to Tim Jordan for able assistance in preparation of the new visual and filmic material that appears in this book as well as on the website associated with it; and Janice Stockard, for her insights as the new co-editor of the Case Studies in Cultural Anthropolgy series. Finally, I remain most grateful to George Spindler and his late wife Louise for their incisive editorial advice and for their long friendship. I alone assume responsibility for any failings in this book.

Introduction

The Sambia referred to their ritual complex of youths inseminating younger boys as a secret marriage—"The boys are married to the flutes." The "flutes," in this mysterious equation, referred both to a young warrior who had the power to play the flutes and to his sexual maturity—signified by his penis, which in the ritual was symbolized by a bamboo flute (glans penis) placed inside a larger flute (penis). No wonder the Sambia regarded men as the sexy and beautiful gender and objectified them as sexual objects. The ritual teaching exploited the symbolic equation of penis with mother's breast, with the boy sucking a youth to obtain his semen. In the Sambia belief system, the penis and semen as "male milk" substituted for mother's breast and her milk, believed to have the power to grow the initiate into masculinity and manhood. Younger initiates aged 7 or 8 and up, and older bachelors and young men from their mid-teens up to their early 20s were the sexual actors in this highly scripted sexual culture. Once the young men married women and produced children, however, homoerotic insemination was tabooed. "Marriage" between the two boys thus represented a transitional sexual and social relationship, albeit one that lasted years and was filled with power and weakness, connecting childhood with adulthood, sex between males with sex between men and women. Boy-insemination was predicated on the assumption that as the boy gained the strength and prowess of the youth, the village warriorhood gained a new warrior full of strength, pride, and prowess.

I once referred to this symbolic complex in Melanesia and New Guinea as "ritualized homosexuality" because I assumed that this was the "homosexuality" found everywhere, including within Sambia male ritual contexts (Herdt 1981, 1984). But unlike "homosexuality" in our society, this same-sex behavior does not last throughout life and is not seen as antithetical to masculinity—quite the contrary. Sambia could not imagine an outcome in which two people of the same gender would have a sexual relationship as adults for their whole lives. Moreover, the Sambia do not possess the concepts "homosexual," or "gay," and they do not understand the idea that two men or two women could be culturally recognized as sexual partners. For all these reasons, I concluded, "homosexuality" was the wrong concept, even when it is ritualized (Herdt 1993). Now I refer to this whole ritual complex as "boy-inseminating" rites to highlight what actually happens (older boys orally inseminate younger boys) and its particular meanings for the Sambia. As you will discover, Sambia sexual culture channels attraction through several distinct forms of sexual behavior, each having differing motives and meanings, which are not opposed but rather complementary in Sambia thought.

On the broader stage of history and culture at large, the semen beliefs of the Sambia and their ritualized boy-insemination practices were once present in a broad range of societies, from ancient Homeric Greece through the early Roman

Empire, Renaissance Italy and the Circum-Mediterranean region, and a variety of nonwestern culture areas (Greenberg 1986; Herdt 1997) as well as other historical culture areas that extend to the early Modern period in Western Europe (Halperin 1990, 2002: 48–80; Herdt 1991a, 1991b, 1999; Rocke 1996; Trumbach 1998; Williams 1998). Was this social practice more of a ritual or more of a sexual act? We have to understand that this is a Western dichotomy; a concern of ours, not of theirs. Fundamentally, boy-insemination was a sexual practice due to its expression through fellatio and its homoeroticism in ritual context that merged sexual pleasure with the demonstration of power by the older youth, not unlike our own society prior to the modern period, before "homosexuality" took center stage as a sexual identity (Herdt 2003). It is through these contextual and local cultural meanings that we begin to understand the complexity of all sexual behavior—including gendered sexuality (and transgenders) in our America's diverse society.

Boy-insemination rites were once widespread, although by no means common, in pre-colonial Melanesia. Melanesia is a vast area of enormous cultural diversity: over 2,000 different languages and 1,000 distinct cultures. The best indication is that 50 or 60 different traditional cultures historically practiced boy-inseminating as part of sexual development (Herdt 1984, 1991a, 1991b, 1993). The early decades of colonization and Christian missionary zeal destroyed most of these customs—and ritual secrecy was virtually destroyed by the waves of culture change that accompanied late-20th-century market economy capitalism (Foster 2002; Herdt 2003). In cross-cultural perspective, Sambia ritual practices belong to this culture-specific pattern of initiation rites, secret male cults, and small-scale patrilineal villages involved in rampant warfare among men and sexual antagonism between men and women. These groups live primarily in southwestern and coastal New Guinea and among the adjacent Anga area where isolation and recent contact preserved the boy-inseminating practices.

Secret initiation established a life-long "marriage" to a female ritual spirit and, by extension, to her instrument of power, the sacred bamboo flutes. Her name was *"Aatmwogwambu"* (female flute spirit, also associated with the wailing of babies and the croaking of frogs at night). She was aggressive, jealous of beautiful girls, vindictive toward women, and angry toward the initiates until they obeyed her command to suck the youths. In short, she was the guardian of the men's secret society and the critical supernatural partner of the men in keeping control of the social order. *Aatmogwambu* demanded obeisance and loyalty from the men and protected the flutes' secret by punishing with death anyone who dared to spy upon the rituals. She ensured that boys never again came close to women and, indeed, would mistrust and even despise the women they once loved as a result of their traumatic conditioning during the ordeals of the men's secret society. The flutes and their spirits were thus huge forces in culture-building that glorified homoerotic relations between the warrior-youth and boy-initiate. "Being married to the flutes" was a floating sign of conditional masculinity and the misogyny it fed upon across the course of a man's life, and things remained that way until colonialism ended warfare and secrecy, ushering in a sexual revolution.

*   *   *

I first journeyed to live with the Sambia in 1974 when I was 25 and green to New Guinea. Nothing was known of their language or culture at the time. Negative stereotypes and folklore depicted them as murderous guerrilla warriors, thieves, and worse. I found their aggressive reputation to be warranted. Yet I discovered a private side of them never hinted at in the racist stereotypes: their gregarious warmth and friendliness. This is not surprising. Their enemies were terrified of them. In public the Sambia men put on a showy and aggressive front, but in private and with friends, they revealed their talkative hospitality, humor, and common sense—two sides of their personality directly related to the two different worlds they share in, the men's and the women's.

Warfare was officially stamped out six years before my arrival. The warriors have lived in peace since then. How has it affected them? Their war raids are gone. They can no longer use violence to redress wrongs or seek revenge on distant enemies. Gone too are the constant bow-and-arrow fights between neighboring hamlets within the Sambia Valley. This cultural pattern of fighting had been the key contest of masculine "strength" to see which warriors and villages were the strongest. The suffering of war and the ever-present fears of attack were over. And yet, in 1974, everywhere I visited among the Sambia and neighboring tribes, men still carried their bows. The initiates who lived in the men's houses were still being trained in the martial arts. They were expected to learn the ways and ritual lore of warriorhood. Today the boys no longer practice warrior games or are trained to be aggressive fighters. Cash cropping for 20 years has made women ever more powerful and supported their new roles with Christianity and as churchgoers.

Figure 0.1 Gil Herdt and five initiates at the Marriage Ceremony, late 1975

Historically, Australia managed the old colonial government of New Guinea. After World War I and the defeat of Germany, Northern New Guinea, Germany's former colony, became a mandated territory of Australia. England's former colony, Papua (Southern) New Guinea also became a part of the single territory, Australian New Guinea. Until the 1920s the Highlands were believed to be uninhabited. Gold prospectors exploring the hills, however, discovered myriad tribes, some in the tens of thousands, in great valleys there. The Australian patrol officers went to each interior part of the country to stop warfare and establish administrative posts. The Sambia were one of these—the last Eastern Highlands populations to be contacted and controlled in the late 1950s and early 1960s. No outsiders were allowed into the area until about 1968, when it was officially "derestricted."

The search required taking successively shorter flights, first to Port Moresby, the capital of Papua New Guinea; then to Goroka, the capital of the Eastern Highlands Province; and lastly to the Mountain Patrol post, a small administrative center with a tiny grass airstrip high in the mountains. From there I walked over three mountain ranges. The Australian officer found some men to lead me and loaned me the native interpreter, a Sambian man, because I did not speak the language. I began my first patrol of the whole area, which took weeks of walking, to visit each tribal group. The Sambia were the last group I visited before selecting a village in which to live for two years.

After these weeks of patrolling and that one last long hike, three days from the patrol post, we descended into the first Sambia village. It was Nilangu, which later was to become my home. People were dressed entirely in traditional garb. Only a handful of men spoke NeoMelanesian (pidgin), the local trade language. They knew I was coming because such news spreads like wildfire through the area. Crowds were all around. The war leaders looked fierce with their bodies painted and bows in hand. But so many people smiled and seemed open and friendly. The village occupies an extraordinary location, at an elevation of 6,000 feet, literally perched on a mountain ridge like an eagle's nest. It was beautiful, an anthropologist's dream.

I wanted, right then and there, to unpack my bags and settle into Nilangu. People greeted me and we shook hands. The village seemed like it could be a home. The men's clubhouse caught my eye; I walked over and peered into the doorway. And then, to my amazement, out blasted the Beatles' song, "I Wanna Hold Your Hand." Oh hell, I thought. Had I come all this way to find the same old junk of civilization, in these sad tropics, thousands of miles from home? I stepped back, disbelieving and exasperated.

But I was wrong. The radio was a fluke, its owner the only man to return from coastal work with a music box. (It broke in a few weeks.) Everything else seemed traditional: the men who went hunting, the women in the gardens, the initiates hiding behind their bark capes from the women. Kanteilo, the hamlet elder and aging war leader who was to become my village sponsor and "father," stepped forward. He showed me around, pointing out things. He gave me bananas and corn to eat; the old fox was buttering me up so I would stay. I was impressed and intrigued with what was to me an odd mixture of rugged individualism and personal warmth. He could turn on the charm whenever he wanted to.

But Sambia warmth is real and was reflected in the way the men loved to talk and sing together. On patrol, as we climbed up and down jungle mountains and through swamps, the men never tired of chattering. They would prop up each other's dwindling energy at the day's end by singing in unison as we slogged up one last mountainside. In the clubhouse the talking was more intimate and cordial but no less constant. They asked me a thousand questions, and I was exasperated at being unable to communicate.

While on this patrol I heard a rumor that the Sambia were planning to initiate their boys—it was late 1974. Because of this I set up camp there. Would I get to see their marvelous initiations? I asked the Nilangu villagers if I could live with them. They were thrilled; it meant status, money, medical supplies, and who knows what other riches to them, for, with my tennis shoes and kerosene lamps, I was obviously rich. Smoking my pipe and sharing food dispelled the other rumors that I was a missionary or government patrol officer (see Figure 0.1). Everyone helped construct a house in the center of the hamlet, using local trees, bamboo, and grass thatching. Until then, though, I had to live in the men's clubhouse.

The clubhouse was a Spartan place where I hung my hat for a month until my house was built. I slept there, ate what others ate, and began to learn the language. The place was damn uncomfortable: fleas, constant smoky fires, drafty, and noisy. It was difficult to get a good night's sleep, especially when a large, ugly flying fox bat kept flapping up to the house late at night to feed on a nearby banana tree.

The new initiates in the men's house were the focus of my first study. How did the rituals affect them? What did it change inside of them: their emotions, masculine identity or self-esteem, their identification with rituals and associations with their age-mate peers? Could rituals alter their feelings about themselves, even at unconscious levels, such as in their dreams? I knew that it would take a long time to grasp these problems because they require a deep knowledge of the language and culture. As I learned NeoMelanesian, I began simple talk with others. Then I began to learn the Sambian language. In about three months I was having detailed conversations; in six months I could understand some ritual talk; and in 10 months I was fluent enough to interview in-depth without a translator. But even so, when boys told me of their experiences, how could I know how much their stories matched the real ritual events? Or, if they had had idiosyncratic experiences, how was I to understand how typical were their experiences, including their sexual behavior? I will return to these problems later.

These were the questions that worried me on the day of my first initiation experience, December 1974. A marriage ceremony was to be held in our village. The fourth-stage initiates (there were six of them) between the ages of 18 and 25 were to be released for the first time in years from ritual taboos. In the hours before we went into the forest for secret purificatory rites, the men decided to wait in my new unfurnished hut while the rituals were being prepared. The youths to be initiated were nervous. So was I, but for a different reason: I didn't know if I would be accepted. Should I go with them into the forest? Would they let me—a stranger—accompany them to their sacred ceremony? What would I do if they said no? But they put me at ease. Weiyu—who has since become a close Sambia friend—asked me if I would join in the ceremony. Several older men disagreed; but my sponsor, Kanteilo, the main elder and big man, said it was "all right." Soon I found the youths talking among themselves, expressing how they felt about what was to happen. It seemed natural—their talking, their anxiety and shame, and their great anticipation. Here was a backstage sharing of experience and thoughts that surely reflected the men's subjective identities. They were, they said, scared to see the women after avoiding females all these years. But an hour later there they were at the secret rituals, being instructed in heterosexual coitus, the taboo on adultery, and the highly secret ritual practice of drinking white tree sap to replace their semen. When they spoke of women, the older men were angry, even repulsed; for example, when they said the word "vagina," they spat compulsively. I was stunned by their strong misogyny and amazed to learn that they secretly drank tree sap. My friends' initiation thus constituted my own initiation as a field anthropologist: What on earth did all this mean?

Sambia are preoccupied with the differences between maleness and femaleness. Men perceive these differences to be the product of nature, essential forces both in natural species and in humans. While Sambia believe femaleness to be innate and to inevitably result in adult female reproductive competence, they understand maleness to be a weak and tenuous essence that does not naturally produce adult masculinity. Unless men intervene with ritual procedures that protect boys from female influences, boys stay small and weak and ultimately die. Only through inseminations that artificially create maleness are boys believed able to attain adult manhood. The process begins in the initiation rituals described in this case study. Born from the trauma of separation from mother and secret threats, homoeroticism is seductive, powerful, and sometimes cruel. For some 10 to 15 years, Sambia boys engage in insemination practices, ideally on a daily basis, first as the fellator (insertee) and then as the older fellated (insertor). At marriage (usually between the ages of 18 and 25 years), youths become bisexual for a time, albeit unknown to both women and younger initiates. With fatherhood, however, boy-inseminating should cease; men should become exclusively heterosexual in their sexual behavior. The cycle begins again when a new crop of boys is initiated into the ritual cult.

Why were the Sambia so worried about boys that they felt they needed to initiate boys so young? As we shall see in Chapter 5, they emphasized the age of 10—an absolute barrier or boundary to make the life transition, changing from being children to being warriors. So much were they preoccupied that I have referred to this transition as the "magical age of 10"—a special meaning in Sambia sexual culture that unless the boy achieved ritual change by that age, he would die (McClintock and Herdt 1996; Herdt and McClintock 2000; Herdt 2002). It turns out that many other cultures, including the United States, also attach special importance to this age, at least implicitly. In a nutshell, the evidence suggests that sexual attraction and sexual identity are formed around this time; thus the stakes for a society to change identities and relationships are very high, especially if a people fear that their sons will not become masculine, will fail to be fierce warriors, will become homosexuals, and will fail to reproduce the society. Time has shown that such fears are usually not warranted, but that is in hindsight. In order for us to understand what really was at stake for the Sambia in the grand cycle of their ritual initiations we have to look into their social world and what war did to it, and then trace the changes that have occurred in their environment and sexual culture up to the present. By doing so we come to a point of much greater respect for the role of the individual and the power of social change to influence what we think of as natural—sexuality.

Although this case study has been substantially revised, the field observations and my presence in the rituals remain largely unchanged. My presence in the initiations was not extraneous or peripheral; I was not a cold machine—an unfeeling robot who witnessed the ritual nose-bleedings I will describe. It was my self, my feelings of shock and concern and understanding, that emerged as I recorded the events that made this study possible. My feelings resonated with those of the Sambia themselves—their shock, fear, anger, and sorrow in the rituals. Did they sense this? Is this part of the reason they trusted and permitted me to be the first outsider to see their secret rites? So I sometimes will describe my reactions to the events to serve as a bridge for you to understand how the rituals created feelings in all the participants. These emotions are at the very core of the phenomenon we want to understand. By inserting my subjectivity into this case study, however, you should not think that what you will read is fiction or poetry. The extreme view of reflexivity suggests that objectivity is not possible. I am not going to that extreme. My view is that with training and discipline we can study the feelings of others and ourselves as a part of the culture in which we work. This view represents a shift in our awareness of how to study culture. By studying this side of initiation—its power to create a new identity in people—we better understand the mutual interaction between the ethnographer's experience and how it emerges from long-term and sensitive relationships with informants. This process is what has always interested me most (Herdt and Stoller 1990; Herdt 2003).

Although I knew that Sambia practiced ritual initiation, I did not know about their secret cult. Indeed, they hid the homoerotic activities from me for some months. I did not expect them to be secret sharers in that ancient tradition—now virtually vanished elsewhere in New Guinea—of boy-insemination. These practices surprised me, even as a trained student of anthropology; they were unlike anything I have ever read. They sometimes disturbed and even shocked me, for as a stranger and as a young single male, I felt alone and vulnerable. But I was trusted by my friends and gradually, step by step, admitted into the initiations and told of the secret myths. In these ways I became a participant-observer of Sambia initiations. My empathy and curiosity and friendship admitted me to the rituals. Those attitudes also influenced my rapport with individuals, making this report far richer. I was permitted into the initiations on the condition that I not allow the women and children, or the outside authorities, to learn the true identities of the persons and events. Over the years many conversations with Sambia have helped me understand their concerns about this. Hence, all of the names in this book are pseudonyms, and certain background details are altered to protect people. Likewise I was allowed to make a film of the Sambia initiations on condition that women and children would not be able to see it during their lifetimes. I have kept my promises.

*   *   *

What do sexual identity and sexuality as a whole mean in the context of culture and society? How does growing up in a particular society influence sexual beliefs and practices—the framework of sexual culture? Does society actually "control" or "influence" the sexual desires of the individual? And finally, is "homosexuality" (attraction to and desire for sexual interaction with the same gender) universal? These are the questions that frame this study. Among the Sambia we shall see the incredible role that traditional warfare and the culture of masculinity in the men's house played in sexuality and gender.

Homosexuality is a western idea that by 1870 was being transformed from sin to perversity to disease as it became visible in the late 19th century. The notion of being exclusively attracted to the same sex was a radical and subversive idea. However, we must not forget that William James once regarded heterosexuality as a perversion on the grounds that exclusive attraction of the opposite sex was also abnormal. In a sense this paved the way for the invention of "heterosexuality" as an idea, and then individual heterosexual identities, by the 1890s. *Homosexuality* was coined first—people notice what is exceptional and label it as deviant before they get around to naming what is obvious and normative. Soon, however, the idea of individual sexual identities, heterosexual or homosexual, inside each person grew in popularity. Indeed it was this historical formation that enabled the politicalization of sexuality and the creation of new sexual identity movements, such as the Free Love movement among heterosexuals, and the homosexual emancipation movement, in the late 19th and early 20th centuries. The next hundred years were built upon these historical, cultural, and psychological ideas.

Moreover, sexual identities such as the transgendered (people who are neither male/female or heterosexual/homosexual and seem to enjoy the ambiguity of both genders/sexual positions) did not even exist until about 1990! It was on the basis of sexual identities that the gay and lesbian social movement was created in the 1960s.

Because nonwestern societies such as the Sambia do not recognize western concepts of individual identity states and sexual cultures, they typically handle same-gender attraction through divergent social practices, including ceremonies and rituals, and very different sexual life ways from our own. In fact, prior to colonization, peoples like the Sambia thought of sexuality in terms of family and kinship, not identities. Nevertheless, they may provide for the expression of homoerotic or bisexual attractions. Individuals may engage in same-sex play or discreet relationships as part of a culturally accepted life way, for example, in adolescence and before marriage, the Sambian way. Or they may be initiated into a special role, such as shaman or priest, that exempts them from traditional gender and sexual norms, at least for a period of time. However, with very few exceptions around the world, sexual cultures express the expectation of social marriage, with economic and social activities designed to produce and support children (Herdt 1997). Homosexuality, in this frame, is not universal, "natural," or "normal"; it is culturally relative. Conversely, an opposite attitude often prevails, that is, that only heterosexuality is normal and natural, also known as *heteronormativity*. And one further linked idea is relevant: *compulsive hetero-sexuality,* (coined by Adrienne Rich 1980) meant to indicate that people, especially women, are expected to act as if they are attracted to the opposite sex, marry, and produce children without thinking about or questioning their desires or sociosexual relationships.

Several additional concepts will help to provide a new tool kit in rethinking sexuality and gender among the Sambia. Sexual culture is the first concept—this construct means the system of cultural meanings of sexuality (such as the mean-ing of fellatio between older and younger males) and the social practices of sexuality (such as when the first sexual intercourse between males and females in marriage is oral sex, in which a woman fellates her husband).

Sexual identity is the second concept—the intentional sense of being or hav-ing a socially constituted form of sexual preference and desire around which your whole identity is built, for example, heterosexual, homosexual, gay or les-bian, queer, transgender. It was on the basis of sexual identities that the gay and lesbian social movement was created in the 1960s.

Sexual orientation is a third concept—specifically defining the habitual pref-erence for one gender or the other, and sometimes for a particular form of sexual technique, such as oral or vaginal sex with others. Whereas sexual identity is a social construction of the society, a social difference, sexual orientation seems increasingly recognized as an internal psychological and biological prop-erty of the individual, that is, an individual difference largely impervious to social change and social influence. Thus it is generally agreed by scientific authorities today that while an individual's sexual identity can change over time, as the great American sexologist Alfred Kinsey (1948) believed, sexual orienta-tion is durable and cannot be "cured" by psychotherapy, as Freud (1935) con-ceded, or even dramatically influenced by religious conversion experiences (Murphy 1992).

Sexual attraction is the fourth concept—desire for sexual contact with another, which may include his or her beauty, his or her body, sex appeal, and other forms of liking and wanting to be close to or stay with someone of the same or other gender.

Sexual life way is a culturally constructed course of expressing sexual being and gender roles in a particular society. It suggests that each sexual culture pro-vides its own plan or "cookie cutter" blueprint for how the individual's sexual-ity will unfold across each epoch of development, from childhood to adolescence, adulthood, middle age, and elderhood. Part of these life ways are the sexual subjectivities that resonate inside the individual. They may be asso-ciated with sexual scripts (Gagnon 2004) that provide the "lines" and "roles" for people to play, as if they were performers on stage, in a sexual culture. Sexual scripts help provide the necessary beliefs and meanings to accompany each of these stages of sexual development as well as the changes that occur from one life stage to the next, for example, from childhood to being an adolescent—the great transition Sambia initiation provides in secret rituals. The sexual scripts have three primary dimensions: intrapsychic—what goes on inside a person's head; interpersonal—the guides to intimate relations in dating, courtship, marriage, extramarital relations, and so on; and cultural—the specific and often gender-specific rules and beliefs for playing out a role in a particular sexual culture, institution, and social event.

These concepts will help to prepare us for observing the Sambia and understanding their remarkable sexual culture—its means of dealing with individual sexual expression often through fierce social regulation and imposing order upon random variation and unique life events, largely to adapt people to warfare. They also help us to link these understandings of sexuality and gender to our own society and our own lives—the larger reason for studying other cultures and their sexual life ways.

1/The Mountain Setting

Sambia are a rugged mountain people whose remote homeland is one of the world's great remaining rain forests. The entire tribal population is spread over a territory hundreds of square miles across a remote corner of the Eastern Highlands Province (see Figure 1.1). The landscape is rugged and isolated: high mountain ranges soaring to 11,000 feet (the same altitudinal range as the Swiss Alps) pitched between swift natural river systems, an uneven green canopy as far as the eye can see. Surrounded on all sides by jagged peaks of the impressive Kratke Mountains, Sambia territory was impenetrable except by mountain trails as recently as 1979. Hamlets are built in the elevation range of 3,000 to 6,000 feet. Taro gardens are cultivated up to about 7,000 feet. Pandanus nut groves are tended and harvested to an elevation of about 8,000 feet. Men hunt in inherited clan territories extending to peaks of 9,000 feet and more, an eerie no-man's-land of dense vegetation, fog, and perpetual silence. Rainfall is heavy at 150 inches a year. The rainy season creates ever-increasing wetness over nine months of the year, whereas the brief dry season (often confined to a few afternoons in June) is broken by morning fog and sudden cloudbursts near dusk.

A turbulent land it is, whose terrific rain and dreadful fog were once referred to as "Frankenstein country" by the local *Kiap,* or Australian government patrol officer, a young man who could abide the biting fog only by taking cognac in his morning tea (he retired to Queensland to sell life insurance). Though lush and forbiddingly beautiful, the area seems anomalous because of its alpine climate rain forest almost dead center on the equator, creating unusual climatic conditions. These include extraordinary temperature changes each day: cold, hot, rainy, sunny; occasional earth tremors, landslides, and creeks that flood constantly in the monsoon; spectacular rain and electrical storms creating veritable light shows at night, with thunderbolts reflecting off mountains miles away beneath a dark cloak of glittering diamond stars. Against such a backdrop one feels acutely the smallness of the human element compared to the vastness of nature. No wonder Sambia refer to themselves as squatters in the nest of the proud harpy eagle (a clan totem), as cousins of the tree-dwelling possum.

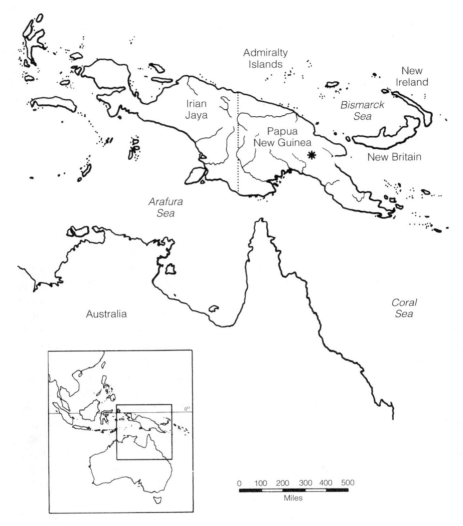

Figure 1.1 New Guinea and off-lying islands

THE LANDSCAPE

To understand the local economy and settlement patterns, we must grasp an image of the landscape. We can do no better than the mental map of Sambia themselves, a folk image of their geography. Through this map we will see how three basic pursuits—food gathering, residence, and defense—are organized.

Suppose we take a bird's-eye view of the Sambia River Valley; what do we see? Very little differentiation in flora or fauna. We notice the high mountains with their green carpets soaring above the ever-constant river, which dominates the landscape of the valley floor. In between the peaks and river, garden patches intermix with bands of grassy meadows. And, of course, there are the hamlets, easily recognizable from great distances by stately groves of feathery mint-green bamboo growing in and around them.

The valley can thus be viewed as a series of five concentric circles of ecological zones climbing from the river to the mountain peaks, thousands of feet above. Each of these provides valued resources, outlined here:

Wunyu-wulu (riverine land). This zone refers to banks and marshes of watercourses, primarily adjacent to the river on the valley floor, so it is at the lowest altitude. During the monsoon the river sometimes rages and overflows its banks. These narrow, muddy flood plains provide rich soil for pandanus fruit and banana trees, taro, and the cane reeds women use in making grass skirts. From the riverbanks, freshwater eels are trapped; when smoked they provide delicious treats. In the dry season some areas of the river are dammed to catch the local scavenger fish, which are also smoked and eaten. Children love to play in small creeks by day, and women hunt frogs in them by torchlight at night.

Wungul-kwaku (habitation area). Here we have the hamlet living space and its adjacent gardens. When Sambia use the term *wungul-kwaku,* they have in mind "cleared areas," swept clean and without vegetation, such as the small central plaza space in the center of the hamlet wherein children play and elders chat or do busywork. Village habitations are built hundreds of feet above the river bottom, on mountain ridges, to prevent surprise attacks. One can thus look down and across vast distances from the hamlet. Huts are built in a line formation and are fortified against attack by tall, concentric barricades of bamboo groves, cordylines (waxy-leafed trees of many colors, sometimes called palm-lilies), wild sugar cane, and various trees. Bamboo groves are also the resting places of hamlet spirits *(aatmwogwambu)* who protect the village and are associated with the ritual cult. Gardens of sweet potatoes, sugar cane, and European-introduced vegetables such as corn and green beans surround the village. Nearby mountain streams provide sweet drinking water; lower in the valley these creeks demarcate clan territories, gardens, and the riverfront property.

Angoolendoowi (edge land forest). The middle area of mountainsides beyond and above hamlets forms a random patchwork of secondary forest and occasional grassland. Here the virgin rain forest has been cleared for garden land. Initiates like to hunt small game here. Some pandanus, areca or betel nut (which is chewed and is mildly narcotic), and other special trees are planted around gardens for their foodstuffs. Today, this zone is the prime area for coffee growing, which was introduced in the 1970s as a cash crop. Small plots of taro are planted here and there. But the larger individual and communal gardens are the key food supply. These yam and taro plantations are also used for ritual feasts. Pigs occasionally forage nearby, although Sambia keep few domesticated pigs. Ramshackle pig-herding huts are built nearby for older women who take on this chore. More common are the garden huts that provide alternate residences for families during planting and harvest times. Finally, the higher grounds of edge land forest provide flat spaces for sacred ritual dance grounds during male initiation, and every hamlet boasts one of these.

Koonai-wumdu (pandanus nut forest). Above the edge land forest we move into deep rain forest. Only men and older initiates usually venture here to hunt; at harvest times, however, men take their families to live temporarily in pandanus-nut houses, which are sturdy cabins constructed of pandanus materials. Nearby forests have mixed varieties of oak, pine, beech, and other broad-leafed trees sheltering thick vines with beautiful forest orchids. All pandanus trees are individually owned and tended by men. Their nuts are highly valued and taste like coconut. Sambia regard them as protein sources equivalent to certain meats, to mother's milk, and to semen, as we shall see. "Harmless" cold swamp bogs are used for taro gardens. Some bogs, however, are believed to be inhabited by evil nature spirits that can engulf men and are very much feared. Possum-hunting parties operate out of the pandanus-nut houses too. Pandanus groves are perplexing places, silent and fogbound with enormous trees—eerie and jagged monstrosities growing in deep-forested swamplands that extend a mile or so up into colder cloud forest country. In this zone, men say, the elusive cassowary (an ostrich-like bird) can be trapped, and here she mingles with fierce male forest spirits *(ikeiaru)*. Both these creatures are respected and even feared, and occupy important roles in Sambia mythology.

Kai-wumdu (high forest hunting territory). Great expanses of wild growth slope upward to the peaks above the pandanus. The area is perpetually foggy, so it is damp with mossy surfaces and thick undergrowth. Gnarled and crooked cedar and other trees are festooned with liverworts and lichens. Limestone outcrops create rock shelters and shadowy caves that Sambia dread—the hiding places of ghosts and forest spirits. Village clans as a group own large tracts of this forest, for which they will wage war to protect their exclusive hunting rights for possum, cassowary, and birds. To travel here one must crisscross high and treacherous tree bridges, often wet or mossy. Hunting lodges of poor construction provide temporary shelter during times of ceremonial hunts. Though miserable abodes, perpetually cold and damp and without barriers against the terrible leeches that thrive in this zone, men may spend weeks in them. The possum they catch and smoke here are crucial for ritual feasts. This high roof of the world is indeed a kind of masculine testing ground unknown to women and children.

POPULATION GROUPINGS

The patterns of population and settlement of the Sambia and their neighbors are similar throughout the region. Here I will concentrate on only the Sambia, while in the next section we will examine wider regional patterns. Today Sambia live in six different population areas organized around river valleys. These populational clusters are *subtribes*. Each is made up in turn of one or more social units referred to as *phratries,* composed of different hamlets.

Phratries are social units that group people according to their common geographic territory, an image of common origin and fictitious ancestors, shared ritual customs, and identity. In some cases there are minor dialect differences between phratries. Nevertheless, Sambia of all six subtribes speak one language and recognize other speakers as similar to themselves and distinct from neighboring tribal groups. Each phratry is composed of two or more hamlets, which, in general, vary in size from about 40 to 150 persons.

The end of warfare has created several large *composite hamlets* (based on the merging of two previously separate hamlets) like Nilangu, my fieldwork site, which numbers about 160 people. In all there are 10 phratries and some 40 different Sambia hamlets scattered throughout the six valleys. These phratries range in size from the Yulamwi, with about 80 people, to the Wunyu-Sambia in the Upper Sambia Valley, with 421 people. These river populations are the focus of a person's social affiliations and interactions throughout life. Each valley's hamlets are usually within sight and earshot of each other; by contrast, valleys are separated, depending on the particular area, by the mountains and by walking distances ranging from three hours to two days. Within the social universe of each valley, marriage and initiation co-occur, so ties of kinship, marriage, and/or co-initiation link men to each other. Within these clusters in the past, hamlets often fought against one another in ritualized bow-and-arrow fighting; while when necessary at other times, they united in defense against attack by outside groups. However, in the Sambia Valley and one other valley, the social situation is more complex due to the presence of three different phratries in the same broad valley. Traditionally, then, a river valley population has a string of neighboring hamlets with their own common forest and riverine territories, which also share ritual dance grounds and fight grounds.

Sambia River Valley

The focus of this ethnography is the Sambia River Valley and its hamlets (see Figure 1.2). To understand the Sambia ritual initiatory cult, we will want to study how the valley is internally divided. The Sambia River Valley is a long, thin, partially deforested habitation zone, falling between two mountain chains, the Green Mountains and the Blue Mountains. The Sambia River headwaters flow from the northerly Papuan Vailala Divide, a 10,000-foot mountain pass that separates the Sambia from their neighbors, the Wantuki'u tribes. Politically and ecologically, the valley can be divided into an upper and lower area. The Upper Sambia Valley contains two different phratries: the Wunyu-Sambia on the western bank, with six hamlets (total population 421); and the Seboolu on the eastern bank, with four hamlets (total population 411). In the early 1970s a new settlement sprung up on the valley floor near the first local Christian mission. This mission is about a 45-minute walk from my fieldwork village. The Middle Valley has a small phratry, the Yulami (total population 98), the original inhabiting group mentioned previously—remnants of the hunters and gatherers chased out long ago. These three phratries together number 930 persons in all, and they constitute my major research population.

The population density of Sambia is low, between four and five people per square mile. However, the density dramatically increases if we consider only the landmass that is ecologically utilized. The Middle and Upper Sambia Valley, for example, is an area whose total exploited land base is about 24 miles (6 km wide by 10 km long, or 60 km^2). This area mass yields a population density of just

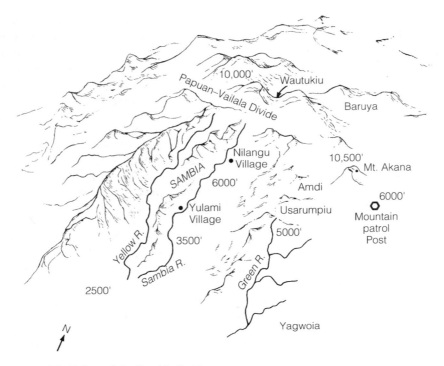

Figure 1.2 Tribes of the Sambia Region

over 38 persons per square mile, a truer population density picture. This helps us to understand why the land near existing hamlets is also more coveted and fought over. Even assuming this higher density, however, Sambia have vast unused forest preserves for future use.

An hour farther south of the Yulami over a steep mountain range is the Sambia River Delta, which is, more properly speaking, the drainage basin of the river. This area is inhabited by the Moonagu phratry, with six small hamlets (total population about 300). The Moonagu are distinct from the Upper Valley and traditionally have had few social contacts with them. But they trade and exchange marriages with the Yulami people, and in 1975 due to social changes, they joined the initiations we will study shortly.

Farther afield, Sambia are linked as one of seven societies formed with their immediate Anga neighbors in the Mountain District, the most southerly political division of the Eastern Highlands Province. It covers an area of about 8,000 square miles and has a total population of 12,000 people, quite a low population density (Brookfield and Hart 1971: 96–124). Of the other Anga tribes, only the Baruya people (Godelier 1969, 1986) outnumber Sambia. In regional politics, Sambia and the Baruya were the local kingpins in war (see Figure 1.2). Although separated by middlemen tribes, each bordered four of the five remaining Mountain District tribes, so they were always involved in shifting alliances with smaller groups in between themselves. Thus, the Amdi tribe would attack the Usurumpia people. Sambia would aid the latter, with whom they intermarried, whereas the Baruya would support the Amdi tribe. And so it went. On unconditional terms it was considered dangerous, or in most cases (as for the Amdi and Sambia) suicidal, to travel through these neighboring tribal areas.

HAMLET SECURITY CIRCLE

Every society must weigh the dangers of its behavioral environment for children. A boundary of security must be drawn around them. Peter Lawrence (1966) once coined the term *security circle* to indicate the widest area within which the New Guinean felt free and safe to move about. For Sambia this was the hamlet, as the perceived dangers beyond were great. But what we must not forget is that insecurities also existed inside its walls.

Several factors color the nature of the hamlet security circle. First, in the past war was going on and people got killed. Second, women are imported from potential enemy groups, so the insecurity of having "aliens" around—potential spies and collaborators with enemies—permeates village life. Third, the hamlet is tiny and insulated, a fact that makes living in close quarters much harder when conflict breaks out. Fourth, everyone knows everyone else, typically since birth, which precludes privacy and the emergence of selfhood free from village regulation, yet ritual secrecy creates gaps and fears in women's and children's lives. Fifth, there has been a high infant mortality rate and constant sickness in the area (there was no modern medicine until recently). Sixth, biological maturation has been extremely slow in the region, with menarche as late as age 18–19, supporting ritual beliefs about the need for ceremonies to "grow" the body.

The Sambia social world, in short, is very small. In the valley with its population of about 1,000, everyone knows almost everyone else, for everyone was named and present across the stream of life. These people have grown up together and know one another intimately, so that what is hidden emerges in gossip or in the shaman's visions. Members of the group are all around; neighbors are known too. For children, the ancestors' identities are like this too. Some of their exploits are known from myths, like those surrounding Namboolu and his wife Chemchi, the great founders and busybodies of Sambia mythology. The greatest war leaders, shamans, and gardeners have renown throughout the region.

Neighboring hamlets harbor stereotypes about others, images that reflect the habits and predictability of village clan totems. Thus, Nilangu men are fierce fighters with claws like the harpy eagle, their totem. Pundei are sorcerers and shamans, to be feared like their totem, the blood plant. These animosities and stereotypes remind us of legendary feuds between the families of Romeo and Juliet in feudal Italy, where the fact that people knew each other and fell in love made their hatred and social opposition the more poignant and fatal. The point is that hamlets are like tiny islands whose relations of marriage, politics, and ritual create a fatalism characteristic of tightly knit roles and societies.

The feeling of security in the hamlet is real. It is hard to convey this feeling to Western city dwellers. If I could transport you for a moment to the village on

Figure 1.3 Two Sambia boys, Songei village 1975

a warm, dry-season night with a full moon, you would see what security and happiness truly look like when they are *lived*. You would see naked children laughing in the extraordinary silver light as they dash through the hamlet playing tag, even late at night. You would see the orange glow of fireplaces through friendly and wide-open doors. Dogs bark and cicadas sing; the old people gab. Kanteilo draws chuckles of amazement when he announces, at his advanced age, that he will set off tomorrow to trade bark capes way over in Wantukiu tribal country. Smoking and betel chewing relax people, who turn to gossip, to local news, to stories—the old men always ready to spin tales about war and adventures of the past, the children always ready to hear ghost stories that make them wide-eyed and giggly with excitement. Maybe there will be a songfest, for Sambia love to sing. Not everything is ideal: The sexes remain divided, and there is perhaps a marital spat mixed into the evening's events. But these are usually temporary and soon forgotten. It is the feeling of being at home and being safe that pervades and warms.

We should recall the physical setting of the hamlet: a narrow stockade containing a few huts encircling a tiny plaza on a narrow mountain terrace. The hamlet site is lush and green and fertile but tidy in a way that sets it apart from the encroaching forest. The family houses are built in line formation, the men's house situated at the higher end of the sloping ridge. This spot affords the warriors the widest surveillance during wartime. By placing the clubhouse at the top of the residential zone, nearest the forest, men also reduce the possibility of female contact and pollution. Women are told not to walk above the clubhouse, which would contaminate the initiates, war weapons, and ritual paraphernalia. "Women belong down below, men on top," my age-mate Weiyu typically says.

This pat statement, which downgrades women because of their polluting vaginas, rationalizes living arrangements.

An invisible tapestry of spatial taboos and architectural designs separates women from men inside the hamlet, its narrow confines segregated into men's and women's spaces. Zones of female movement are polluted, according to male dogma; since no area is immune to this contagion, everyone is restricted by taboos. A startling assortment of such taboos and avoidance rules curtail the movements of women, initiates, and men. No part of the hamlet is perceived as being unrestricted by sex-related taboos, except for the dusty central plaza (and even this is not neutral during ceremonies). Interpersonal heterosexual behavior is therefore rigidly structured. Women are not at all free to move about as they wish, and initiates are even more hemmed in. Men believe that women may pollute them merely by stepping over, above, or beside them, or by touching their persons, food, or possessions. During menstrual periods women retire to the menstrual hut, which is below the hamlet. Men and initiates completely avoid this area. Likewise, women must not walk near the men's clubhouse or ever look inside.

Like other New Guinea peoples, Sambia are subsistence horticulturalists. Food is plain but usually plentiful. Sweet potatoes and taro are the main staples, and yams are a seasonal feast crop. Many other green vegetables are cultivated too, and mushrooms and palm hearts are gathered from the forest on an irregular basis. Cash cropping for coffee production and the import of expensive foodstuffs such as rice have greatly altered the traditional economy, as we will see. Sambia practice slash-and-burn gardening. After a garden is exhausted, it is left dormant for a few years. Gardening is done in shifting swidden cycles, with garden plots cut out of virgin rain forest and secondary forest. Gardens are cultivated up to two hours' walking distance from the village. All slash-and-burn was formerly done with stone tools. Until recently (around 1980), Sambia probably had to gather wild foods much more than now. Sambia themselves say that the introduction of steel axes has made food more plentiful and easier to obtain.

Sambia historically had simple technology. Their greatest number of implements was the weaponry used in war. Arsenals included stone and wooden clubs, pineapple-shaped clubs, and stone axes, all crafted for killing in intertribal wars. Men still carry bows and arrows wherever they go. There are over 20 types of arrows, according to whether the shaft is straight or barbed, long or short, of hard or soft wood. Bows are made of wood from an extremely hard palm tree. Barbed or hooked arrows are for killing men and pigs. Blunt-nosed arrows are used for killing birds, while multipronged arrows are used to kill wild pigs.

In gardening, however, there are really only two key instruments, and these reflect the strict sex-role dichotomy: stone (and today steel) axes for men and digging sticks for women. Men say it used to take as long as two weeks to fell a large tree with their old-fashioned axes. Nowadays, they can chop down the same-sized tree with a steel axe in only a few hours. Bamboo knives, cassowary bone awls, and other simple tools were also employed in butchering and cooking animals. Grass skirts woven by women and bark capes made by men (from bark of the local mulberry tree) provide the main clothing.

Men and women have sharply defined places in the behavioral environment. Their society dictates that men be warriors and hunters (skill with bow and arrow being the critical sign of competence both in war and the hunt), while women be mothers and gardeners. Men express incompetence in the rearing of children. While these roles are rationalized by social needs, Sambia themselves view gender roles as natural.

All economic activities are strictly regulated on cultural-based gender principles governing the division of labor. Men fell trees and clear brush; women burn off the debris, till the soil, plant, weed, and harvest. Men hunt, women do not. From childhood onward, boys are prepared to use weapons in hunting and war, whereas girls do domestic chores such as babysitting and learn more about gardening. Hunting remains an important economic pursuit even today, for it provides some meat protein as well as the possum meat used for ceremonial gifts.

Both hunting and gardening are intermixed as economic routines year round. But marked climatic seasons—dry and rainy periods—also strongly influence subsistence activities and family life. During the light monsoon the weather is normally wet, so people stay closer to home in the hamlet. During the short-lived dry season, hunting parties are launched and men live for weeks in the forest. When new gardens are cultivated by the whole community, people also live away from hamlets for long periods of time in garden houses. Finally, ritual initiations and trading parties to other villages lead men away from the village. A good deal of time is thus spent removed from the hamlet over the course of a year.

Gardening routines are rigidly sex-typed. Being the main staple, sweet potatoes are the most common type of garden plant. They are planted in large tracts by a nuclear family, or a man and his wives, on the man's own clan land. If the bush is virgin forest, it is much harder work to clear. If it is secondary forest—the site of an old garden—the land will have lain fallow for 5 to 10 years and, though still heavily forested, it is easier to till than virgin land. Men do all the chopping of trees; they climb up and cut off branches. Women are not allowed to do this. Then the tree is slashed around its base, partially burned, and left standing for firewood. All other activities related to sweet potatoes are mainly done by women, as shown in Table 1.1. Other crops, such as sugar cane, allow more gender flexibility as to who does the work.

Part of the reason for the rigid sexual division of labor is that all natural species are culturally categorized as being either "male" or "female"—a common belief throughout New Guinea. Sweet potatoes, for instance, lie in the ground horizontally and are thought to be "soft"—they are categorized as female. Taro grows vertically and is "hard"—it is thought to be a "male" food. Therefore, women tend sweet potatoes while men cultivate taro. In Chapter 4 we will study how ceremonial hunting and ordinary gardening are the differential ways each gender prepares for collective initiations.

Hunting is critical for two reasons: First, it is prestigious and provides prestige food, which traditionally included most meat and was therefore the source of masculine status. Only recently have pigs and pork played a larger role in gift giving and feasts to mark ceremonies. For instance, in 1975, Nilangu—the largest hamlet in the valley—had a total pig population of only 15. Compare this puny figure with the Western Highlands Anga tribe, which has hundreds of pigs in each small settlement, thousands in total (Meggitt 1974). Because the Sambia region is heavily forested and has little grassland, pigs did not thrive well. As possum

TABLE 1   SEX-TYPING IN GARDENING ROUTINES

Routine	Plant	Putative "Sex" of Plant	Men	Cultural Actor Women	Cultural Actor Initiate	Child
1. Scaling trees		———	X			
2. Clearing grass		———	X			
3. Loping off small trees/ branches		———	X			
4. Burning vegetation				X		
5. Digging soil	Sweet potato	Female ———	X			X
6. Weeding						
	Taro	Male	X			
	Leafy greens,	Female	X	X		
	Reeds, flowers	———	X		X	
	Sugar cane	Male	X	X	X	
	Banana trees	Male/ Female	X	X	X	X
	Pandanus trees	Female	X	X		
7. Harvesting	Sweet potato	———		X		
	Taro	———	X			
	Sugar	———	X			
	Greens	———	X			

and similar marsupials are the game men hunt, this marked off the fringe-area Sambia from other more powerful and populous Central Highlands groups. Sambia emphasize possum hunting over pig husbandry, which reinforces the rigid sex-role dichotomy: Men must hunt to provide meat for initiations and marriage exchange since they cannot rely on vast pig herds, raised primarily by women but distributed by men, as elsewhere in New Guinea (see Brown 1978; A. J. Strathern 1972). Historically, hunting was thus a central context for proving manhood.

There are three main types of hunting: the hunt with bow and arrow, trapping, and the scaling of trees to roust possum and bag them. There are no natural predators in Highlands New Guinea except man, who hunts and kills many species. Only the cassowary and wild boar are of any real danger to men. Bow hunting is mainly used for birds. Trapping is done by snares or spring-traps, which are the only means of catching the elusive cassowary—so powerful and quick a bird that it eludes the bow. Trapping for possum, eel, and birds is respectable enough. In the case of possum hunting, what is most daring and masculine is to catch the prey with one's naked hands. This brings the greatest prestige. Men watch their forests daily so they know the ins and outs of game, including their lairs and trails. Possum are nocturnal mammals that forage high in trees. Men scale trees—some over 100 feet tall—aided only by vines. Then they grab the possum or roust them to the ground, where another hunter clubs them. Traditionally, a marriage gift of possum meat requires long ropes of dried possum (cured for preservation over weeks in the high forest), some ropes being 20 feet long, which hold between 30 and 60 possum. No wonder these hunts require months of daily possum hunting for the bachelor, his clansmen, and age-mates (men initiated together, who call each other *ginyoko*). We shall see later how ritual initiation encourages boys to be strong hunters and virile men.

The sexual polarity of Sambia economic roles is a powerful fact in the behavioral environment. Men spend most time with other men, and women and children are more often together. The sexes economically complement rather than cooperate in this division of labor. Perhaps because of the long-standing identification of one sex with certain routines, the opposite sex comes to envy them their power in that domain. The striking thing is a tendency for many activities to be restricted to one sex or the other. Even after decades of culture change, this holds true.

SOCIAL STRUCTURE

The hamlet is the key unit of social structure. In most matters—such as war, hunting and gardening, marriage arrangements, and property disputes—men look to their hamlets and find mutual interest and support there. Hamlets have their own troubles, of course. Squabbles over gardens, adultery and marital arguments, not to mention petty gossip; all these have created problems for peaceful coexistence. At their worst, the disputes led to fighting and a rupture in the hamlet, with the disgruntled faction (usually a clan or clan segment) forming a new hamlet elsewhere. But that has been rare. Sambia still view their hamlet as home and a haven protecting them from multitudes of enemy groups and evil spirits.

Hamlets have women's (or nuclear family) houses *(aambelangu)* and one or two men's clubhouses *(kwolangu)* associated with rigid taboos of all kinds. My village, Nilangu, for example, had two men's houses during the period of my fieldwork. Women are felt to be polluting, especially their menstrual blood. Since they can transfer the pollution, they cannot ever enter a clubhouse or go near its male initiates. Women must travel only on specified female paths inside the hamlet, whereas initiates must travel only on physically elevated male paths. Families live in women's houses. In Nilangu, the women always had to take the lower, muddier path inside the village, and they complained about it. Adult men sleep and eat in the male space of the women's house. Their wives, unmarried daughters, and infant uninitiated sons sit in the female space. Women should not interfere with men's activities either, and they are forbidden from touching men's heads, weapons, and ritual ornaments. Somewhat older boys sleep in their fathers' male space.

All initiated unmarried males reside in the men's clubhouse and must avoid women (and to a lesser extent, children) at all times. The clubhouse is the real nerve center of masculine activity and secrecy because ritual, warfare, and hunting groups operate from there. During such times men leave their wives and sleep in the clubhouse. This creates a barrier between fathers and sons until the boys are initiated. Boys and women are kept in the dark about some men's activities, especially ritual events. All male informants disclaim knowledge of secret

Figure 1.4 Initiates huddle for taro feast (Sambia Valley initiations, 1975)

rituals before they were initiated. It is as if there are two worlds in their child-hoods: that of the men and that of the women.

The Sambia men's clubhouse is so typical as to be distinctive of male sexual culture in New Guinea societies. One sees similarities, even striking resem-blances, between the male organization and ceremonial behavior surrounding men's clubhouses everywhere on the island. Gender segregation is part and par-cel of this powerful institutional pattern (Read 1955). Yes, it is true that some cul-tures differ in ritual beliefs regarding male cult life; that some groups emphasize warfare much more than others, as, for example, the aggressive Mundugumor versus the peaceful Mountain Arapesh (Mead 1935) in the great Sepik River basin, far north and west of the Sambia region. And some societies place a larger emphasis on sacred art in the clubhouse or on mythology told by men, or the women may play a more prominent role in the symbolism of certain male cult rituals (see Herdt 1982). Yet these differences must not blind us to the cultural patterns that men share through the institution of the clubhouse. These include military training, supervision and education of boys in the masculine realm, the transmission of cultural knowledge surrounding hunting magic and warrior folklore, the organization of hunting, some separation or recognition of the differences between men and women, the socially sanctioned use of ritual paraphernalia and musical instruments such as flutes and bullroarers, and so forth. These distinctive customs anchor the men's world in the club-house throughout Melanesia.

The division between men and women in the Sambia hamlet is based also on kinship. A hamlet is organized by the core of its male patrilineal kinsmen (reck-oned by genealogical descent from father to son) who were born there and are expected to always reside therein. Hamlets are internally segmented into smaller descent groups. The largest unit of hamlet grouping is the great-clan, which consists of all persons who trace genealogical descent to a known, fictitiously named ancestor. The great-clan is usually named after the founding clan of the hamlet. Its members can also be dispersed in other hamlets. Great-clan leadership is vested in eldest males of its founding clan. The hamlet is made up of one or more great-clans, and these great-clans are subdivided into two or more component clans (*iku,* for tree). Clans link persons who can actually demonstrate descent from a known, real ancestor (one to three generations back, according to Kanteilo extensive knowledge).

Clansmen usually reside in the hamlet of their father or, less commonly, that of their father's brothers, biological or more distantly related, who may reside in a neighboring hamlet of the same phratry. Hence, patrilocal residence—living in father's village—is very high among Sambia, with more than 80 percent of Sambia males residing partrilocally. Clansmen share collective property, especially garden land and pandanus and forest preserves, as noted previously. But the individual clansman also has his own personal property (such as garden plots, pandanus groves) inherited from his father.

Sambia have a kinship system that stresses generational relationships. Clansmen refer to one another as "brothers" and "fathers" and "grandfathers," and women as "sisters" and "mothers," such that the children of the same generation refer to each other as "brother" or "sister." Hamlet playgroups of children are thus reared as if they belong to a large extended family. The numerical size of clans and great-clans depends on the hamlet's size and whether the clans are localized in one hamlet or dispersed. Female clansmen do not inherit land property, although they have "use" rights in certain lands. Women are seldom utilized for reckoning descent because they often move out of the hamlet upon marriage. In sum, a hamlet's clan groups are united by an image of common descent as brothers who support one another in economic production, warfare, and ritual, as well as in marriage.

The clansmen of a hamlet are allied in matters of warfare and ritual, ideally linking them to (usually neighboring) hamlets that belong to the same phratry. Phratry members are descended from a single, fictitious ancestor, making them "brothers" or "age-mates." Namboolu is the most famous mythical ancestor (Herdt 1981). He came from Kokona; so all his descendants share a common origin. Furthermore, the separate clans of a phratry participate in a structure of rituals, some of which they own as intangible property. Next, and related to ritual identity, is the wearing of a common style of male grass sporran, or grass apron (a kind of grass skirt like a kilt, which in males covers only the genital area; in females, the grass forms a true skirt). This is a sign of their phratry membership and an emblem of ethnic identity in intertribal relationships. In times of war, hamlets of a phratry can call on each other for assistance. These facts reveal how phratry organization is linked to ritual initiation in many ways.

Neighboring hamlets in a valley tend to jointly sponsor collective ritual initiations. These occur every three or four years and are first focused on the construction of a large cult house (called the *moo-angu*). The cult house is a production of the locally involved men of the clans of these hamlets, usually at the behest of their elders and war leaders. It is always built adjacent to a dance ground *(korumundiku:* dancing, *korumu* + bonfire, *diku).* Although each hamlet has a separate dance ground, collective initiation is usually celebrated on a neutral dance ground associated with all the hamlets of a phratry and situated at a distance from any one of them. This collectivity of neighboring hamlets within a valley, which usually join to co-sponsor bachelor initiations, is a dance ground confederacy (or simply "confederacy").

The confederacy is thus a political and ritual grouping of local hamlets that cooperate politically on certain occasions and suspend their intermittent fighting long enough to initiate together. Sometimes such groups feud with others of their own phratry. Hamlets of different phratries, however, fight more frequently and with more bloodshed and vengeance. Still, their joint initiations make their sons age-mates, members of a regional age-set. As adults, some of these men marry their age-mates' sisters and daughters, so they become in-laws, sometimes enemies. Male age-mates not only share in ritual secrets but they also exchange sisters and clanswomen as pawns to opposing hamlets to obtain wives. No wonder men fear women: Their wives often come from enemy groups. Kinship and intermarriage, joint initiation and warfare, all are factors in the functioning of the confederacy.

Within the Sambia tribe are two types of confederacy. The first consists of only one phratry, in one valley. These hamlets, to reiterate, believe they share common descent, geographic origin, and ritual customs. We best call this unit an intraphratry confederacy. The phratry itself is identified with one of its own dance grounds, and it internally organizes collective initiations only by and for its member hamlets. This form of initiation usually occurs in settlements such as the Moonagu phratry in the Sambia River Delta (see Figure 1.2), geographically isolated from other phratries. The second type of confederacy is more complex and powerful, such as the magic-political Sambia River Valley. This is an intraphratry confederacy incorporating hamlets of two or three different phratries. When peace permits, these groups jointly initiate their sons on a single dance ground, which thus crosscuts phratry boundaries (see Figure 1.6). Over the past 60 years, Sambia claim to have held many intraphratry initiations. From the 1940s until pacification, however, warfare increasingly blocked these performances. This changed in the 1960s, as we shall see. It seems, then, that intraphratry confederacies are less stable than the smaller intraphratry organizations. Yet in both types of confederacies, the initiation program coincided with unpredictable war and peace.

Despite a tradition of intertribal warfare, the Sambia and neighboring Anga societies shared important cultural and linguistic patterns, and they all were probably prehistoric migrants from around Menyamya, in South-Central Papua, more than two centuries ago. Sambia themselves look to an archaic ritual center there called Kokona as their actual ancestral, as well as spiritual, "origin hole."

In 1976, I did a long patrol leading to this area to visit Kokona, and I discovered the extraordinary contradictions in secrecy and sexuality in the area (Herdt 2003). Ten Sambia went with me. We saw the basalt pillar outcrops Sambia associate with their sacred myths. Neither my friends nor their fathers had ever visited this place, and they were in awe of what they had previously known only from legend. They were also fearful of the alleged cannibal ways of the local tribes as well, fearing attack by the local people—ancient enemies— the group associated with the original cause for migration generations ago. Old wounds heal slowly. Besides, the Menya were cannibals (Sambia never were), and Sambia distrust headhunters, even those who now wear T-shirts.

The results of this common heritage of regional traditions can be seen in social organization throughout the Mountain District tribes: identical house forms, residential patterns, dress, nearly identical material culture; strikingly similar socialization and sleeping patterns, behavioral gestures, and body language; and ritual, marriage, leadership, illness, and mortuary customs that are much alike in form and content. Most impressive of all for this case study is the universal presence of men's secret societies in all these Anga tribes, extending throughout the Mountain District all the way to Menyamya and farther south. My reconnaissance patrols over the years have convinced me that a basic, archaic ritual complex is common to all these tribal groups (see Herdt 1993). It involves both secret male initiation and boy-inseminating practices.

RELIGION

Sambia are close to death, and their omnivorous spirits are never far behind. Forest and hamlet spirits are different from ghosts. Their brooding ghosts, nameless spirits of the dead who mercilessly strike the living to devour their innards, are truly dreaded and frightening shades. Sambia hate them, and they sadly mock themselves with the proverb: "We are their meat, their possum and pig, the helpless prey of our ghosts." Ghosts are believed literally to eat the corpses of the deceased. In dreams all images of people eating are interpreted as ghosts eating human parts; the meat, though disguised as pig or possum, is really the corpse of a targeted person. For the dreamer to partake of this flesh invites feelings of cannibalism, sorcery, and soul-death upon awakening. And people never quite forget this hideous image. Sambia are no friends of their ghosts, nor are they at peace with them (any more than with each other). Ghosts also hover close to hamlets they lived in as humans, sometimes frightening children. By contrast, hamlet spirits are deceased prominent females and forest spirits are bygone big, or esteemed, men thought to be generally protective of the village.

Neither in life nor in dreams can ordinary men control spirits. Only shamans can do so. Sorcerers can say incantations over the skull and bones of one's ancestors (or deceased kin) to conjure up their ghosts to level sickness and death against one's enemies. Yet because these shades are unruly and unpredictable, Sambia are reluctant to practice the sorcery for fear it will turn back on them. Even shamans can only exorcise or outwit the ghosts. Spirits have a greed and envy surpassing men's. At times of death, which bring mourning and wailing for the loss of loved ones, the new ghost is feared for its anger. Sambia believe sorcery or spirits supernaturally cause all deaths. So the ghost tries revenge, extending the human norm for blood revenge after death. Indeed, at such times I have seen people travel alone or to their nightly toilet in genuine fear.

Ancestral forest spirits are not as vicious as ghosts to their own kinsmen, but they still are to strangers. These souls of deceased big men guard clan territory. They are said to be envious of any hunter's catch, and many a folktale tells how a lone trapper met an untimely death through the deceptive cries of spirits. Children enjoy such ghost stories with wide-eyed interest. Through these stories they unwittingly learn that their male cross-cousins (from neighboring hamlets) are ambivalent and tricky figures with divided loyalties—sometimes changing from spirits into men—who are never to be fully trusted, as their fathers well know from past battles.

Only the female hamlet spirit, the *aatmogwambu*, whose cries are supposed to animate the sacred flutes, is a protector who alerts her hamlet to enemy attack. These spirits are thought to be the souls of prominent deceased women of the hamlet. Notice the differences in the sexes of these spirits. Ghosts are believed to be of both sexes; ancestral forest spirits are almost universally conceived to be only male, and hamlet spirits—as one would expect because of the close association of men with forests, women with hamlets—are normally female. Sometimes people say forest spirits are married to hamlet spirits. Hamlet spirits are named and "owned" by individual clans, in association with the spirit's dwelling place on clan property, which it guards. Although ghosts seem evil and other spirits punishing and angry, at least they make men thankful to be alive, and they help explain the otherwise unknowable.

In greeting death, Sambia reveal a characteristic vitality that is cloaked in masculine bravado. Men and women alike break into soul-wrenching sobs at the news of death. At no other time does this occur, and it is otherwise unacceptable for a man to openly cry. Brothers gradually succumb to piteous wailing and out-bursts of anger, eventually ending in the frenzied destruction of the gardens of the deceased and a feasting on his food crops. Meanwhile, the widow and female relatives and some male kin roll in mud to express their sorrow. In a day or two they have exhausted themselves. A hunt is then organized by the sons and brothers to provide gifts of meat for the funeral guests and grieving kin. Finally, with warrior aplomb, all of these sad sentiments are hastily laid to rest at the funeral, a month later. A simple sacrificial act of placation of the ghost, with food offerings, is transformed into an aggressive and noisy chase by men flaunt-ing phallic bamboo poles mounted with bullroarers, in hopes of banishing for-ever the now evil ghost from its own homeland. The attempt is always futile; the ghost is here to stay. Yet this ceremonial bluster typifies the dramatic way in which Sambia confront feelings of loss and death in their lives: Beginning with wailing, they turn their exhausting lamentations eventually into anger, only to recover themselves in the most masculine act of self-assured pride. Are they not trying too hard and protesting too much that in spite of their grief they are in fact masculine?

This attitude toward the dead has its parallel in men's views about death in battle. Most Sambia men are terrified of death, as you can see in their eyes when they discuss the subject. The smallest cuts or colds are cause for concern, and yet Sambia have a remarkable capacity to endure great pain. Squeamish but obstinate they are. Sickness, pain, and death are for them no strangers; in war-fare they are expected. To endure the possibility, men have created mental tricks for drumming up a paradoxical stance in doing battle: turning resolve into reck-lessness. For instance, a great secret of the men of one hamlet is their consump-tion of bitter, bright red juice (consciously compared to menstrual blood) immediately prior to battle so as to inject into themselves aggressive abandon in the battle-charge, which does frighten enemies. Thus they defend themselves against fear and create fierceness for battle.

What is difficult to grasp is the personal glory, which is a valued end in itself, of being successful in war. This glory entails something else: a capacity to regard one's opponents as inhuman, according to the degree of hostility in the fight. At their worst, Sambia have an extraordinary ability to think of true enemies as tar-gets divorced from any sense of humane empathy at all (Read 1955). But we must remember that many other New Guinea peoples are alike in this regard, nor are we Westerners so different, as recent wars have shown. This suggests my main point here: Warfare creates cruelty and preoccupation with the present. Sambia are oriented to the present. They confront the past, the spiritual world, or the future only as pragmatic matters, rarely as reflections on the existential potentials of life itself. This pragmatism is necessitated by the pervasiveness of warfare in their behavioral environment.

No account of Sambia religion is complete without studying its shamanism, a complex subject mentioned in later chapters. Shamans mediate between this world and that of the spirits. They have the power to heal; to move into trance states; to summon unto themselves their spirit familiars in many forms and shapes; to be possessed by them; and through these beings—while in a trance—to ascend to the realm of the ghosts where they say they can see and hear and feel through the senses of their tiny human counterparts, to engage the spirits and outwit ghosts, and thus retrieve the "stolen" souls of their sick patients over whom they sweat and suffer. These miraculous feats, in states of "magical flight," distinguish true shamans from other healers or sorcerers, who are also present in Sambia society. For here, too, *jerungdu* creates unequal powers in shamans. Thus the shaman is a hero, a person whose great strength is used unselfishly for the good of the group.

I have always felt that their shamans, who sometimes are eccentric and ratty and even crazy, provide great relief to Sambia, the hope of escaping the dark forces of their evil spirits and horrible sicknesses that lead to death. Shamanic cultures are a heroic complex in human society, an archaic and simple way—although one riddled with complex states of mind like trances that we still little understand—of easing suffering and providing encouragement to those who must will themselves to live. Hope is provided for those who survive the prob-lems of constant war and for those who cannot bear to have survived when their loved ones were so capriciously carried off in death's cruel arms. Sakulambei is such a hero. Like other male shamans, he can perform healing ceremonies both in women's houses and in the clubhouse. Women shamans, such as Kaiyunango, can only perform in women's houses. Yet she too is no less a heroine in the eyes of women and some men.

Male shamans were also critical in warfare. Much of the reason for this was once succinctly put to me by a renowned war leader. In doing routine geneal-ogy collecting at a distant hamlet, a borderland village near hated enemies,

Figure 1.5 A shaman in trance during healing ceremonies

I discovered an inordinate number of shamans (deceased and living) compared to Sambia society at large. When asked about this a war leader (then about 50 years old) said of his community:

> We live near the Amdi—our enemies. They raid us. Who can foresee their attacks? Who could help us? Shamans' dreams foretell raids. . . . If they see [dream] particular enemy warriors, we know those men will die before us.

The shaman was an oracle, then, whose allegedly infallible advice no doubt foretold and even stimulated military activities. From their own divinations and dreams (and those of war leaders and elders), shamans tried to predict the success of a battle or an impending attack. This was their duty as they learned it in initiation rites. Male shamans also offered supernatural purification for warriors by performing healing ceremonies in the clubhouse. Each warrior received protection, and this surely comforted men who faced an early-morning battle. Their persons and weapons also needed cleaning of residues of female pollution. Such traces made warriors weak and vulnerable, for men feel that the "smell of women" attracts arrows to them like a magnet.

After the battle, male shamans did even more. They performed ceremonies to cleanse the blood of slain enemies from the weapons and bodies of living warriors. This purge lessened the possibility of reprisal attacks by the ghosts of their victims. To sum up: A shaman could heal, oraculate, and provide for the magical strengthening and cleansing of warriors. Shamans are colorful figures who require more description, especially women shamans, whom we will study later.

Figure 1.6 Mokeiyu initiation dance, Sambia Valley 1975

Tali and Kanteilo once told me an old myth that explains how Sambia followed the east-to-west movement of the sun from their ancestral territory at Kokona, long ago, to the present-day valley. The sun bore them pandanus fruit and arrows but no stone war clubs. They could not defend themselves! A strange oversight, for Sambia refer to the sun as "our father," the provider of all things—except for the first war club. They had to acquire such weapons from neighboring tribes. Why is this? Sambia needed their neighbors because legends say they fled their ancestral home following a great war, only to enter the valley and war against its true owners, the Yulami. Soon they were at war with their neighbors too. In short, war was perpetual. Perhaps this myth mirrors the fact that Sambia always had two different types of warfare going on: the one, with bow and arrow; the other (more deadly) with stone clubs, applied to other tribes, against whom they killed and raped. Remember that Sambia men were not considered masculine until they had killed a man and stolen a woman as one of their wives. And perhaps it was not until they came to the Sambia Valley that their environment forced them into just as deadly intratribal war, using stone clubs as weapons against neighbors. This was a harsh reality, yet this is how Sambia associate their origins with ancient warfare and their need to be strong to survive. Therefore, in that timeless realm of ritual, the old fear of a necessity for war still reigns, a theme we shall see reflected constantly in the next chapter.

2/Warfare and Cultural Life

You are asked to grant as a fact that several generations ago—225 years, in fact—bands of fierce warriors and their families, perhaps refugees of a great war in Papua or perhaps fed up with too much war, ventured from the Papuan coast across unknown swamps and mountain valleys to a new mountain fortress, there to chase out a handful of indigenous hunting and gathering people, and settle. They were small in number, unorthodox, and weak, ancestors of the present-day Sambia. Their cultural creation was an exceptional sexual culture adapted to a world of constant war.

Warfare was the ultimate reality, transcending and influencing everything else in the sense that none controlled its impact. The fear of war breaking out at any time conditioned an aggressive and sometimes paranoid masculine world-view, the misogyny with which men related to women, their religion, and cultural institutions at large.

The pioneers founded tiny hamlets atop steep mountain ridges for defense. Using stone axes they hacked out the jungle, cleared land, and planted the first gardens. Until the harvest, hunting and foraging provided the only food. Death from sickness, accidents, and famine eliminated many, and Sambia say only the strongest survived. Their famous ancestor and culture hero, Numboolyu, lived, loved, and warred during this time. Legends say he founded the great cultural institutions, including the initiation rites; performed miraculous feats; and fathered many children. He survived his peers; indeed, the name Numboolyu means "he who outlived others in a great plague." Two villages were eventually founded and soon they were at war. Thus began present-day Sambia society.

"A WAR IS GOING ON"

Sambia made being a warrior and war leader, and being aggressive and "top dog" in battle, the supreme measure of a man's place in the world and the status and prestige of his social relationships in it. This meaning system, and its associated mythology, what the great French anthropologist Maurice Godelier

(1986) refers to as the "Great Man" complex in New Guinea, still underlies much of Sambia masculinity and society after decades of change (Herdt 2003). For war had always been, as far as Sambia had known, chronic, widespread, and destructive. Warfare appropriated much time and resources: Men spent much of their lives keeping watch against surprise attack and preparing for it (for example, by making weapons), not to mention the long periods in battle and on war parties. Masculine prestige came from one's reputation as a warrior. In so many ways, great and small, men competed with one another for the social praise they constantly sought. Hence, from the time of their youth, men tried to establish their reputations as able marksmen, hunters, and war leaders (*aamooluku*).

A war is going on: This idea, a powerful feeling—call it partly fear and partly perception—created vigilance bordering on paranoia, the psychological sense that war could break out at any time. Many are the stories of children and adults telling of their first memory as fleeing the village as it was invaded. Political assassinations (either actual or attributed to sorcery) were common-place. War leaders dominated the scene. When they happened to be shamans (*kwooluku*), their magic and spirit familiars made them doubly powerful. Women needed armed guards to escort them to their gardens for the same reason. Children could not play outside the hamlet since parents feared they would be easy targets for payback killings due to the strong value on blood revenge. Men watched their interactions with their wives closely for fear of sorcery practiced by the women in sympathy with their enemies should war break out. When such violence can erupt at any time, one remains constantly on guard.

Sir Kenneth Dover (1978: 122), the great scholar of the Ancient Greeks, once referred to how Spartan communities were organized "permanently like an army in training," a description that captures the essence of Sambia village life. Sambia grew up with a deep anxiety about having to defend their homesteads with nothing but courage and stone weapons. From childhood onward the hamlets' warriorhood, constant battles, and war tales molded masculine education. This unpredictable environment promoted a defensive and anxious style of parenting reinforced by perceptions of one's own parents: of one's mother, who clutches one during assaults on the hamlet; and of one's father, who leaves the household to fight, returning with wounds or glory, or not returning at all. The suspiciousness infects one's father, who is also wary of one's mother, since she is "naturally" polluting and comes from a hostile hamlet. Beyond the hamlet, who is not regarded as potentially dangerous? The problems surrounding these preparations plague everyone, but they are felt most deeply by men. Even today men are the more suspicious Sambia citizens. In both group situations and individual relationships, a wrong or an insult (imagined or real) can provoke quick violence. Without written laws, police, or courts, men must rely on their own might and their supporters in defending themselves. The grudges of the past smolder and die slowly. Men are sensitive to abusive language, which makes people cautious even of their words for fear they may unleash violence, or that other secret treachery, sorcery.

Beyond the hamlet, all groups were potentially hostile. In such a world the Sambia, like all Melanesians, as Theodore Schwartz (1973: 161) once suggested, must determine "[w]ho can be trusted? The question is crucial for any culture."[1] This question permeates many Sambia stories about the past. In the behavioral environment of historic Sambia society, fear of attack always surrounded travel and everyday life.

The need to rely on one's wits, brawn, and stone weapons creates a watchful anxiety among Sambia men that is alien to most middle-class Americans. Is it not difficult for the middle-class–comforted American to appreciate the effects of this gut-level anxiety, which, after years, becomes a constant murmur in one's insides? (I am sadly reminded after 9/11 and the disastrous attack on the World Trade Center in New York that terrorism has created a new awareness among us of the sense that a war is always going on.) But think of close brushes with death, as from accidents, and how these make us watchful about the feared situation of the accident for days afterward.

The unpredictability and constant need for preparedness make men aggressive in their worldview. Perhaps this is an inevitable response to both "projected and perceived enemies." People develop a social paranoia that becomes a "variable made constant, *a principle that cannot be relaxed*" (Schwartz 1973: 163, emphasis mine). This idea helps us to calculate what the experience of chronic war might have been like. When something is stressed so much, it invades every part of life, gradually creating—from routine conversation and activities—the warrior values that permeate one's outlook on society and the universe. Let us now turn to warfare, the concept of strength, and the associated male values that Sambia identify with the complex of war.

JERUNGDU AND THE MEN'S WORLD

If we would gauge the inner workings of Sambia society through the strivings of its men toward an ideal of masculinity—a state of being both chosen and necessary—we would discover that Sambia belong to that group of warrior cultures that stress ideas about strength. We then must focus our sights on understanding their single most powerful concept: *jerungdu.*

Jerungdu is physical (biologic) strength, the supreme essence of maleness in body, personality, and spirit. The concept subsumes hardness and resolve, bravery and warlike exploits, among its connotations. *Jerungdu* means the strength to do battle: not just to defend oneself, one's family, and property but to prove or reaffirm the fact of one's masculine powers. Like a silent power behind the throne, ideals of *jerungdu* embody the essence of a masculine state of being, a

---

[1]Schwartz (1973: 157) states further: "The paranoid ethos in Melanesia derived from the uncertainty of life, from the high mortality rate and short life span, from the many births and relatively few surviving children. It depended on the uncertainty of the yield of productive activities. Perhaps more fundamentally for Melanesia the paranoid ethos related to the extreme atomism of social and political life, to the constancy and omnidirectionality of war and raiding, to the uncertainty of village and clan cohesion. In the Melanesian behavioral environment actuality and fantasy are mutually supportive. The effect is the same: the individual both projects his hostility upon his environment and realistically perceives it there. Projections that find confirmation in actual interpersonal hostility remain projections." Out of such conditions come suspiciousness that pervades their thoughts and even their dreams.

guide for rhetorically typecasting all others, and the socially necessary way to behave. *Jerungdu* speaks to the hard reality of male existence.

Even though *jerungdu* is believed crucial for the creation and maintenance of masculinity, it is an outstanding problem of male development that this state of being is not natural or innate; it must be achieved. We must understand this belief in its social context.

Jerungdu is a bodily essence, a substance akin to life force. At bedrock, it is semen *(kweikoonbooku)* that bestows this power. *Jerungdu* is thus a substance uniquely male, produced and transmitted only by men. Here is a simple example. My informant, Tali, when talking about *jerungdu,* said this: "A woman—she has no *jerungdu.* A boy has none. That [*jerungdu*] of a man—semen—they have none of that." Semen creates what Sambia call the "hard" parts of human anatomy: bones and muscle and skin tissue, as well as the brain, spinal column, hair, and fingernails. *Jerungdu* is observable, too, in the virile qualities of large physique, taut skin, shiny face and nose, and sharp eyes. The secondary sex traits of puberty likewise stem from semen (not from sperm: Sambia do not recognize conception, as we know it). Semen stimulates the growth of these masculine qualities, which, together with the capacity to ejaculate and the willingness to do battle, constitute the culturally shared gender signs of *jerungdu.*

Above all else, the ideals and sentiments of *jerungdu* lead to dominance behavior: Males must constantly strive to seem manly. In its simplest form, this is because society—one's parents, siblings, and peers—demands that a male demonstrate his strength to reap the benefits of being a fully masculine adult. It is also because a man believes his life force and existence hinge on possessing abundant *jerungdu.* This is why the individual is motivated to dominate in warfare and in sexual intercourse. Sambia men (like men elsewhere) rely upon their culture—values, symbols, and myths other men accept—to justify their action for the sake of their own *jerungdu.* And there are conflict, sour grapes, and cruelty in Sambia life as a result. Yet there are also care and pageantry in Sambia relationships.

I use *dominance behavior* as a descriptive concept in relation to *behavioral outcomes:* the subjective principle that, as a result of his interactions with others, a man should be perceived as more masculine and stronger (possessing more *jerungdu*) than they are. Dominance is necessary to defend the community and accomplish what needs doing. For these reasons, *jerungdu is* not only the key principle of all masculine behavior; it represents a principle of the male cult that can never be relaxed.[2]

MARRIAGE AND SEXUAL ANTAGONISM

Marriage among the Sambia was a challenge of politics and war, often involving a political arrangement between groups who were hostile. *Sexual antagonism* is the term that has been applied to this complex sexual and gender politics in New Guinea societies (Langness 1967). Sexual antagonism complicated

---

[2]Throughout the text, *jerungdu* and "strength" are used interchangeably in this sense; other connotations will be annotated as appropriate.

virtually all gender relations and made marriage unstable. All men and women had to marry and have children to be esteemed as whole people. Men had far more rights than women in this political game, but men as well were traditionally assigned a wife for marriage. Men who came from powerful villages and clans had the upper hand. Historically women were in short supply among the Sambia, since polygyny allows powerful and senior men to take several wives at the expense of weaker men. Moreover, there was a preference for the firstborn to be a boy, and female infanticide was practiced. Adding to this problem, wives must be obtained from outside one's clan and preferably beyond one's hamlet. So this means women must be traded—sometimes against their will—with other, often hostile groups, in unstable political circumstances. Virtually all marriage was between people in the valley, for intertribal marriage was very rare. Two forms of marriage contract predominate: infant betrothal and brother–sister exchange; the other type, bride service, is a weak third.

Infant betrothal *(ichinyu)* was the most honored, complicated, and traditional marriage practice. It is an old-fashioned custom based in the giving of meat gifts to a woman at the birth of her daughter. Infant betrothal once accounted for upward of 40 percent of all marriages in Upper Sambia Valley hamlets. Today, it is unusual and has largely been replaced by bridge wealth marriage, as explained later. Traditionally however, infant betrothal was common as a means of alliance between the component clans of a hamlet and between more stable and allied villages. It created political alignments of in-laws between these neighboring hamlets. The rule is that a woman obtained as a wife through infant betrothal must be replaced—her daughter or another woman returned by the man recipient or the donor clan group—in the next generation. Besides this expected reciprocity, infant betrothal warms up relations between affines, as in-laws are expected to provide food gifts, render assistance, and avoid direct battle with each other in warfare. More broadly, it tends to solidify intrahamlet unity and moderate interhamlet relationships. However, the question always remains: Will such-and-such group give us back a woman in the next generation?

Brother–sister exchange contracts *(yandiandi)* were less valued socially than infant betrothal, though sister exchange is the more pragmatic and numerous of all presently existing marriages. The principle is simple and less troublesome politically: Two individual men (usually acting in concert with their clan brothers) arrange to exchange their sisters (biological or classificatory) as wives to each other. But if for some reason one of the men objects to marrying the woman offered, then he may proceed differently. He can negotiate with a third party to obtain a different woman, trading the woman of the donor group to the third party to conclude the exchange and have a wife. Sometimes, then, as many as six clans are involved in sister-exchange marriage. If there is a discrepancy in the ages of the women's brothers, an exchange is concluded with the older man's promise of his sister later to come to the immature male. For example, a marriage-aged man may arrange to marry the older, marriage-aged sister of a boy; the older man then promises to give his younger sister (or another substitute clan sister) to that boy for marriage after his puberty. This introduces the uncertainty of future conditions, as in infant betrothal. The ideal is for men of equal age to have an immediate transaction (though often discussed for months or even years in advance) with no further obligation on their part. The advantages are obvious despite the lack of pomp and ceremony accompanying infant-betrothal marriage.

The third form of marriage contract was bride service. If a man was desperate, had no claims on infant girls or available sisters (or willing clansmen to help him with such) for obtaining a wife, he could ingratiate himself to an older man with daughters or sisters in the hope (not promise) that eventually one will be given *(yashyotwi)* to him. This is an uncommon practice. For one thing, Sambia men are too proud to ingratiate themselves easily. When it occurs, however, the expectation is the same as for infant betrothal: Eventually, the recipient must return a daughter or other marriageable woman to his father-in-law's group.

Though most rare of all, wife stealing was a pervasive male fantasy. If one was man enough and brave enough, he might try to steal the woman of another group. Wife-stealing inside the valley was rare but not unknown; indeed, it was so unusual that I would omit it except for its glorified mythology: Men feel that, among the best of warriors, it should be counted a caring ideal for them to someday, somewhere, steal the woman of an enemy after doing him in. Wife stealing was thus a male fantasy of ultimate conquest. (In Upper Sambia hamlets I knew of only a handful of such wives taken over the last two generations.) There is a big payoff for the risks, of course: What is stolen need never be returned.

Since the mid-1970s another form of marriage has been introduced: bride wealth. A man and his clan mates will "pay" for a bride. In a few short years this practice dramatically increased in frequency, to become the norm, as discussed in Chapter 6.

Not only the character of Sambia social organization but also the ideals of masculinity are deeply wedded to this structure of types of marriage. The structural currents are twofold: Obtain a wife by infant betrothal and take on a *delayed-exchange* obligation in the next generation; contract a brother–sister marriage and this *direct exchange* requires no further obligation. Either case holds an implied willingness to create social bonds with an individual and/or his group. Sambia refer to this longstanding relationship between neighboring hamlets as *ninbuninyaalum* ("sister's husband, my in-laws"). Later we will see how ritual homosexuality reflects such alliances. In many ways marriage relationships provide a "push" to Sambia society and its individuals along a path toward intergroup stability. Yet, the violence of war and the concept of *jerungdu* are factors of dominating that tend to pull apart and destabilize the society. For instance, what will become of the boy whose older brother-in-law promised him a wife in a sister-exchange contract but fails to deliver? Will the boy as a man seek revenge, which leads to warfare? The awareness of this "push" and "pull" in Sambia masculine behavior is a definite concern in growing up and in being initiated.

Masculine apprehension is also embedded deeply in male-female relationships, which are highly associated with the economic division of labor. Men feel that maleness is a higher, cleaner, better essence of nature than femaleness; women are only there. Women feel the men are too aggressive and somewhat lazy, yet men must be reckoned with. Masculinity is both a social framework of perceptions and a cultural way of acting, and these emerge in two contrary settings: the women's houses and the men's clubhouse.

Femininity is associated only with the women's houses and the menstrual hut. Women have their own world, which is secret in some respects and off-limits to men. Ritual and military activities derive from the clubhouse, which forms a barrier between men and women. Women are responsible for supplying most garden food, especially during time of war. They were in the past no doubt cynical of these arrangements, since nowadays some women scoff at the men's preoccupation with old war tales. Even men recall that they tired of the constant fighting that disrupted gardening and hunting, making food scarce. But it is the nature of female essence that motivates men's antagonism toward women.

Men cling to a view that masculinity can be depleted: a belief that the male body runs down and wears out, due to the notion of a short supply of semen, *jerungdu*. Women extract this, sapping a man's substance. Through intercourse a wife is believed to draw selfishly on her husband's substance, redoubling her own strength. "No wonder women are healthy and outlive us," men say. And recall that wives are of other groups, often from potential enemy hamlets, so they cannot be trusted. Yet only a wife and children bring personhood and full masculinity. Here we have a basic tension that is central to the male ethos.

Women's sexuality has mysterious origins diametrically opposed to that of men's. Men have body strength sapped to produce children, which depletes them, inducing weakness, old age, and death. On the other hand, men feel women bear children and yet remain strong and vital, outliving one and then another husband, to remarry without remorse for insatiable sexual desire and longevity. Note that this view pertains to *marriageable* women; mothers and sisters are not feared in this way. However, the men generalize: They not only regard women as hostile, even evil, but ironically they see females as inferior, even though women's natural powers enable them to procreate and outlive men. We will study these contradictions more fully in the following chapter.

A wife thus brings a man maturity, food, a home, and heirs, all necessary for full manhood. A wife is a man's sexual property, as other men recognize. She draws him into social relationships with others, including in-laws. Relationships to in-laws are demanding and also rewarding. Children bring full adult status to both husband and wife, but that is not all. Sambia do not live only for the enjoyment of their offspring, yet one finds it difficult to imagine them without the bright faces of their children, who so innocently break through the heavy formality of men and women. Sambia look down upon a barren woman and later in life pity her for her condition. Men deny sterility in themselves. Jealous male suitors who commit sorcery on the female to spite the marriage are usually blamed. Yet men also recognize barren women as full-time sexual partners, something a nursing mother cannot be. No woman goes unmarried for long. But some men do. And without the advantages of marriage, men are nothing. The qualities of Sambia male-female relations may be seen as consequences of warfare, sexual antagonism, gender stereotyping, the male concept of *jerungdu,* and the aggressive behavior deriving from its socialization.

MASCULINE VALUES AND GENDER STEREOTYPES

A company of warriors has but a handful of ruling stereotypes. This restrictiveness is understandable: Warriorhood requires hard standards of conduct that keep the ranks in line. Moreover, military rules create *esprit de corps;* they also maintain allegiance to the military club by creating a safe haven for masculinity (Tuzin 1997). Such stereotypes affect the wider society, although their restrictions fall hardest on men since women here do not fight in war. Military orders and such standards are common in most New Guinea Highland societies (see Herdt 2003; Knauft 1999; Koch 1974; Langness 1972; Meggitt 1977; Read 1954; Sillitoe 1998). Such stereotypes manage Sambia social behavior and have many consequences. Gender stereotypes also dictate attitudes about one's position in sexual intercourse. Masculine stereotypes, whether in serious rhetoric or personal jokes, control the degrees of sexual freedom in Sambia society.

The gender stereotypes are thoroughly structured in men's thinking, speech, and institutions. They can be described in two ways: as a set of characteristic gender identity states, *ways of being* male or female; and as a set of distinctive gender statuses, *ways of acting* masculine or feminine. Three verbal categories of being stand out most: *jerungdu,* being strong; *havaltnu,* being equivalent (symmetrical, competitive); and *wogaanyu,* being unmanly (weak, passive). When applied as judgments to others' behavior, the gender stereotypes have strong effects. They occur in both male and female thought, but are most marked in males. Such labeling is usually specific to particular acts in a situation, so it characterizes the situational behavior of individuals rather than their permanent state of being. When a boy shows fear of a masculine act like climbing trees to hunt possum, for example, he will be called *wogaanyu.* Besides this, there are two prominent male-gender role models: the *aamooluku* (war leader) and the *wusaatu* (rubbish man). Ideal types they are but no less powerful because of that. There is a third type, too, the *aambei-wutnyi* (female kind), meaning a gentle man, who is akin to our label of sissy; but it is seldom used, being a "quiet category." These labels and sex-role types crosscut all other social, kinship, or ritual status terms among males, from small boys to elders. So the identity categories apply to all males regardless of their age, rank, ritual status, and reproductive status, and are powerful mechanisms for self-control and social regulation. What is the cultural logic of these gender stereotypes?

The essence of *jerungdu*—the state of being physically strong—is observable in one's behavior and everyday deeds. In its highest form, *jerungdu* is like our notion of prowess in battle; in its crass form, it means to be a big and strong man. Yet *jerungdu* also aims men toward masculine competence (as defined by Sambia culture) in hunting, ritual, and sex. It drives men to be the strongest, bravest, and best. Stated simply, *jerungdu* means pure masculinity.

Havaltnu, meaning "to be the same", provides a more complex counterpoint to the concept *jerungdu. Havaltnu* can be translated as "like kind" or "equivalent," according to the speaker and the context. Age-mates are believed to be *like kind.* Indeed, we would not go far wrong in seeing age-mates as *sine qua non* persons who must be equivalent. The same idea applies to female age-mates too, though not as rigorously. Equivalence stems from age-mates being of the same sex and having been born in the same time period, therefore being roughly of the same physical size and capacities. These characteristics give rise to an expectation that age-mates should be biologically and socially alike.

Initiation formalizes this standard. Age-mate A is expected to match age-mate B in all accomplishments; so this norm creates competition between them. By contrast, if A's achievements (including physical growth) are not matched by B in scaling trees or marksmanship, then B is socially diminished by comparison to A in the eyes of others. Hence, there is always a tension between age-mates because they face constant comparison.

That men can be ridiculed in everyday life for their masculine failings testifies to the relentless stress placed on conformity to male ideals. Brief mention of the third verbal category, *wogaanyu*, will highlight this point. *Wogaanyu* has a wide range of negative connotations specifying that various acts are unmanly and therefore shameful *(wungulu)*. Physical weakness, fear, laziness, and neglect of ritual or age-mate obligations are all discrediting acts that are labeled *wogaanyu*. Cowardice is most shameful of all. To call someone *wogaanyu* is an insult in face-to-face encounters. It can provoke anger, shame, or both in the accused, depending on the status and social bonds between the two men. A father or brother can admonish another man in a way an age-mate dares not. The war leader and rubbish man provide the opposing models for this evaluation. Boys and men are evaluated using these stereotypes; if found lacking, the stigma of the *wogaanyu* accusation falls on them. Even a young war leader's failures could be labeled this way, if another dared to brave the accusation, tantamount to an insult that could lead to a duel. Yet the accusation need not be made directly. For men, like women, gossip, and their private judgments find currency among them and put pressure on public opinion. Envy and jealousy are no doubt at work in this informal social control process, for when someone grows too strong or too weak, people's words help keep that person in line. Being a war leader or simply being male, therefore, demands scrupulous attention to face-to-face interactions at all times, lest a man's behavior betray any sign of unmanly weakness.

Somewhere in a male's development, the signs pointing to a boy's being a war leader or a rubbish man change from being temporary labels into more binding stereotypes. The symptom is no longer odd-man-out; it is what usually happens and becomes expected. Constant acts labeled *jerungdu* by others transform a man into a *strong man*. Being consistently brave in battle leads to being called a *war leader*. Continued acts of weakness lead others to call someone a *rubbish man*, which is defined mainly by being afraid of fights. Therefore, weakness and strength are ultimately judged by perceptions of a man's prowess in battle. Boys are expected to model themselves after the war leader and to despise the rubbish man. I am speaking of idealizations, not actual behavior. In reality, Sambia recognize that men are weak or strong, rubbish men or war leaders, without usually saying so. Here, personal and kinship sentiments intervene, for one may note that a paternal uncle is a rubbish man and still value him affectionately as a hamlet elder. (In the culture of my childhood—midwestern America, c. 1955—a similar contrast was made between "musclemen" and "sissies," between weakness and strength.)

War leader (aamooluku) is a label assigned to fight leaders, skilled hunters, and virile men, and he is a highly romanticized figure, a Great Man. All true warriors are believed to be potent in a double sense: The obvious one is that warriors are surefooted and efficient in manly endeavors. The other sense is of a kind of liquidity or abundance of body fluids—sweat, mucus, blood, urine, and especially semen—which are noticeable and symptomatic signs of *jerungdu*. Sambia believe the war leader has a generous seminal emission every time he ejaculates. Yet please note—this male essence is contained within a hard, tough, pointed, lean body, taller and bigger than most. Sambia say that the war leader even has an erection going into battle! The war leader should be physically big: broad shouldered and barrel chested; with taut skin, sharp eyes, abundant body hair, and a small waist, abdomen, and buttocks. (A male infant born with body hair is felt to hold promise of being a Great Man.) The war leader as a boy is distinguished by his sharp shooting; love of hunting (birds); being pugnacious, easily angered, and quarrelsome (he enjoys fighting with other children); and, appropriately enough, a tough quietness. This quietness—the Sambia word is *mangu-tetnyi*—has qualities of arrogance, tight-lipped pragmatism, proud carriage, and humorlessness. Initiates are punished for laughing in public, and men rarely crack jokes except in private with their cronies. War leaders do not chatter or make idle conversation, that is too feminine.

There is a distinctly antisocial flavor in the extreme form of these traits. Swashbuckling and fearless, war leaders enjoy aggressive confrontations and battles. In their religious belief, Sambia hold that deceased war leaders become the fearsome forest spirits, the *ikeiaru*. Rubbish men never become that. War leaders are proud. They cannot bear being shamed, and they become arrogant and withdrawn when ignored. They may be silent in the presence of elder authorities, but they are cagey and distrusted by equals. Here is an apparent paradox I have noticed in several war leaders: Though usually quiet, they are demonstrative when greeting me, grabbing hold of me, offering big smiles (empty smiles) and sticky praise, touching my body, searching me (frisking me). Sambia, too, note this: The war leader "butters you up," but later, in a battle, "It's you he'll aim toward killing," they say.

But there is a less extreme form of this ideal. Sambia refer respectfully to their older war leaders as the "mother of our hamlet." This image conveys the sense of how the war leader "guards the doorway" (the entrance within the barricades) to the hamlet and is its true protector. All of a war leader's aggressiveness and spite—his *jerungdu*—is to be aimed beyond his group toward enemies. In this sense, too, older war leaders who have proven themselves can relax more as others come up through the ranks.

Lastly, war leaders are womanizers but of a special kind. They do not love women—they lust for conquest and use of women as objects. Bearing the very face of manliness, they prefer men and the company of men. They are thought to have been rapacious fellators as boys (hence, they possess abundant semen and *jerungdu*). As bachelors, they do not leave boys alone and enjoy using younger initiates as an erotic outlet whenever the need presents itself. They are also felt to attract women easily, copulating with wives as soon as it is possible

them. Imitating their seniors, boys label one another as weak or strong, as rubbish men or war leaders. Thus, initiates are being prepared for battle.

It was a dangerous step toward adulthood that led initiates directly into bow fighting. Eventually they fought against peers, sometimes those from nearby hamlets with whom they had engaged in the earlier games. Usually this began when they were second-stage initiates. Instructed and supervised by father or brothers or war leaders, the initiates were praised for "standing strong" to protect the hamlet. When the heat was on and the battle thickened, however, they were removed behind the front line of the older, experienced warriors, all except the best of them, the initiates who would distinguish themselves. With experience and age, they became better bowmen and took risks, until finally the bow fight had become for them the reality of their fathers, a military game whose essence was competition for strength. Each boy's opponents were the youths who helped initiate the boy; sexual contact was appropriate only with them, and eventually he could seek a wife among their groups. Each of these spheres—ritualized fights, ritualized homosexual fellatio and initiation, and marriage—became a part of the contest for manhood.

Underlying each one of these activities is a stylized masculine protest: *"Mi aatmwunu tokwuno, mi aambelu-maiyo!"* ("I am a man, not a woman!") In such terms elders still coach the meaning of the warrior decorations first placed on boys at initiation. This then returns us to the political context.

Despite this harsh declaration, the need of men to rationalize local war fatalities indicates that local groups sought to contain warfare. The presence of a local fight ground was a key symbol of the regulation. The fight ground parallels the confederacy dance ground; they are only a few hundred yards apart in the Upper Sambia Valley. Both are signs of ritual relationship: Neighboring hamlets were opponents, as well as some of them in-laws. The men were initiated on the same dance ground at the first-stage initiation and became members of an age-set. They had conflicting loyalties: first to their clansmen, then to in-laws, and usually last to their age-mates in other hamlets. Boys owed their primary allegiance to fellow clansmen. Fighting could take place between any of the hamlets, but the most frequent and deadly bow fights engaged nearby hamlets of different phratries.

Numerous marriage relationships between two hamlets create a political alliance between the in-laws. I mean by "alliance" nothing more than this: Individual men aided and were indebted to their male in-laws in those hamlets, so the more in-laws in two hamlets, the greater their reluctance to feud with each other. One norm prevailed in bow fighting: A man should not shoot an in-law. In-laws often helped each other in battles, especially when their own hamlets were uncommitted third parties to fights elsewhere. In time, marriage created kinship bonds (nieces, nephews, aunts, uncles, and cousins) that helped soften animosities when they flared up. But such alliances are unstable because bonds of blood are stronger than marital bonds for Sambia. Their weakness politically was the weakness of the confederacy itself. In the Sambia Valley these marital alliances, like the initiation confederacy alignments, crosscut phratry boundaries. Hamlets of the same phratry and confederacy were least likely to fight with bows. Conversely, hamlets of different phratries without in-law ties were most susceptible to fights. Finally, aligned hamlets were a potential refuge in case of attack or when fighting erupted inside the hamlet.

When a bow fight escalated into a broader engagement in the valley, Sambia called it a "big fight." Killings were more likely then, and leaders made plans for ambushes and raids. Shamans provided protection for warriors in nightly ceremonies and practiced lethal sorcery upon the enemies. Women and children were hidden in the hamlet stockade.

There were two reasons why a bow fight got out of hand, and both pertained to bloodshed. First, big fights nearly always sprang from a fatality. The slain warrior's group would demand blood revenge. Second, the scale of fighting broadened as both sides called on other hamlets for support. In the Sambia Valley big fights were (like confederacy initiations) invariably interphratry conflicts that evolved from bow fighting between two hamlets of different phratries. They too could begin over a variety of reasons, such as adultery, property disputes, or insulting conduct.

Even in the narrow sweep of the Sambia Valley, big fights were serious enough to provoke attacks on neighboring hamlets. Over the past 40 years, Nilangu hamlet has been besieged twice like this, whereas Pundei suffered at least half a dozen separate assaults. Killings from group attacks and individual ambushes did occur. Nilangu is nearly impenetrable because of its high and isolated location near forestland; its warriors also had the fiercest reputation in the area, were the most sought-after allies, and successfully defended the hamlet, which has never been invaded. Pundei is less defensible, however, because of its broad ridge exposed on two sides and its vulnerable trails exposed to attack by the neighboring Wantukiu tribe. It has been invaded twice in recent memory. In seven drawn-out big fights between phratries, at least one man was killed in each, and sometimes as many as four or five people were killed, including at least two known instances of women being killed. (This does not include other warriors who died later from wounds.) How long did such big fights last? They lasted from a week (one instance), to a few weeks (two instances), to several months (two instances), to over a year (one instance). Fighting did not occur every day, but it could erupt at any time. This possibility kept men prepared.

Bow fights were historically common. Australian patrol officers noted that between 1960 and 1964, at least a dozen reports of fights occurred, and this is surely an incomplete record. Intertribal raids were more rare. I do not have a complete total because they were also launched by different Sambia hamlets outside the valley, but my own local count indicates at least 10 major raids over the past 50 years.

After these big fights broke out, each side sought help from kin and in-laws in other hamlets. Men of ancestral phratries were brought in. Supporting war parties from the outside usually numbered no more than 25 men. These seem like small reinforcements, but remember that such forces still exceeded the warriorhood of many Sambia hamlets, which might count no more than 10 adult male fighters. The foreign and indigenous warriors fought together as a single line. The former usually stayed in the men's house of their kin. The men of one's phratry or ancestral phratry, therefore, were potential military reinforcements, and hamlets counted upon them at wartime. Phratry alignments in this sense served to check aggression by men of another phratry.

Yet the involvement of alien warriors also escalated the conflict into a bigger fight. When one side called on its supporters, it compelled its opponents to do likewise. The escalation in the use of outsiders was more destructive because these men, as strangers fighting enemies, carried deadlier weapons. Why did imported war parties always carry stone clubs and axes, the armaments of deadly raids? A young warrior from an ancestral (outside) phratry, for example, could use the battle as a means of confirming his manhood following third-stage initiation. This is indeed how Sambia Valley men regarded their own war parties that supported external allies. Alien warriors, even though they were Sambia tribesmen, felt little compunction about wounding fellow tribesmen to whom they were unrelated either as kin or age-mates, which increased the chance of killings. Only when the outside recruits left could the scale of fighting be reduced. External supporters were therefore a key source of military strength but also a catalyst for the proliferation of intratribal warfare. One historical example will illustrate this process and serve also to clarify the behavioral environment of war.

Since earliest contact (c. 1957), Sambia were known as troublesome and warring, feared by surrounding tribes despite their small numbers. Like similar Anga groups on the Papuan Coast, they were feared because of their secretive and deadly guerrilla raids, after which they disappeared into forests, making it impossible to catch them. Australian patrol officers failed to hunt them out, since whole villages hid in the forest when the police forces appeared.

Eventually, after several years of contacts with neighboring tribes, the government decided to use dramatic displays to frighten the Upper Sambia hamlets. An Australian man, Patrol Officer D. K. Gordon, took it upon himself to personally stop the warfare among the Sambia. He began by jailing Kwol, a fierce Nilangu warrior captured in battle. Gordon wanted to intimidate the man's fellow warriors, so Kwol was jailed, the first Sambia to hold this dubious distinction. Even today Kwol still gripes over his treatment. Gordon's warning went unheeded, however. This led to the last big fight between Upper Sambia, which I will describe here because it was well documented by Gordon in 1964.

Fighting persisted among Sambia communities throughout 1963. Men did not fully comprehend the implications of Kwol's earlier jailing that year. By April 1964, Gordon learned of more fighting in the Sambia Valley. During a regular reconnaissance patrol, he accidentally stumbled on a raging battle (which began the day before his arrival). He wrote that there had been "four recent outbreaks" of warfare in the Sambia Valley during the weeks before his visit. He witnessed fighting in which the Seboolu phratry was pitted against the Wunyu-Sambia phratry. This interphratry conflict had occurred many times before. Gordon noted of one big fight, moreover, that Nilangu and its phratry sister hamlet were allied against Pundei and its sister hamlet. Gordon personally counted 10 woundings in that battle. Again, he mentions that a "different battle" (but otherwise unexplained) had recently taken place between Wunjepti and Kwoli, two other nearby hamlets in the valley.

Gordon questioned the warriors about the cause of the Upper Sambia battle. Their reports left him incredulous. They spoke of a "theft of customs" and "washing with water," statements that puzzled him. Many years later I asked the parties involved how the war began. They say it originated from the imitation by the Pundei (Wunyu-Sambia phratry) men of their distant Great River Valley cousins (at Laki hamlet on the Great River Drainage Zone), who were taught to wash themselves with soap and water. Native evangelists working among the Laki at the time preached that to become like Europeans, the Sambia must learn to wash. (Traditionally, Sambia did not bathe or wash with water, and older people and most women still do not do so.) The Seboolu people practice a traditional purification ritual requiring water to be briefly lapped on the body. They thus perceived the actions of the Wunyu-Sambia men as a serious infraction of the norm that groups may not perform the rituals of others. In addition, the Wunyu-Sambia men worsened the injury with insult by asserting that their washing made them "more manly" than the Seboolu. This bravado resulted in the violence. Meanwhile, Gordon devised a scheme: Through a sequence of complex moves, he tricked the warriors into assembling and then he handcuffed them. This resulted in permanent peace.

A reconsideration of this 1964 report sheds light on the interplay of Sambia masculine values and warrior behavior more than 40 years ago. The fight began over the "theft" of Seboolu phratry ritual custom by their opposing phratry. But Sambia on both sides now recognize that this big fight resulted from outright misunderstanding, exacerbated by boasting and pride.

To sum up the incident: The Wunyu-Sambia men (of Pundei hamlet) openly imitated their Laki hamlet kin in an aggressive way, taunting their neighbors. The Seboolu men responded to the perceived insult with a bow fight, mistakenly interpreting the washing behavior as a theft of their ritual rights, an understandable but sad comedy of errors. This escalated the fighting, pitting the phratries against each another. And to worsen the situation, the Wunyu-Sambia men castigated their Seboolu opponents as rubbish men. Such double insults drew a wide-scale call to arms. In their eyes, the Selpoolu men felt that they had only one real choice: Either they raised their bows, revenging their pride; or they passively accepted public humiliation. They chose violence. Sixteen men were wounded in only a day of skirmishing, but they preferred open war, even death, over domination by their enemies.

The bloodshed of big fights wrought chaos in interhamlet relationships that only a truce ceremony could remedy. Truces were infrequent and usually short-lived. The ceremony is customarily held on the fight ground, which suggests several things. Though men of nearby hamlets should avoid killing, deaths still occurred, which escalated the fighting. The parties could then use the truce to halt the fighting, restoring balance with compensation payments. The ceremony itself was simple enough: The war leaders and warriors on both sides shook hands, exchanged equivalent amounts of cowrie shells, and then spat ginger (mixed with yellow root) on one another's faces and torsos. This latter gesture dispelled the ghosts of slain warriors, since ghosts dislike the pungent smell of ginger; moreover, the ginger is here transmitted through the saliva of their own kinsmen, whom they would not strike. This implies, furthermore, a degree of mutual trust; one's saliva contains an aspect of one's soul substance, so there must not be lingering fears of retaliatory sorcery. In a more complex truce, ritual sacrifice using meat gifts was required. If the measure of human deaths was unequal, then compensation payments were paid. Groups were reluctant to stop fighting before blood revenge was exacted, for compensation was poorly developed and an unsatisfactory substitute for the slain, which often had to be accepted from a position of weakness: After the Sambia fought for long periods, food grew scarce because gardening had not been done. And no doubt the initial excitement of the conflict had gone.

The truce was a stylized armistice that contained an important message about local political cooperation. It allowed women to return to their gardens and initiates to go to other villages to meet with age-mates and have sexual contacts with bachelors. Peace permitted the elders on both sides to cement marriage commitments or negotiate for future ones. Finally, large-scale war and peace had unforeseen effects on the collective organization of initiation by neighboring hamlets, since effective interphratry collective initiations required peace.

Lastly, and most deadly, there was intertribal warfare. The war parties of Sambia who journeyed to enemy tribes did so to kill and destroy. This brand of war was the most serious of all. It was waged against true enemies, called *iku-mamulu,* "man-eaters." Killings were an expected part of guerrilla raids. Enemy women were sometimes taken as captive brides. Other women and children were put to death in dawn massacres in enemy hamlets. Sambia marauded most of the tribes surrounding them and were attacked in retaliation. Thus, at various periods over the past 50 years, wars have been fought with the South Fore (west), the Baruya (northeast), the Amdi (east), the Yagwoia (southeast), the hinterland Papuans (south), and the Western Wantukiu (north). The conflict never really stopped, since no concept of truce applied beyond the valley. The most hated enemies were the Amdi, a Baruya-speaking tribe who were, legend says, the cause of the original immigrations into the Sambia Valley; and the Fore, whom Sambia fear by association with sorcery and cannibalism (see Lindenbaum 1979). The following is a brief tale of one such raid.

Around 1938 a war party from the Sambia hamlets journeyed to the Moonagu hamlet area, in the Sambia River Delta. They were recruited to raid the Matnu hamlets, a distant Sambia-speaking phratry. The Moonagu men wanted revenge for the insults of some Matnu men. The Matnu called the Moonagu "boneless and spineless children." The two sides briefly lofted arrows at each other. Then the Matnu retreated a day or two downstream of the Lower Green River. The Moonagu then recruited about 20 men from half a dozen Sambia Valley hamlets (including 6 from Nilangu). The Sambia men assembled with Moonagu age-mates and distant in-laws in the hamlet of Yuvulu.

The next day this war party slipped into the mountains south and for two days walked downstream of the Lower Green River, a swamp-infested, desolate area famous for its difficult walking, the worst of its kind in the district. They carried their food and slept without fire for fear of being detected. At dawn on the third day the warriors spotted a Matnu hamlet called Chegumulu. They dressed in full warrior regalia to "look like firelight" and strike terror in the unsuspecting villagers. The greater the element of surprise and fear, they felt, the likelier they were to succeed. Arrows were shot through the barricades. The warriors then swarmed inside and immediately bludgeoned several men. Then all of the houses (about 15 in total) were raided. Most of the people inside were killed. Two or three men and their families, however, managed to escape out the back. The men's house was surrounded, and the Sambia ambushed the occupants who tried to escape after it was set afire. The remaining men and initiate warriors were killed (they numbered 12 to 16 in all). Most of the women and children were killed. But 10 of the women (some of whom had babies) were taken prisoner. The bodies of the dead warriors were looted for decorations and weapons. Finally, the entire hamlet was burnt to the ground. Most of the party returned to the Moonagu hamlets.

But a contingent of the warriors tracked the Matnu refugees. The reason is understandable: They wanted to kill the refugees to ensure against the possibility of their future reprisal attacks. They followed their trail over the mountains for a day, to the Lower Green Valley. The Matnu stragglers were there given shelter in a small and distantly related hamlet, Boolu, in exchange for giving two of their women as wives. When the enemy warriors approached Boolu, they were thus greeted with arrows. One of the attackers was wounded before they abandoned their efforts. Meanwhile, back at Yuvulu hamlet among the Moonagu, the captured Matnu women were divided as chattel among warriors of the participating groups. The Moonagu men took seven of the women; the remaining three went as wives to Sambia Valley men. One of these women went to the dead war leader, Mon, of Pundei hamlet. Such are the stories that characterize how Sambia used to live with war.

THE SAMBIA PACIFIED

The bitter wars just described left scars and old scores to settle in the Sambia Valley, and these were still smoldering at the time of first contact with Westerners in the late 1950s. The Australian colonial government sought to pacify all New Guinea groups, and when necessary, it would forcibly intervene to stop warfare. However, these armed colonial attacks were also the undoing of Sambia masculinity in its traditional form. Particularly severe and dramatic for the Sambia was the Australian patrol's assault during the last major warfare. Here is the account of these momentous events, as told to me by one of the warriors involved:

> Another battle flared up, this time between Nilangu and Moonunkwambi [a now extinct neighbor hamlet]. Shortly before, the initiations were held again. Weiyu's age-set was made a part of the cult. No sooner was it done than another battle started, this time with Nilangu torn apart because the men took different sides in an argument over game stolen from a river trap. [This was in 1962.] That argument led to the last great battle. Many men were wounded. It seemed as though it would turn into a big war when the red skins—the government patrol officers—appeared. They seemed to ignore the fighting and went away. But in a few days they returned with a great line of black-skinned police. They built a hut [government rest house] over near Kwoli hamlet and made a speech. A distant Kaimeru man—a Sambia who'd gotten to be a government interpreter—was his translator. They said they wanted to put the men's names in a book, so we were all to assemble the next day. But we were tricked: the

police circled all of us, took our weapons, and put us in handcuffs. It was terribly humiliating.

Forty men were chained, endured a two-day's walk to Mountain Patrol Station, and were jailed. (They were treated as, what is the right metaphor? Savages? Animals?) When one man wanted to defecate, the whole line had to stop and wait for him. This was so shameful for the Sambia, who are terribly shy about toilet training. They had no food. They were kicked and sometimes beaten. In jail they were treated little better. In a few weeks they were released and warned never to fight again. That was in 1964. War was done with.

Several years later some missionaries arrived. They were strange looking and acting, and they wanted to learn the Sambia language. They lived down by the river and made a settlement of their own (KwatSambia) in time. People distrusted them at first but soon came to like them; they never hurt anyone. Moonunkwambi hamlet was abandoned and its people moved into Nilangu, the former pseudo-enemies now living together peacefully. Two years later Mountain Patrol Station was built. Some Sambia helped build the airstrip. Six years later, I arrived in 1974. Nilangu seemed idyllic. People were friendly and war was a living memory. People were glad it was gone. Three initiation cycles have been held since that time. Moondi's was the first in 1968. The next year, 1975, the full initiations you will read about, were performed. They lasted weeks and wore me out. New Guinea was decolonized that year, and it became Papua New Guinea, an independent state. The Sambia individuals you will meet in the following chapters all derive from this culture of war and they adapted themselves to it through the creation of a unique sexual culture, with rituals that enabled people to adapt. Thus the Sambia you meet in the next chapter have undergone a profound transformation of culture in their lifetimes. But for the oldest among them, war still remains the defining reality.

3/Sambia Social Individuals

To know the people of a culture as social individuals is to understand something of their emotions and meanings, their loves and hates, their dreams and fears—in short, what makes them human. Now, looking back over 30 years, it seems incredible that the Sambia were so accessible to me from the start as teachers, friends, and colleagues, not just as actors on the stage of ritual. For me, as an anthropologist, there is a great joy in this part of the project that we call "fieldwork."

In this chapter I will examine the lives of some of the the key people to chart how individual Sambia have grown, matured, come of age, lived out incredible lives, and passed on. Such a process parallels on a different plane how Sambia society itself has been undergoing dramatic transformation into the 21st century. While this case study is focused on Sambia ritual and sexuality, we cannot ignore the distinctiveness of individuals—outstanding war leaders and shamans of yesterday, remarkable men and women and their extraordinary virtues as fathers and mothers, sons and daughters, and leaders of the new culture emerging in the globalizing world of today. In previous chapters we have observed how the setting and male ethos affected pre-colonial warfare, which in turn conditioned gender, sexuality, family life, and adaptation to a climate of war. These factors took shape not only in the great institutions of Sambia society, such as ritual initiation, kinship, and religion, but also in the personalities of its citizens. In this chapter we shall meet some long-time informants, friends, and neighbors, observe how their lives have changed, and sadly mourn the passing of some of them. A portrait cannot do justice to the richness of a life, any more than the newspaper or the web can plumb the depth of diverse realities today, but for those who seek a deeper understanding of these and other Sambia people I have written more extensively elsewhere (Herdt and Stoller, 1990; Herdt 1997, 1999; Herdt and Stolpe 2005).

You will get to meet a few Sambia women and men via cameo portraits. I have selected them to contrast traditional and changing culture and social structure, and the part that each of them plays in Sambia society. These include: the elder, Kanteilo, who is now deceased; the senior female elder and traditional woman shaman, Kaiyunango, who remains the most powerful woman in the village; Penjukwi, a strong woman, who has moved to the coast; my close friend Weiyu, a thrice-married man who is now a village elder; Sakulambei, a powerful shaman and a hermaphrodite whose life has revealed remarkable resilience, and who managed to arrange his own marriage and socially father a son; Moondi, my closest informant and friend whom I observed in his transition growing up and having a family, who is now also deceased; and Danny, a young Sambia man whom I have known since he was a boy, who embodies the new and changing ways of Sambia masculinity in change.

We will concentrate on a few key psychosocial characteristics in each person's life, beginning with Moondi, since his biography reveals the incredible challenges of male sexual and gender development in traditional and changing culture in Papua New Guinea today.

MOONDI

Moondi—who hailed from Nilangu—was such a smart and intelligent guy, and so articulate. The eldest child of a family of eight, he was born about 1960. His father was mild but respected, one of the so-called "gentle" men among Sambia (Herdt and Stoller 1990:246ff). His mother, Kaiyunango, profiled later in this chapter, is an unusually strong woman and a renowned shaman. Moondi's parents were highly successful in the time when I conducted fieldwork. Moondi himself was extremely intelligent and affable, typically of short (about 5'2") and stocky stature but good looking and, as was traditional, tough and durable as steel.

Moondi was popular and well liked, but he had the reputation of being impetuous, a "hothead," even his friends liked to say. In fact, it was this trait that landed him in trouble many times, including his being jailed later in life for adultery with another man's wife (a criminal offense in Papua New Guinea). I first met him in 1974 when he was a second-stage initiate. He became my main young interpreter on very subtle issues of meaning with initiates, who distrust older Sambia men. No one could ever replace him.

Moondi's was the last real generation to have experienced warfare in their childhood. Moondi liked to tell stories of fearful events (1960–1965), for instance, of his mother fleeing with him as a child into the forest when the village was attacked. And his mother told me the same stories independently of him—lending credence to his sense that "a war is going on." These feelings do not go away; they are like scars on one's soul, scars later compounded by initiation, scars that inflect sexuality and gender.

Yet Moondi thinks of his childhood as having been relatively happy. His parents squabbled, and he mostly sided with his mother. This pattern is common. He was initiated with his peers into the ritual cult when he was about age 8. He was smaller than other boys, and he says he was hazed and bullied more than others for this reason. Initiation was terrifying: the beatings, the nose bleeding, and the homosexual fellatio. This was a harder time for him than his childhood, he has always said; lonely and sad. He missed his mother and younger siblings and resented his parents' allowing him to be initiated. But eventually these feelings passed. He became an enthusiastic fellator and was sought out as a sexual partner by many bachelors. He lived in the men's house this way until late 1971.

Then Moondi left the valley and went to a small mission school a day's walk from home. He was among the first Sambia boys ever to be formally schooled. He became a nominal convert to the mission. This life was hard and lonely too; he was often hungry, without help from others. But he learned quickly and advanced. A year later he was transferred to a bigger school far away. At the end of that year he returned home for a visit. He became very ill, however, and had to drop out of grade school. So he fell back into village life because he was home, food was plentiful, and he was back with his own people. I arrived at this point. Moondi proved to be a gifted translator and field assistant, for he was among the few who could speak to me in pidgin. I liked him and we became friends. We agreed that if he would assist me for a year, I would help him return to school. Then the 1975 initiations were held, and it was time for him to be elevated into bachelorhood, third-stage initiation. He resisted fiercely but finally gave into the pressure. That story is told later.

Moondi helped me until late 1975, when he did return to school. He was successful and graduated from government primary school at the Patrol Post in 1977. This was a high achievement. When I returned to the Sambia in 1979, he was back in the valley and he assisted me again. We were glad for each other's company, for many of his age-mates and my friends had left the area to work on coastal plantations. Moondi was betrothed to a woman during this time, a premenarchal girl. The marriage was arranged, but Moondi approved of it; he had seen her from a distance and liked her. He liked her family too. During this time he still engaged in homosexual activities with younger boys. But his thoughts turned more and more to girls, and in time he lost most interest in boys. He left the area in 1979 to live and work in Port Moresby. He married his betrothed in 1983 and took her to the city. They had their first child in 1985.

The last segment of Moondi's brief life was lived there in the setting of rapid social change and global capitalism in the 1980s and 1990s. He found it hard to get employment for a while; he had a lot of time on his hands and was dependent upon his Sambia kin in Moresby to feed his family, a humiliating experience. He was jailed for three months for adultery with a woman—adultery is still punishable by imprisonment in Papua New Guinea. Soon thereafter Moondi was employed by a leading gold mine in the Papuan region, for which he worked in the mines for many years. This was a tough life that offered release in drinking beer and having casual sex, and Moondi had problems with alcoholism for a while. I worried that he might contract HIV, which was just beginning to be reported in the region. However, in the course of these years at the mine he managed to save more than K$33,000 (more than US$40,000 at the time), an astounding sum greater than all the monies probably circulating in his own village at home. When I saw him for the last time in Port Moresby, he was good; he had mellowed out. He refused a beer and said he was now following a "cleaner" lifestyle. Only a couple of years later Moondi was dead of an illness by his mid 30s. I am not sure what did it—malaria, tuberculosis, HIV, or something else. I miss him.

KANTEILO

My sponsor and supporter in the village was Kanteilo, a wiry old fox of about 60 years who was the leading elder during all the years of my early fieldwork. He spoke no pidgin and had never been away from the Sambia world. He represented the old ways, tradition—what Moondi grew up with but which is now changing so quickly. Kanteilo was a colorful and significant actor on the local scene. He was born in a now-defunct village not far from Nilangu that was one of the two original homestead villages in the whole valley. His father was a well-known war leader, although Kanteilo surpassed him in reputation. Kanteilo remembered his father well because he had a superb memory. Indeed, he was my key genealogical informant, and he recalled for me countless names spread over hundreds of genealogies. He took pride in this phenomenal memory, and he was known for his wide knowledge and interest in historical matters. His memories have always checked out, so his stories have helped me to reconstruct old wars and past events.

Kanteilo was married five times. During my fieldwork, he lived with his last wife, a barren widow. They had a comfortable marriage. He had several children from his previous marriages, including two sons I know well. Neither of them, however, has Kanteilo's charisma or his charm. He loved to talk, to tell stories, to impress and cajole with jokes and flattery and little gifts of food. His nickname meant "the good man," indicating his generosity and wisdom.

Yet he was not always so. In his prime, Kanteilo was a real fighter, a war leader, a womanizer, cunning and daring. He fought in many wars and battles and loves to pull back his bark cape to show the battle scars on his stomach. He was not above treachery; Kanteilo had to use his keen intelligence and guile to

Figure 3.1 Gil Herdt and Kanteilo, Songei village, early 1976

outlive his peers and survive the war raids that took him to distant lands. This hardens a man, whose vision grows sharper, pragmatic and cold. But he was no savage. We should not put him into the same heartless category as Mon, the great and rigid war hero in Pundei, Sakulambei's father. Indeed, Kanteilo's influence eventually surpassed that of other renowned war leaders such as Mon, who lack qualities of compromise and wise rhetoric. You cannot be too bitter and strong and still be an acknowledged elder among Sambia.

Kanteilo was a man with both a serious and a funny side, each developed in good measure. The seriousness was gained first through initiation into the warriorhood and then through warfare itself. His marriages seasoned him too. Kanteilo was a defender of the old customs, especially traditional initiation and marriage. He rose to the occasion of ritual teaching with flair. and passion. To the end, he still commanded respect and could hold audiences quiet. His abilities to calculate and plan helped him organize things; for example, he remembered the ritual magic spells. Yet his funny side constantly came up. For instance, he loved to yodel at dawn—a social right of prominent men. When I first lived in the village, Kanteilo often slept in my house, near the fire. He did this to keep me company, to gain prestige from association with me, to enjoy my food, and to teach me about the culture. He would arise at dawn and yodel loudly, waking everyone, which used to annoy and amuse me. Then he would chide us for sleeping past 5:00 a.m. He loved to sing too. Kanteilo was a character. But the side you will see is the elder taking charge, affirming traditions and reminding others of their responsibilities.

Kanteilo lived to a ripe old age, succumbing to illness in 2000. Right up to the end he remained engaged in the thick of village life, as expected of an elder. He was the very last of his generation.

KAIYUNANGO

The life of Sambia women is not easy, and yet Kaiyunango has shown what is possible given the will to gain esteem. A senior and highly respected woman of 60 or so and a remarkable shaman, Kaiyunango is in many respects atypical. Her influence and power stand her out from the crowd. She is looked up to by younger women and listened to by elders. I knew her first as Moondi's mother, for I got to know his family well. She surprised me by seeming to run the show in their family, until I realized that she was the most powerful woman shaman and that her husband, Moondi's father, is a mild man. Over the years I have gotten to know Kaiyunango in her own right and have interviewed her many times.

She was born in Nilangu, the daughter of the most important man in the village of the previous generation. He was a war leader and shaman, a founder of the village and an age-mate of Kanteilo's. His adult children are now all prominent people: three are shamans—Kaiyunango, her sister, and a brother. But Kaiyunango is acknowledged as the greatest power. Her shamanic traits first came to her in childhood. She had dreams that her father interpreted as signs of her calling to be a shaman (see Herdt 1977). Her mother, one of her father's three wives, was a minor shaman too, and she taught Kaiyunango magic. Kaiyunango saw her father do many healing ceremonies and says she wanted to do them too

Figure 3.2 Kaiyunango—a high-ranking woman shaman, Sambia Valley 1993

when she grew up. When she was a teenager a crisis befell her relatives, and only she was available to heal. This was her first shamanic performance and it was successful. From then on her skill and fame grew throughout the area.

She married Moondi's father in her late teens and was soon pregnant. Her husband fled ambush and fighting between relatives in his own village area on the other side of the valley. Kaiyunango's father and other men like Kanteilo suggested he settle in Nilangu. This allowed her to remain in her own village rather than move to her husband's. Consequently, she has family and friends to support and protect her, which I see reflected in her greater confidence and security compared to other women. She has had 10 children in succession, 8 of which are still living. And yet, even today, Kaiyunango remains youthful, vital, and striking—still attractive as the beauty she surely once was. Her youngest is now an adult, but she continued to brag, as a "strong" Sambia woman would do, that she was not too old to have more children right up to her menopause!

When ceremonies begin, Kaiyunango is usually to be seen. Like other women she provides food and female items expected of her. She is an excellent gardener and provider for her family. Moreover, she is extremely generous—a virtue Sambia expect from older women (they dislike it when they do not see it). Yet this alone does not stand her out from her woman age-mates. For that she has her shamanic role to thank and her reputation as a healer. At the women's ceremonies she takes a central place, teaching and talking. She helps as a midwife in the delivery of babies as well. It is a tribute to the men's esteem that they allow Kaiyunango to do healing ceremonies with male shamans in a hut near the cult house at the start of the initiation cycle. The men could not allow her to touch the initiates for fear of the usual pollution or allow her into the cult house itself for the same reason. That she can perform at all in the vicinity of male initiation is remarkable: Here we see an expression of her "strength" at work, an expression of a pattern Sambia would label masculine—and, therefore, an aspect of her womanly activity that transcends the usual male-female dichotomy in Sambia culture. As you will see in the accompanying film, she remains vital, a woman who defends the old customs of sexual modesty and ritual teaching among women.

SAKULAMBEI

In a society that so much values masculine performances, in which ritual and myth place highest value on the penis, semen, and many progeny as admission into adult masculine personhood, hermaphroditism could hardly be a condition more anomalous or sensitive. Hermaphrodites are Sambia intersexed persons: biologically hermaphroditic males treated differently from birth, who have microscopic penises. Sakulambei is such a person. He was born about 1953 and warfare raged throughout his childhood. Though assigned to the male sex, he was labeled a hermaphrodite at birth because he had a tiny penis and an odd-looking scrotum. Like all identified Sambia male hermaphrodites he was assigned to the male sex because people knew that later sexual differentiation in the genitals would occur around puberty.

Hermaphroditism is a mystery to Sambia. That it has magical associations is understandable. When a people are so preoccupied with keeping the sexes apart, it is not surprising that sexual ambiguity would fascinate them, for it blurs sexual boundaries. But mysterious or magical, hermaphrodites are stigmatized. Saku, no different in appearance from other hermaphrodites at birth, has made himself

Figure 3.3 Sakulambei, in full warrior regalia at third-stage initiation, 1975

different. He is at present the most powerful living shaman. I know of no other Sambia hermaphrodites, past or present, who became great shamans. Saku's achievement is unique (see Herdt and Stoller 1985).

Saku has a history sad and yet triumphant. His father rejected him in childhood because of the hermaphroditism. Life's cruel joke was for Saku to have been born the son of Mon, the terrible war leader of Pundei. At age 5 or so, Saku's mother died. His mother's brother, then the most powerful shaman and sorcerer in the valley, took him in and reared him as a son in another hamlet. He truly loved Saku. And when, like Kaiyunango, Saku had dreams and visions in childhood, his uncle knew that Saku would be a shaman. Shamanism is strong in Saku's family. As a child, Saku says his first spirit familiar used to come and play with him out in the gardens. Perhaps this was like what psychologists would call a child's "imaginary companion," to replace his lost mother and father. Later Saku says he saw the familiar in dreams, and he still sees him and other familiars in his trance states. Children teased Saku. They made fun of his genitals and humiliated him, saying he was a girl, not a boy. Few of his childhood friends helped him. But Weiyu, his cousin, always defended him.

Saku's social development was otherwise normal until puberty. He was initiated with his age-mates. He was an active fellator for years. Second-stage initiation was normal too. But after that, the elders and his father passed him up. Their attitude was, "Why waste a good woman on *him?*" This hurt him deeply. They did not initiate him into the bachelorhood, so Saku persisted in the homosexual fellator role longer than normal. He became a shaman though, mainly through his uncle's influence. In 1975 he arranged his own third-stage initiation, years behind his mates. His uncle also got him a wife. During this initiation he was also formally installed as a full shaman, and thereafter he quickly became more powerful. He has managed to hold onto his wife in spite of many problems associated with his stigmatized sexual condition. His uncle died in the late 1970s, leaving Saku the most powerful man shaman. He often performs healing ceremonies together with Kaiyunango.

The masculinity and identity of Saku are therefore complex. His shamanic powers have been thoroughly blended into his identity, such that it is hard to separate the one from the other. His sense of himself is neither absolutely masculine nor feminine but rather hermaphroditic. His courage in earning the status of shaman and in overcoming his childhood difficulties rings clear in his proud bearing and defiance of others who gossip about his inadequacies. His feeling of power thus derives from the conviction that "I am the shaman Saku, whose identity is strong." In this sense, then, Saku has *created* his own self. This is, in all of us, a necessary part of development, but in Saku's case it was an act of heroism against great odds. We will see more of him later.

PENJUKWI

The wife of my late informant, Nilutwo, Penjukwi is an attractive twice-married "strong" woman, who has reared four children over the years I have known her. She is remarkable by being one of the first women in the Sambia Valley to have

Figure 3.4 Penjukwi and her newborn, late 1975

attended for a few months a mission school in the early 1970s, before it failed
due to a scandal involving sexual relations between the boys and girls. In the
old-fashioned sense of it, Penjukwi is what Americans once would have referred
to as a "tomboy" when she was young because she liked to climb trees, accompany her father more than her mother, and roam around with young boys around
the village. Born about 1955, she was the first born of her mother, who was the
second most prominent shaman, and her biological father, one of the so-called
"gentle" Sambia men, from the village Kwoli, across the valley. Her father died
when she was 12; her mother remarried, as is common. At this point she grew
increasingly close to her paternal uncle, Yanduwaiko, a fascinating guy who
became one of the first official translators of the government and whose worldly
influence no doubt moved Penjukwi to grow up expecting and enjoying social
change.

As she served as my key informant and interpreter with women, I got to
know Penjukwi, and encouraged by Robert Stoller (my postdoctoral mentor), I
interviewed her in depth and created a life history in her own words (Herdt and
Stoller, 1990, Chapter 6). As we became closer, Penjukwi confided things to me
that previously only men had shared. She talked of her childhood sexual play
with a boy when she was about 9 or 10 (see Chapter 5, where you will understand the importance of this age), breaking a taboo. She spoke to me of her
infatuation in her mid-teens with a young, handsome Sambia bachelor—she
fantasized about him for a long time after and wished to marry him. By 1973,
Penjukwi had her menarche, around age 18, which was normal for those times.
This precipitated a crisis, as the men from Nilangu village plotted to marry her
or steal her, if necessary, as a rumor floated that Penjukwi was going to run
away to the coast with the young man of her dreams. Whether true or just a

rationalization to spark them into action, the men abducted her and threw her into a hut with a much older man, Nilutwo, the famed cassowary hunter (Herdt 1981: 142ff). Nilutwo was instructed by the elders to rape and subdue her, and after some days, they were released from being interned and guarded. It was traumatic and a dreadful beginning, even by Sambia standards. I met them four years later. Penjukwi had a daughter and then a son.

In 1979, Nilutwo fell from a tree while hunting, broke his back, and died soon after, leaving Penjukwi a young, attractive widow. Her uncle invited her to the patrol post for a time, and she lived there with her children for a few months. She continued to elude the men, including Weiyu, who had always been attracted to Penjukwi, but she spurned them all. She enjoyed her freedom and hardly wanted to be saddled with another unwanted husband. She had to be careful in what she said, however, because it was rumored that she had sorcerized Nilutwo, causing his death; and it was also rumored that she had a lover at the patrol post. Her personality blossomed during this time; she had a lightness and joy that I had not seen before. In subsequent field trips I was able to see her again in the village and then at Port Moresby, continuing the conversation. She had met a Sambia man who for years had lived and worked on the coast; they married and she began a new life. It was quite noticeable that she was able to "boss" him around, and being a bit older, never previously married, and obviously taken with her, he seemed to accept her in all of her new-found independence. Penjukwi found the life she wanted away from the village, not with her fantasized lover but nevertheless a lot more on her own terms, a new kind of woman.

WEIYU

A striking combination of an older guy who incorporated social changes into his life while continuing the customs of his ancestors, Weiyu was a close interpreter of my own age, and he is my best Sambia friend. I have known and worked with him since 1974. Weiyu was among the first people I got to know well. His marriage ceremony occurred only a month after my arrival in the village. He stood out from his peers: He was taller, more verbal, gregarious, and (by Sambia standards and my own) handsome. He liked to show off, to be seen as acculturated when it counted; but when dressed in warrior garb (which was rare, for he usually wore Western clothes), he cut a dashing figure. Women liked him and he knew it; he is still a lady's man, a Don Juan. He liked sex with boys too—in fact, he likes sex in general. More blatant about that than other Sambia men; his coastal experience was a big factor in making him more sexually aggressive. Weiyu and his cohort of fellow initiates invited me (in December 1974) to join in their initiation shortly after my arrival. I was honored; the experience made me—by age (I was 25, about their age), by subsequent identification by other villagers, and by common interests (being bachelors)—their age-mate.

Weiyu's childhood was unusual. His true father was a renowned and feared shaman of Pundei village (Nilangu's sister hamlet). He was said to have been a physically powerful man, too tall and strong, impressive and reckless (Weiyu does not remember him). Some 20 years ago he was murdered by his own clan brothers in an infamous massacre that set off a war between Pundei and Nilangu.

Figure 3.5 Weiyu, in full regalia for the marriage ceremony, Songei village 1975

Weiyu's father was simply too brazen and reckless: He openly flirted with women; let it be known that he was having affairs with other men's wives, using his powerful sorcery knowledge to keep men afraid of him; and—the unbearable and insane sin—he claimed responsibility for the (sorcery) deaths of several people. He was disposed of in an ambush, hacked to death by a gang of warriors. One of them was Mon, Saku's father. His widow fled with her two children, Weiyu and his older sister, to Nilangu, where their in-laws gave them shelter. A Nilangu big man, Chemgalo, who was himself an older widower, took Weiyu's mother as his wife. He adopted Weiyu and, with unusual kindness for that day, gave Weiyu the advantage of full social rights in the village. Shortly before his initiation, Weiyu's mother died. He has been cared for since by Chemgalo's eldest daughter (his stepsister) and Chemgalo himself, who never remarried.

The wound opened by Weiyu's father's murder never healed. His father's only biological brother (himself a powerful shaman) also fled Pundei and never returned. This man still mutters that the murderers will pay eventually through his sorcery powers. Sambia is a society that honors blood revenge, yet Weiyu's father has never been revenged. So Weiyu grew up with a fantasy, sometimes quietly expressed today, that *he,* the son, carries the burden of knowing that there has as yet been no revenge. Little wonder that his wonderful old paternal aunt, Towianderei, his deceased father's sister, an ancient who possessed great sorcery powers, refused to give Weiyu her knowledge before she died some years ago. I heard her myself say to Weiyu, "You'll seek revenge if I give you the powers—it will just bring trouble." This awareness, and a quiet, romantic identification with an amazing father cut down and never known, is burned into Weiyu's masculinity.

Weiyu's marriage following social change was also odd. He and his wife were the first couple (to my knowledge) to have chosen each other. They were mutually attracted and went against others' wishes in marrying. There is also a sense that Weiyu's wife is socially inappropriate for him because they are too closely related through marriage. They have been at each other's throats for years. Both are jealous. Weiyu is flirtatious and an exuberant fornicator whenever possible. (As a bachelor he frequently had sex with boys and was even sometimes unscrupulous, having sex with male cousins such as Moondi, who are supposed to be tabooed, Moondi says.) He outgrew boys and concentrated on women, whom he prefers. Weiyu is, nonetheless, misogynous. He has had many fights with his wife. (I know he beats his wife, but I have never seen him do it. She has also beaten him.) Though they have a house, gardens, and two children, their marriage is not successful or satisfying. Weiyu's mother-in-law did not want them to marry. She seems to feel that their chaos is the result of marriage inspired by romance, not by custom. Though other men share feelings of misogyny with Weiyu, and they may sometimes fight, they do not—nor do most other couples—persist in the vicious combat that characterizes Weiyu's marriage. One is tempted to suggest that their romantic beginning is the cause of their conflict, making them the first "luv'" marriage well ahead of the present-day popularity of these changes, but that is too simple.

Weiyu represents, in a paradoxical way, old-fashioned phallic masculinity. It is paradoxical because he has had outside life experience other men lack. Yet his sense of self is so much more like Kanteilo's than Moondi's. The elder, like Weiyu, is an old-fashioned warrior, the kind of man made famous by Sambia stories.

DANNY

Danny was 5 years old when I first met him in 1975. His father had recently died, leaving his mother a young widow with two small children, in Pundei hamlet (Weiyu is Danny's uncle). The impact of the loss of his father trailed Danny throughout his childhood, as his mother did not remarry, making food and shelter more difficult to come by. He is gregarious and innovative, and aspires to be a leader among his people. Because he was never initiated properly and because he did not have a father to pressure him into traditional ways, he took the name "Danny" when he was young, in part due to mission influence, in part due to a radio program involving a namesake. What distinguishes Danny's development, then, is that it has been primarily governed by social change, not tradition, unlike Moondi's development.

In the early 1980s the Sambia staged a truncated initiation that enabled Danny and his cohort to gain some knowledge of first-stage initiation and the men's secret society. Warfare was now only a memory. The men's houses were largely abandoned by that time; and the Sambia had stopped teaching about nose bleeding, for fear of being criticized by the missionaries, and boy-insemination, due to the men's inability to maintain social control. Thus, Danny did not grow up with these traditions, nor did he have pounded into him the fear and misogyny of women experienced by older males. He sought a new pathway to development through school, knowledge of Western ways, money, and the influence derived from these things and the NeoMelanesian language. Danny was, in short, a product of a society pacified and undergoing dramatic development.

Figure 3.6 Danny—a "new" Sambia man, Sambia Valley 1993

Danny asked me to help him get to school in the mid l980s, and I was glad to do my part. Like Moondi and a couple of other young people, the payment of school fees was a huge burden to their families, and I was glad to help out, indeed, obliged to do so, as a *wantok* of their fathers and mothers. Danny was able to attain Form Six (sixth grade) before dropping out and working for a time in Goroka. He returned to the Sambia Valley and began to plant coffee gardens and garner other local *bisnis*. He gradually grew interested in a young woman of the community who, like him, had had schooling, spoke Neomelanesian, and represented a new generation. Her name is Ginny, and she is an attractive, modest, and genuinely sweet person who is obviously smitten with Danny. They formed what Sambia call a "luv" marriage. This is a new way of being married that involves living in a square house with a tin roof, not a traditional round house, freeing them from having the segregated gender spaces of old. Such marriages were unknown when Penjukwi was growing up. They are reported to sleep in the same bed and even to kiss, ideas truly shocking to their elders. As you will see from the Sambia film accompanying this case study, Danny speaks of some of these changes in his own voice, espousing his own vision of a future in which he is a community leader.

These are the Sambia individuals you will meet in the following pages. They are social beings, because the powerful forces of culture and history have obviously shaped them. Their stories help us to understand their motives and behavior in the text and in the film that accompanies the initiation ceremonies. As social actors they are at the center of their society, along with their age-mates and kin. And now that you have met them you must be aware that they are not ordinary people at all; they are the inheritors of a rich cultural tradition that they are adapting to, and in some cases changing, making them participants in a unique social reality and cultural history.

4/The Men's Secret Society

Warrior societies throughout human history have employed initiation rituals to create standards of masculinity and special requirements such as taboos to recruit, train, and maintain the solidarity of males. This was common in pre-colonial Papua New Guinea, and the Sambia were no exception. Indeed, their local warriorhoods created an extreme emphasis upon the achievement of being a Great Man through the ordeals of ritual initiation, prowess in hunting, and the war raids that followed. But the Sambia also made of their secret society a safe and homosocial harbor for the creation of an alternative reality that denied the importance of women, created a pure hierarchy of males, and produced a kind of secret masculinity. A secret form of boy-insemination was a critical part of this world. Through the rituals and taboos, Sambia attempted to regulate not only the sexual behavior of boys but their attractions and desires as well. The problems that this secret cult created for the men, its power relations, sexuality, and tensions between the genders and generations are all part of the story of the secret society.

For the Sambia the ordeals of manhood were part of a political union of neighboring hamlets, a kind of ritual confederacy, that performed collective initiations (called *iku mokeiyu*) together every three or four years. This series of ritual events and processes is the grandest of all Sambia society and takes months to complete. We should think of this initiating group as a religious cult, for the clubhouse has the blessings of female and male spirit beings; mystical powers associated with medicine bundles and magical formulas; and fantastic ceremonies, some public but many others secret, expressing the sacred core of Sambia society.

The ritual elders and war leaders arranged a cessation of war and raiding with one another sufficient for cooperation to induct a new crop of boys into the men's secret society. They halted war temporarily for the political and religious purpose of having to transmit the sacred rituals to the next generation and the urgent need of having a large body of men and resources from the larger Valley in order to reproduce their own men's house, producing a new cadre of warriors to replenish their local ranks. The initiation system thus created age-graded and ritual-ranked status positions, akin to generals, lieutenants, and soldiers. As you will see in the following description, fears of warfare and armed conflict erupted at every turn of the initiation cycle, suggesting a temporary halt, rather than an end, to the sense that a war was going on among the confederacy villages.

This secret society teaches the warrior ethos to boys and transmits to them through ritual and sexuality the power called *jerungdu*. Sambia men believed that *jerungdu* was empowered through the oral insemination of boys. Additionally, they used phallic symbols, especially the secret ritual flutes, to empower men and support the secret of the male cult masculinity. The men's club celebrates the male body, which, as Maurice Godelier (1986) has remarked, is the sexy and beautiful object in Papua New Guinea. Much of this cult's power derives from its arcane and strict secrecy, or, to be more precise, from the way in which the men use secrecy to support their misogyny; and to accomplish military, ritual, and sexual aims through the creation of an order of being that they viewed as higher and more pure than the messy, polluted business of living with women and children (Herdt 2003). While the account you are about to read is an ethnographic account detailed in the mid 1970s, nevertheless, the CD-ROM provided you contains the ritual performances of the period 1990–1993, suggesting that this rich and vital tradition remains alive in the social memory and experience of Sambia today.

INITIATION FOR STRENGTH

The main goal of initiation is to make boys masculine and to "grow" them into big and strong warriors. Taboos are needed to help them "grow," regulating what they eat and drink, where they walk and with whom they talk, and where they sleep and eat, ensuring that they avoid all pollution from women and children. This regulation is accomplished by moving boys from their mother's house and the women's domain into the cult house. This abrupt move is a shock to them, and they lose their childhood freedom and innocence. Pre-initiates are immature and unmasculine, for they express female traits such as shyness and crying, and they do female tasks like babysitting and weeding. Most of all, they have lived so close to their mothers that they are believed to be totally polluted both on the inside and the outside of their bodies. In this sense they belong to the female world, though they are not female. To enter the men's secret society they must be purged of all this pollution and these "feminine" traits, requiring a radical change. They must learn new things, but they must also unlearn old traits and ideas so that they can truly feel in their gender identity: "I am *not* feminine; *I am* masculine." Such developmental change we call radical resocialization.

The transformation in their bodies and minds from boyhood to manhood is hyper-tough and sometimes brutal, but entirely necessary, as the men saw it. *A war is going on:* this is the perennial idea that underlies initiation. The whole secret society is oriented toward the constant struggle to triumph in war.

How are boys to acquire the strength to be warriors? Here the dilemma for Sambia in thinking about *jerungdu* is twofold. First, the male body is believed

Figure 4.1 Two shamans purify first-stage initiate (Sambia Valley initiation, 1975)

incapable of naturally producing semen, so it must be externally acquired. This means that *jerungdu* itself is not an intrinsic capacity of male bodily functioning but must be artificially introduced via insemination. Second, semen can be "lost" (ejaculated) and, along with it, the *jerungdu* that it sustains. Therefore, ritual measures must be taken to artificially replace what essence is lost to prevent weakness and death. No semen, no *jerungdu*, no masculinity. Overcoming these masculine challenges is the long-term goal of Sambia secret initiations. This entire process I call *ritualized masculinization*. Oral ingestion of semen—boy-insemination—is critical to the development of *jerungdu*.

Only after years of insemination and ritual treatment of the body do the key sexual signs of male strength take on physical form, such as through muscles and facial hair. For the Sambia, *jerungdu is* felt to be a real force, not a metaphor or symbol. Fellatio is a concrete means of attaining it. Men are absolutely convinced of their innate lack of semen and of the need for their rituals, and they transmit their convictions to boys in ritual teaching. Because of its contingent qualities I have referred to this cultural belief system as *conditional masculinity* (Herdt 2003).

To understand how deep this cultural belief system goes, let me share an amusing story from fieldwork. Dr Robert J. Stoller, MD, a psychiatrist and renowned expert on sex and gender, visited my village field site in 1979 as part of our collaboration during the time I was a postdoctoral Fellow at UCLA. One day following some interesting interviews I was conducting with Weiyu and Tali on ritual beliefs, Dr Stoller asked me the simple but obvious question: How can your Sambia men explain that I grew up to be a masculine man who is married with four sons but has never drank semen? My friends huddled together, and they responded quickly that Dr. Stoller has had the advantage of "drinking cow's milk his whole life," and that was obviously a semen substitute (Tali, Weiyu, and most Sambia heavily cream their coffee and tea with milk, sometimes having more milk than coffee!). Stoller replied that he did not drink milk (that is, he was lactose deficient). Not to be outdone, Tali immediately challenged him by saying that he noticed Stoller liked cheese (from a can, provided at lunch), and isn't cheese from milk? Stoller conceded, and Tali cinched the point: "You needed the 'white stuff' [kwei-koon-booku, semen, here also an allusion to the collective pool of semen in Sambia imagination] as much as us!" All of us laughed at the triumph of Sambia cultural logic (see Herdt and Stoller, 1990: 141, for the context of this story).

Initiation occurs at the harvest season, ideally under a full moon, when men build the great cult house and utilize the bounty of nature's fertility. Organized by one's fathers, brothers, and clan elders, the ritual is done by the most loved and admired people in society. Even one's mother takes pride in the event and in her son's accomplishment. For despite her husband's demands, her workload, the heavy gardening responsibilities expected to ensure the success of the event, her other babies' needs and her own—and notwithstanding her ambivalence in losing a son's companionship and help, or her occasional opposition to the idea of initiation, which sometimes provokes nasty quarrels with her husband—a mother surely recognizes that this is the course a son must take, that the hamlet needs her boy as a defender. Where mother loses a son, father gains a comrade. And mothers say that they need their sons to be big and strong one day, to make gardens and go hunting, replacing what they will lose when their husbands die—and they expect to outlive their husbands, as is true in many societies.

The pre-initiated boy, then, is seen as polluted from the womb, mother's food, and saliva. Being constantly in touch with the contaminated skin of her breasts and body, a boy is dependent on mother for protection and warmth; her body remains too much of a haven for him. There is more than a hint of femininity about him; he even wears the same type of grass apron as females. He is undisciplined and bawls and throws tantrums when unable to get what he wants. At such times men are openly hostile to boys, taunting them till they cry, saying "Go back to your mother where you belong!" Men cannot forget that their sons are carrier of feminine pollution, so they watch them lest they pollute men, their weapons, or their own bodies. Such considerations come to mind when men discuss the need to initiate their maturing sons.

THE ECOLOGY OF INITIATION

The Sambia cylindrical system is based on the solar cycle and seasonal climatic changes. The sun's fertility effects are especially important to the Sambia. They credit the sun with many of their harvest blessings because the sun is another power in nature that has *jerungdu*. So in their own meaning system, magical beliefs about the sun are woven into practical harvest activities and initiation. The sun comes at a period of natural abundance. It signals, for Sambia, the impending maturation of root crops (yams and taro) as well as sugar cane and banana, planted in the preceding agricultural season to be used in initiation, then at their peak. Certain ritual trees and plants are also in bloom and are used for ritual decoration. More importantly, the pandanus trees—first the fruit tree species and then the nut tree species—reproduce and ripen, becoming available for harvesting in response to the sun's natural warmth. Both types of pandanus are crucial for initiation rites. Possum appear in greater numbers and are most easily hunted in the dry season, and their meat is consumed during the rituals. So this is a time of fertility, of plenty, of renewal.

The sun is experienced sensually: not as an abstract planetary body or as a meteorological force of physics, and not only as a pleasant change into dry weather but also as a vital being, a masculine power that unites nature and society.[1] The old-fashioned term for this idea in Victorian anthropology was *animism* (from Latin, *anima,* "soul"), which is appropriate so long as we stress the Sambia view that this force has regulative control over the cosmos and human order (Whitehouse 1995). Sambia elders refer to the power with sayings such as "The sun gives us everything" and "The sun is our father." Indeed, the archaic word *akumú* ("father sun") is sometimes used in this metaphoric kinship sense. Its imaginative association with the native word for the sun season, *atamdu,* seems certain. In myth, the sun is depicted as male and is masculinized, while the moon is sometimes said to be male or androgynous and is spoken of as "the mate of the sun." Furthermore, the myth of pandanus fruit tells how the sun provided this red phallic fruit and war weapons at the very founding of Sambia society (a tale symbolically reflected in second-stage initiation). Men themselves refer to the qualities of the sun's power as *jerungdu.*

Finally, the initiations represent a message that the communities involved (the local confederacy) are healthy and thriving. Staging the collective rites means that during the preceding year a political agreement among hamlet leaders had been reached to initiate; so either peace is at hand or a truce was imminent. The same understanding also made it possible for initiates to travel to other villages for the purpose of homoerotic contacts; the boys were supposed to enjoy safe passage back to their village during times of war.

Planting the gardens was the first step in planning. Ecological conditions must be good for crops, since abnormally wet or dry years deplete the harvest; during bad years, initiations done the following year were meager. Sambia believe that local droughts affected past ritual cycles, although no one could recall one that was postponed due to food shortages. (Warfare, on the other hand, clearly has interrupted past initiation plans.) Nonetheless after the initiations

---

[1]There are special conditions of cloudiness and light in the Highlands, since, as Brookfield (1964: 25) noted of the atmosphere: "The air is different, with less water vapor and solid particles, and hence more rapid heating and cooling" (see also Brookfield and Hart 1971: 17). Bowra (1957: 23), in a classical work on Attic Greek poetry, made a more romantic point: "What matters above all is the quality of the light . . . even in winter the light is unlike that of any other European country, brighter, cleaner, stronger. . . . The beauty of the Greek landscape depends primarily on the light, and this had a powerful influence on the Greek vision of the world."

I observed, a mild famine did occur in the Lower Sambia Valley in 1976, and food was scarce throughout the area. Hamlet leaders blamed the situation on the 1975 initiations, saying that sponsoring the feasts had exhausted gardens and prevented them from planting enough new crops before the monsoons began, indications that initiation has a significant economic impact.

THE INITIATION CYCLE

The Sambia are intent on initiating boys before they reach age 10. As I will explain in Chapter 5, Sambia intuitively understood that to control gender and sexuality, they had to channel the attractions and desires of boys away from women toward the bachelors, and they had to do so before the boys were too big. In this way, the secret society regulated virtually all areas of subjective and behavioral development from middle childhood through old age. Without exception, every male is initiated, even the blind. The first initiation places one in a fixed age-set for life. It also creates age-mate ties to males throughout the valley. There are six initiations in all, leading to full manhood. These initiations and age-mate bonds get intermixed with kinship and political relationships, as shown in Table 4.1.

The overall initiation system has two interlocking subsystems. The first subsystem consists of *collective* initiations done by the hamlets acting together: first, second, and third-stage initiations—performed as a set; and a second subsystem. These always occur following the communal construction of a great cult house,

TABLE 4.1   INITIATION AND THE MEN'S SECRET SOCIETY

Age in Years	Initiation	Ritual Grade	Status Rank	Sexual Behavior	Categories Used in This Case Study
0–6			child	neuter	child
7–10	First-Stage (choowinuku)	kuwatni'u	initiate	semen recipient	initiate
11–14	Second-Stage (imbutu)	kuwatni'u	initiate	semen recipient	initiate
15–18	Third-Stage (ipmangwi)	nungenyu	bachelor	inseminator	bachelor
17+	Fourth-Stage (nuposhu)	aatmwol-chenchorai	newlywed	inseminator	youth
Late teens	Fifth-Stage (taiketnyi)	aatmwol-chenchorai	newlywed	bisexual	married man
Early 20's	Sixth-Stage (moondangu)	aatmwunu	adult	inseminator/ women	married man
Mid 30's+man		aatmangootu	big	inseminator/ women	elder

whose name, *moo-angu*, incorporates imagery of feeding *(monjapi'u)* and breast milk *(aammoonalyu)*. The second subsystem completes adulthood: Fourth-, fifth-, and sixth-stage initiations comprise the transition from adolescence to adulthood. These are *individualized* rites, performed as needed by each hamlet separately. Unlike the collective rituals, they are performed as needed.

The collective initiations are held in a fixed sequence in the early dry season. First the cult house is built. Then third-stage *(ipmangwi)* initiation is performed for youths aged 14 to 16 or so. These boys are thus elevated from second-stage status. Please note: *They are initiated first to help older men in hunting and in initiating boys.* A few weeks later the second-stage *(imbutu)* initiation is held for boys aged 11 to 13. They too assist third-stage bachelors in helping initiate the youngest boys. The first-stage initiation *(choowinuku)* is then held last, for boys aged 7 to 10. It must be done soon after the *imbutu,* Sambia believe, since second-stage initiation leaves them without first-stage initiates in the men's house, which people feel is "bad."

Following collective initiation is a period of several months' living in forest houses for the new initiates of all ages. It is a liminal world, betwixt and between the normal village and the forest, filled with secrecy and the yearning for the alternative cultural reality that Tuzin (1980: 85) described so well for a similar ritual phase among the Ilahita Arapesh (who have transvestites and the imagery of boy-initiates as "adolescent girls" during menstruation). A makeshift hut is constructed for initiates called the "rat house" because first-stage novices hunt large forest rats to smoke and present as return food gifts to elders and their ritual guardians, who earlier hunted possum for the boys' feasts. Boys are strictly forbidden during this period from seeing or interacting with women or children, who, in turn, are tabooed from entering this area of the forest. Homoerotic activity is at a peak here, as is the hazing of younger boys. Thereafter, the boys return to the clubhouse of their own hamlet where they reside for years, until they marry.

The second subsystem of initiations begins several years after the third-stage collective rite and depends on a youth's maturity and the elders having obtained a woman for his marriage. Then, the youth's own clan-hamlet hosts a marriage ceremony *(nuposha)*—a lavish affair, such that the village likes to have several age-mates married at the same time to pool resources for a common ceremony. The public sees the grooms in their elaborate ceremonial dress, as shown in Figure 4.21. Then, the men go off into the forest again to stage secret ceremonies for the youths, while far away, women hold their own secret ceremony for the brides in the menstrual hut. During this period the couple may secretly begin to have sexual relations, with the bride sucking her husband. Menarche triggers a man's fifth-stage initiation *(taiketnyi),* which is held in secret again. Only now are vaginal sexual relations permitted between husband and wife. After the birth of the first child, sixth-stage initiation *(moondangu,* "new birth") is held for the man. Both fifth- and sixth-stage initiations are done only for the individual man undergoing status changes, due to the "life crisis" events his wife is undergoing. Each of the fourth-, fifth-, and sixth-stage ceremonies is preceded again by long possum hunts, some lasting for months in the high forest. Age-mates are expected to help each other secure bride wealth meat gifts, preferably by capturing possum by hand, for this is a test of real manhood. After menarche, couples cohabitate in their own hut, which concludes the clubhouse residence for the man. After two children are born, no further initiations are done on him or his wife because they have attained full adulthood *(aatmwunu)*.

BOYS' SUBJECTIVITY AT INITIATION

First come piercing cries, mysteriously, as if from nowhere: the message to everyone that the cycle of initiations is coming. From within the men's house, later near the dance ground where a new cult house is being raised, and eventually at the edge land forest, the haunting sounds increase in tempo. Children are told the cries come from old female hamlet spirits. Somehow—never fully explained—the men's secret society has power over these spirits. Their music alerts women of the coming preparations. Boys may be curious or fearful. They are teased with remarks like "The spirit wants to get you, she wants to kill and eat you!" Then mother or father may smile or laugh or be quiet, responses that heighten the mounting tension that intrudes on the household of a boy whose time has come. "The female spirit protects the clubhouse; she's aged, we keep her hidden in an old net bag," fathers tell sons. Boys' responses differ according to their age and personality. Yet they all experience discomfort that in some of them turns into panic at initiation. Unknown to the boys, the ritual flutes *(namboolu aambelu,* "female frog") create this mysterious sound that triggers the boys' fear, signaling an unalterable transition into warrior life.

Several factors contribute to the boys' anxiety at the time. The boys' mothers and fathers begin to talk of how "the boy's time has come." Suddenly too there is a new mysteriousness and secrecy in the way the boys' fathers are acting. The boys know as well that there is no escaping this—there are no exits, and no exceptions are made to being initiated. Many boys fear the ordeals and physical punishment in the rites; and boys are treated as a batch-living group, not as individuals. Once it begins there is "no going home." Only very sick children at the time are allowed to postpone initiation, but this is considered "bad" in many ways. No Sambia man exists who is uninitiated. In the valley, for instance, a mentally retarded man and another who is viewed as permanently insane are both initiated. "Even they have kept the secrets," my friends say with a gleam in their eyes. The male hermaphrodites, however, present a bigger challenge. How does the phallic cult regard these biologically abnormal children with microscopic penises? They initiate them without exception and in this way treat them no differently than normal males. Once I even encountered a blind 10-year-old boy who was initiated in the Blue Valley. The men said: "He is a man; we have to initiate him!" Let us briefly examine these elements of the boys' consciousness before observing the initiation itself.

Boys are kept in the dark about initiation plans. Many are never told they will be taken, though most can guess it. Mothers actually speak about the need for their sons to be initiated and provide economic support after their husbands are gone. Fathers speak of their pride in being able to have the boy enter the men's house. Yet as the parents prepare ritual decorations for the boy, sometimes in secret, mothers also cry and say that they will never see their boys again. Boys hear that a new cult house is going up, yet secrecy surrounds the plans. Some boys ask if they will be initiated; some parents, knowing boys' opposition, deceive them: "Oh, not this time, the next." Such tricks also add to boys' later feelings that they are dupes—that parents, especially mothers, betrayed them—or that adults are to be distrusted. Many mothers comfort and cry over their sons, however; they say they can do nothing to stop the rites. They know initiation will be filled with glory and pride, and that only through this ceremony can the boys "grow up."

Even though there was nowhere to go, many tales tell how boys ran away into the forest to escape initiation. To stay boys? No, these are more than "Peter Pan" stories. I have twice seen boys flee into the forest at initiation. In the 1975 rites, described later in this chapter, three boys (two of them from one hamlet, a third from another) ran and hid to escape. Search parties were sent to find them; they were brought back, and in retaliation they were more severely handled during the rites. In the summer of 1983, another boy tried to escape initiation in the valley while I was there; there are still no exits for them. Why? Because everything that matters most—village survival through the cult and warriorhood—depends on initiation. The elders still insist on this. This feeling that there are no exits is laced into Sambia consciousness of ritual. And the boy's resistance to initiation is part of the social inequality of power relations studied in Chapter 6.

Boys lose their individuality in initiation; they are handled as a batch, an age-set. This group treatment comforts them in the sense that they are not singled out for ordeals. But it threatens them too, for they become aware that no exceptions can be made for the individual boy; not even father can halt the process. The boy child, in other words, experiences the loss of parental protection and security while being forced into the broader social group of the secret society wherein he has to make his own way. This secondary socialization group has its own agenda (to initiate boys), and it will not pamper them, as did their parents.

Finally, there is the feeling that, once initiated, a boy "cannot go back" to his childhood home. He must live in the clubhouse. Yet this feeling extends far beyond his living arrangements. I mentioned prreviously the loss of parental security. More than this, however, boys totally "lose" their mothers, as it were. They are detached from mother, whom they can never again be with—to touch, hold, talk to, eat with, or look at directly. She is off-limits. And what this taboo of detachment represents symbolically is the way the female world becomes generally forbidden. These changes cannot be halted or reversed. Once told the ritual secrets, a boy can never be trusted to be close to his mother again for fear he might reveal these secrets. This dimension of secret knowledge gives the boy a secret identity, shared with father and age-mates. The feeling of loss of mother is compounded, then, by the sense that he can never return to the innocence of childhood.

ORGANIZERS AND SPECTATORS

Who is involved in this unfolding drama? The answer is virtually everyone in the valley. The roles played by elders, war leaders and shamans, bachelors, women, and the initiates are very different. So we should expect that their experiences would differ too.

The elders are in command of the initiation process.[2] This is as it has always been, for Sambia is a headless society, without kings or chiefs, courts or councils. Political power rests primarily in the elders' hands. During warfare, though, young war leaders take charge, whereas at other times the elders—former war leaders, for the most part—do so. As a warrior culture, power in Sambia men is vested in a principle expressed by the Latin phrase *primus inter pares:* first among equals. Elders lead by force of personality, by ritual knowledge, by social connections, and by show. Look around at the streaming initiation events, and you see a flurry of activity. Young war leaders parade around, and older ritual experts shout orders directing the crowds or "stage sets" for the pomp of ceremonies. But these are not the true organizers. They are puppets of the elders in the sense that the old men decide what rites are performed, by whom, in what order, and with what magic. This vast magical knowledge, required for mixing feast foods and in saying spells over rituals, is the ultimate source of elders' authority. The hurried younger men are not "calling the shots" in initiation; the elders do this, far removed from the public eye, off in a little hut somewhere, muttering about what to do next. At the critical moment in ritual teaching, when sage words are needed, when authority figures are required to impress on initiates the secret society's power over the sacred, the elders will appear.

The elders' control should not surprise us, for Sambia is an age-graded society. It is not far wrong to call their political system a form of gerontocracy. People's social status generally rises with age. Merely outliving others is an accomplishment, although not enough of one to bestow leadership in itself. For that the elder must organize, make his presence felt in ceremonies, and be able to orate in public. The old men are committed to advancing their own village. This makes them rivals with their elderly age-mates in other villages. Yet, for the purposes of collective initiation, they forget their gripes and join together to stage a grand event. Adult men provide the real manpower for the rites, however. They hunt and build the cult house, harvest the feast gardens, stage key events by placing themselves in long rows as fearsome warriors, and collect food from women to feed initiates and make feasts. The bachelors assisted them in traditional times; they later went together as a war party, after the collective cycle of rites was done. In the meantime, the men's sexual life changes. While preparing for initiation, all heterosexual activity is forbidden. Men cannot copulate with their wives since female pollution is transmitted, via the person of the man, to the boys, whose "growth" would be thwarted or whose faces would turn "ugly and black." For weeks, then, spouses have no sex. Bachelors have homoerotic contact with younger initiates, but the men—married with children—are not supposed to, and most do not. A few break the rules. Other men break the heterosexual taboos, or so it is rumored. When the moonlight dances begin and the crowds assemble, people say there is illicit heterosexual play and even adultery going on in the shadows. It is a time of sexual license, a bacchanalian time, when the normally prudish Sambia momentarily escape their strict sexual code.

---

[2]Donald Tuzin has vividly portrayed this power of the elders' presence as ritual authorities in his stunning works, *The Voice of the Tamberan* (1980) and *The Cassowary's Revenge* (1997), on the Ilahita Arapesh ritual cult in the Sepik River area of Papua New Guinea.

How do mothers and fathers respond? The rituals tend to obscure the role of individual parents. What emerges instead is a collective image of the men versus the women. The antagonism between the sexes is exaggerated by the ritual cycle. For, after all, hostile hamlets are brought together in the same place, the women rejoined with people of their own villages, the men of each village competing with others to see which group is strongest in ritual and dancing performances. Since the parents must be separated during the hunting and initiation activities, their relationship is more polarized, and it is obvious to the initiate that the distance between his parents is greater than ever. A woman is acting both as the boy's mother and as his father's wife. A man is both the lad's father—an initiator—and his mother's husband. What men do toward boys may be interpreted as an action against the boy's mother as well. This is why men forcibly separate boys from their mothers at the very start. Women's responses, likewise, seem to be partially aimed at their husbands and partially at their sons.

The attitude of women about their sons is ambivalent. Women resist the separation (Bonnemere 2004). At the Yulami initiation we will see the ceremonial wailing of the initiates' mothers opening the rituals. Later they aggressively reclaim their sons for the frog feeding on the dance ground. And yet women chastise boys for their laziness as economic providers. Finally, the women identify the boys with their hostile fathers, just as the men identify their polluting wives with their sons. The boys are caught between the two worlds.

Women thus play a definite role, although men think of them mainly as spectators. Women have interpersonal influence in the domestic sphere, extending even to a say over how much time their husbands spend gardening or hunting. In public affairs, however, women have little formal power. The exception, as we shall see in Chapter 6, is a fascinating one: women shamans, an oddity in such a warrior culture. Women contribute food and handcrafted items such as net bags and grass sporrans for the initiates and other kinsmen involved in the rites. Their labor is also crucial at the start when they supply piles of grass thatching for the cult house roof. These are customary female tasks that prepare for initiation. Women dance on the dance ground in the opening public ceremonies and play other minor parts too. But the fact that they are always there, always an audience for whom the men stage the public displays, adds force to the idea that spectators really have more power than we think.

The final category of organizers is the boy's ritual guardian or sponsor. He is called "mother's brother." Not all ritual guardians are actual mother's brothers, although many are. For the others, the title is honorific. At Yulami village, only about a third of the guardians were actual or classificatory mother's brothers. Nonetheless, the warmth in the maternal uncle–nephew relationship is obviously being highlighted. The sponsor's job is to protect the initiate from being beaten too much and to teach him about ritual lore, especially the need to ingest semen. Guardians physically carry initiates through the ordeals of initiation, creating a powerful bond between them that lasts throughout life. The sponsor serves as a boy's supervisor and mentor at first-, second-, and third-stage initiations, wherein the sponsor is ceremonially treated or thrashed along with a boy whom he carries. He also instructs and ritually decorates the boy. Later, at fourth-, fifth-, and sixth-stage rites (if alive and active), the sponsor participates and takes pride in his ward's achievement of advanced masculine status.

The boy's father usually selects the guardian. A man may earn this guardianship right by giving an *ichinyu* possum food gift to celebrate the birth of a child by another man's wife. These men should not be blood kin, which means only men of other clans can bestow the gift. If a female child is born, the possum gift obliges the family to give her to the donor for a delayed-exchange marriage to his own son years later. A male infant's birth creates a different opportunity because a male infant eventually needs initiating, and the gift of possum provides a right to serve as his sponsor. Here, the boy's mother will also have a say in the matter. The father remunerates the sponsor for his services with possum, vegetal salt, bark capes, and the like. The initiate, moreover, later gives gifts to his sponsor over the years and also receives food from him. Another mode of selection is for adult age-mates (of different clans) to act as the sponsors for each other's sons. This arrangement precludes the exchange of gifts between them, and Sambia dislike this method because they feel such fathers are simply stingy or unwilling to hunt or trap for meat gifts. In either case, such fathers are labeled *wogaanyu,* unmanly. More rarely, a father names his trade partner as a sponsor. In short, the sponsor is well known to the novice's father, and they are comrades. Most boys no doubt see this, which is perhaps why boys often identify their guardians with their fathers.

Yet, ironically, the cultural norms governing the initiate–guardian relationship suggest that, symbolically, the sponsor is like a surrogate mother. Initiates are at first respectful and fond of their sponsors. Later, as they mature, they develop a joking relationship. The initiate is, however, bound by strong taboos toward his sponsor that match those toward his mother and women to a surprising degree. He should not, for example, ever say his sponsor's name, a taboo that also applies to spouses. Not until he is an adult can he eat food or drink in front of his sponsor, which applies to women as well. The sponsor holds primary responsibility for motivating a lad to engage in homoerotic activity, but the sponsor and initiate are absolutely forbidden to have sex. Later, when the initiate marries, his mentor will pass on the magic of heterosexual-purification techniques and his wisdom about how to handle a wife.

THE INITIATIONS BEGIN

The planning of the 1975 Sambia Valley initiations was set with the planting of feast gardens. Some of these gardens were being planted when I arrived in October 1974. The cult house was built in early 1975. From April to mid-July there were intermittent months of possum hunting that secured the meat for initiation feasts. Throughout the whole Sambia tribe, several different initiation cycles were done in this period by different confederacies.

I spent 62 days and nights attending the rites for these initiations. I could provide you with an idealized or formal account of the rites, which would tend to standardize the details and be impersonal. Instead, I will concentrate on my eyewitness observations of the events. Initiation ceremonies are elaborate, so we can only examine a few key rituals, touching on the main happenings while skimming the surface of others. My selection of ethnographic data will illustrate the main events and the overall theme of initiation. We will begin with the cult house scene, followed by short sections on third- and second-stage initiation.

All Sambia initiations have a political dimension, as I have said, but the first-stage rites described later occurred in a most highly charged political climate. The Sambia Valley confederacy of hamlets and its men's society crosscut phratry boundaries. In the Upper Valley the opposing phratries have long performed joint initiations, over 20 of them since 1900. Yet warfare has sometimes disrupted this alliance between hamlets and phratries. The ritual cycle performance of 1975 was influenced by historical events in the previous generation, and the initiation itself represented a change in local politics. Only once before (c. 1953) had the particular surrounding hamlets participated in collective initiation. This meant that some of their rituals were still unknown to the opposing phratries. Warfare and sorcery accusations had plagued the relationships between the Yulami hamlet, their Moonagu phratry allies, and the Upper Sambia phratries. This political antagonism did not, however, cause a breakdown in the initiation plans. Indeed, the sheer fact of the performance showed that leaders of both sides recognized peace and the end of war, as seen in men's rhetoric during the ceremonies. In still another way, this initiation shows the general acceptance by Sambia of the political realities of increasing social change in the area.

On the night that ushers in the construction of the cult house, men of nearby hamlets gather in the clubhouse of the host hamlet. They have an all-night songfest and make plans for events of the coming days. There is the usual singing, smoking, and betel nut chewing of all-male songfests. But the war songs and blowing of long bamboo flutes distinguish this songfest from ordinary ones. Local shamans perform a collective ceremony and devinate for omens revealing the success or failure of the impending rites. Despite preparations and rumors, the actual day the rites will begin remains unknown to women and children. The urgent, mysterious power of the flutes announces the beginning of the ritual cycle that night. Initiates have told me how the flute sound alerted them of their inevitable initiation and made them worry about what was to come.

Transition Rites: a characteristic *structure of transitions* can be seen in Sambia initiation rites. It will help you to follow these events if you understand the early insights of the French anthropologist Van Gennep (1909). In his *Rites of Passage,* Van Gennep discovered a set of changes associated with life-crisis events in many societies. He found that people involved in initiations, puberty rites, marriage, and other ceremonies undergo similar status changes. First, they are separated from the group. Usually they are secluded or otherwise treated as ritually special, as if they were more powerful or sacred than normal. Then they are endowed with the status of true marginal beings, who are "betwixt and between" normal states of social living, on the margins of the group. We refer to this special marginal status as *liminal* due to its ritual power.[3] This is a

---

[3]Liminality is taken from the Latin term *limen,* meaning threshold. Victor Turner (1967: 93–94) states: "If our basic model of society is that of a structure of positions, we must regard the period of margin or 'liminality' as an inter-structural situation." This notion depends on Van Gennep's scheme of the *marginal* period of *rites de passage,* when "the state of the ritual subject (the *passenger*) is ambiguous" (Turner 1967: 94).

momentous and dangerous condition. Society itself can undergo change here because the initiates are between different social roles, reflecting on their own identities and realizing new things about their bodies, their past experience, and future social positions. This is why they are confined and kept removed from society. Finally, following these changes, the initiates are reaggregated into society and returned to normal social relationships. But not as before: Their ritual experience has made them different, both in their outward social roles and in their inner identities. By experiencing these transitions together as a group, Sambia initiates develop affectionate friends as well as age-mate bonds, which we shall examine later.

THE CULT HOUSE SCENE

Early in the morning, a large group leaves our hamlet for the cult house and dance ground on the other side of the valley. They include Kanteilo, my elder sponsor; Weiyu; Moondi; and younger friends, males at all ages from the village. I am among them. We take up quarters near the cult house. Other men, some women, and children follow. Soon hundreds of visitors are settling all around us. Tonight the first moonlight rituals and dancing begin. Everyone is beautifully garbed and decorated. Weiyu and Moondi show me around. We see throngs of people from all over, even from other valleys.

A long sequence of nighttime ceremonies is held that first night. The next night these are duplicated, with the third-stage initiates taking prominence. On the third day things calm a bit. That afternoon I went to the cult house and was amazed to see open homoerotic play, which I had not seen before.

How did the men accept me in this scene? This question is basic to all anthropological research. Yet in sensitive settings like this one it is essential to know how and why people accept an outsider, how he or she influences their behavior, and whether they keep secrets. Remember that I had already been in the village eight months. I had lived in the men's house, where homosexual activities were at first hidden from me. I had friends, and several informants had stayed in my house and I ate with them. We had often traveled together. But after four months it was still a scandal when my friend Nilutwo told them he had told me about the secret homosexuality. The men were furious with him. Things were tense for days. What could I do? I waited, and gradually their anger passed. They made me promise I would not tell women and children the secret. As time passed and I was good to my word, they trusted me more. When the initiations rolled around, my friends never doubted I would go to see the secret ceremonies. The men of other hamlets asked about me too. Could I be trusted? A few tried to get me to leave or tried to trick me into missing the ceremonies; but they were exceptional. Most of the people accepted me, for the men with whom I worked always stood up to speak in my behalf. They still do. I was involved in their cult in this sense; I saw the rites and was there when it all happened. Yet I tried to stay off to the sidelines, not wanting to attract undue attention. Some things, like the harsh beatings in initiation, were hard for me to witness. I tried always to describe my own reactions to things too. Thus, I was a participant-observer of the rites, though I did not directly join in or accept as a part of my own personal style all that I saw.

The emotional and sexual tenor of the cult house scene reveals that Sambia society is temporarily in a state very different from everyday life. Norms and rules are turned on their head. Some anthropologists have referred to this as "ritual time": a time with the license to act out normally forbidden impulses, a sort of free "play" within ritual. Turner (1971) has referred to this as a period of "anti-structure" in society, when relationships are open to reconstitution of ideals and exploration of tabooed feelings. We will see the individual counterpart of anti-structure in the liminal experience of initiates later.

The dance ground comes alive at dusk. The weather is cool and clear. Men and initiates are everywhere, although the area is uncrowded. From somewhere, out of sight, flutes can be heard, a part of the male camaraderie celebrating the complete absence of women and children. Homoerotic contacts are rampant here. People are open and unabashed, though they do honor certain taboos. Homosexual activity is governed by rules that match incest taboos: All kinsmen and distant relatives are tabooed sexual partners, as are boys' age-mates and ritual guardians. Brothers-in-law may be acceptable sexual partners, depending on their exact relation to the boy. The mood is festive and light, with initiates running around, laughing, and clowning, an atmosphere as different from the heavy solemnity characterizing formal rituals as is the night from the day. The following are my very first observations of homoerotic play in the dance ground context. Similar things happened in later initiations too.

The cult house is dark and noisy, a mass of bodies and movement and laughter. There are two dozen initiates and older bachelors. None of the new *ipmangwi* bachelors are here; they are in ritual seclusion. The elders have absented themselves. Sambia males feel that it is in bad taste for initiates to engage in homoerotic play in the presence of elders. (Homoerotic jokes or innuendos, however, alluded to by elders vis-à-vis their peers, are appropriate in front of initiates.) So boys usually refrain from homosexual play when near elders or their fathers. In situations like this one, where elders know what to expect, they conveniently disappear. Several men have built a small fire in the hearth. Some adults who are forbidden to engage in homosexual activities are present. They sit detachedly chatting, incongruously calm in the center of a storm. All but one of them can sustain this composure—which feels artificial— as seen by his fascination in watching the homoerotic play. The boys are openly initiating foreplay here. Several sitting near the fire are flirting and hanging onto bachelors. Allusions are made to me watching, but no one seems to mind.

Outside on the dance ground three boys are hanging on to Sonoko, a bachelor who seems to be in demand. He is talking loudly. A short, strange little Wantuki'u tribesman, who is older but still unmarried, is glued to the second-stage initiate Sollu, a pubescent boy from our hamlet. I am amazed to see Sollu, who is surly, hugging him, their arms locked, faces cheek to cheek. The boy actually nuzzles the man's neck, but there is no kissing. (Sambia do not kiss mouth-to-mouth.) Nearby, several small boys reach underneath the older bachelors' grass aprons to arouse them. A tiny initiate says impatiently to Sonoko:

"Come on, shoot me." Occasionally the smiling youths halfheartedly protest that the initiates are pulling on them too hard. In the shadows of the house are several male couples rolling around in the grass. One of them is older, married, and a father, which makes his behavior immoral by ritual convention, but no one pays attention.

Most of the new third-stage initiates are milling around outside. I walk over to join them. Several feet away is their ritual seclusion hut, filled with elders and off limits to the younger initiates. Some of these youths flirt with initiates, though the youths are forbidden to inseminate them until they complete their own initiation. Some smaller initiates look nervous in anticipation of the night's events. Moondi is among this mob, but he appears calm. It is not clear exactly which youths will be initiated; several of them are strangers from outside the Sambia Valley. Two Sambia boys from the village talk with me. Someone hands us baked taro, our first food.

I turn back to the shadowy dance ground where sexual exploits and their risqué sounds are even more outrageous than those in the cult house, which seems to excite the crowd. There is still a faint light outside and I am conspicuous. Several times I hear allusions with mild hostility to my presence, but I try to ignore them. A little later, in response to one of these mutterings, I hear my friend Sonoko say: "That's nothing. . . . He knows." Here—witnessing open homoerotic activities and standing alone, tall, white, Western-clothed—I feel awkward and out of place, more like a voyeur than I ever have, peeping in on a private show. I clutch my pipe nervously and smoke more than usual. There seemed nothing else for me to do if I was to remain and yet ease my tension.

Some two dozen men, bachelors, and initiates are now milling around the dance ground, scattered on the great empty space here and there. Some walk in pairs, others in small clusters of bodies, all restlessly flowing clockwise around the circular ground, as if keeping time with some slow, silent hymn (and there was no singing). Initiates are also horsing around among themselves, playing tag, running back and forth, pushing, pulling, and shoving. In the center are several married men who are oddly detached, circling idly among the others. But there are no initiates with them. Nearby are several young and recently married men (without children yet), including my friends Erujundei, Sonoko, Ooterum, and Aatwo (the latter a hard-bitten man in his early twenties whose father is a war leader). Each of them has one or two initiates; Aatwo is with a boy whom he has long favored. Sonoko has three initiates, who come and go while I stay on the dance ground over the next two hours. The atmosphere remains edgy and exciting. There is rampant sexual foreplay, initiates even competing to hold a man's genitals. From time to time, these couples exit the dance ground into the grass close by, for fellatio; Sambia never permit sex in public. When they reappear minutes later, most walk over and sit inside the cult house.

There is variation in this sexual behavior, but two general patterns emerge. First, most of the couples return to the cult house afterward, some—in blatant public "statements"—entering together, while still physically touching, arm in arm. Others, out of embarrassment (as noted by waiting on purpose, then nervously talking to friends), enter separately, moments apart. Second, a few couples return to the dance ground together but then separate. In some instances the initiate goes to another man, leaving his bachelor on his own or with another boy. Generally, in ordinary life, homoerotic partners will split up after sexual intercourse and go in different directions to avoid notice. Several Wantuki'u men join in, initiates trailing after them. And so does Chemona later on. Like Sonoko, he is very popular with the initiates.

It is the older second-stage initiates, especially the ones recently initiated, who are the most aggressive at this sexual play. Nilangu's own initiates are prominent here: Kambo, Buvuluruton, Sollu, and Dangetnyu. But there are others too. For instance, Merolkopi (Tulutwo's younger blood brother) literally hangs on to Nolerutwo, smiling and petting him. Around 7:00 p.m. I hear the youth say matter of factly to the younger Merolkopi (who stands with two other initiates who want to be inseminated, all pleading "Me! Me!"): "All right, I mark you to shoot." The initiate lights up in a wide smile. Two other initiates keep teasing and pulling Sonoco's genitals, trying to get him aroused. But twice he says loudly: "Stop it, I've already slept [had sex]!"

Thus it goes into the night. On the next night it is the same. And again, at the start of each successive initiation, this free and orgiastic carnival atmosphere is repeated. Never before or since have I seen public erotic behavior of this sort or on this scale. Homosexual play does occur in other secret situations: at night in the clubhouses, and in the forest or hunting lodges. But it is never this blatant, with open foreplay, and it certainly never occurs on such a wide scale within a large group. The closest situation is that of the rat-hunting lodge, which follows first-stage initiation in the forest. Indeed, the repressive nature of Sambia society makes it seem impossible to casual observers that such frenetic energy could be so easily unleashed in males who, except for these several nights—two or possibly three times in their lives at initiations—are renowned for their reserved, straitlaced behavior, abhorring public eroticism. Yet, my most singular memory of that night is the *openness* of sexual play, which shocked me, for it meant there were similar past experiences locked inside the adult men I thought I knew before but would never have imagined out in that crowd. Yet the anthropologist knows that some of the most profound experiences of people are taken for granted or hidden, except on occasions when the reproduction of society reveals more openly the fundamental contradictions of a society.

MOONDI'S DECISION

There are several hours until nightfall and the formal seclusion of the third-stage initiation candidates. My friend and younger interpreter Moondi is one of them. This is a momentous time, when the older second-stage initiates who have reached puberty are expected by elders to voluntarily enter the cult house. Though they are nearly independent, they are still not adults. Social change in recent years has made this a key "pressure point" on youths. Beginning in the late 1960s, bachelors began leaving Sambia to work on coastal plantations far away. They would walk to the patrol post and be flown out. We saw in Chapter 3 as well that Moondi started school in 1971. He saw this schooling as preparing him for an alternative lifestyle, although elders and parents rejected this idea. Moondi had been to a mission school on the patrol post for two years. Then his circumstances and sickness forced him to return to the valley. Eventually he worked as my key interpreter and we became good friends. When the initiations approached, Moondi was dead set against them, as he wanted to continue his schooling. The elders are still doing everything in their power to pressure youths like Moondi to be initiated. Here the issue of there being "no exits" from initiation remains relevant in the face of change. Moondi's generation is at a historic turning point. His situation will introduce the initiations in the context of the changing behavioral environment as it is today.

Moondi appears around noon with his age-mate, Tulutwo, at the dance ground. Both youths are defiant. As the dance ground quiets down in the afternoon, the men's talk turns to the subject of these new bachelors, the men intent on having their will done, and proper induction of the whole set of youths that night. So far I have managed to remain neutral in this conflict over Moondi's initiation without making enemies or compromising my integrity. I want to keep it that way; I am no ombudsman. Moondi's intentions are muddy: He says initiation is not for him, yet at the critical moment he has publicly reemerged. He is a complex young man, intelligent, vocal, and headstrong. Sometimes he is torn between two worlds: the village and the dream of a different life far off in Port Moresby, New Guinea's capital. He is of two minds, not knowing what he wants or what he can have. This day he will decide. The men pressure him. Sitting with Moondi and the men, it is hard for me to silently watch the age-old dilemmas of tradition versus change, of group needs pitted against the individual's will played out again, my friend the pawn, myself an audience. I feel painfully helpless. After some minutes of interrogation, in which Moondi stays silent, I rise to leave. Then so does everyone else.

Down the hill we walk to a hut where I am staying and the drama continues. (Looking back now, I see that Moondi's only real—and final—defense against being initiated was the "authority" of my presence. But he knew I could not stop the men.) Moondi stays physically close to me; his friend Tulutwo stays close to him; my friend Weiyu, as if defending me, walks on my other side. And a mob of men is on our heels.

Suddenly I realize that Moondi is actually afraid the men will abduct him and force him into the cult house. Were a scuffle to ensue, trouble could erupt. What were we to do?

Moondi's father (who is characteristically soft-spoken) pursues us, imploring his son to talk. Oolerum, whom Moondi favors as a mother's brother, speeds along asking me if Moondi would be initiated. The men assume I know what he is up to, but they are wrong. "This is your matter and Moondi's own choice," I said. When they tell me that Moondi said I asked him to go to my house and fetch some things for me, I halt. Now I understand. Unknown to me, Moondi had been using this lie as an excuse. I can neither betray him nor lie. Caught between Moondi and his fate, I sputter: "That's Moondi's affair; I don't need anything urgently. But if he does go, well he can bring back my tennis shoes. *If* he comes back." The men look perplexed. Moondi speeds up (as we all do), actually running just ahead of us, as if the men might still grab hold of him to prevent his escape. The tension is not over.

The hut I am staying in fills up with the whole mob of men. We are an hour's walk from our own village. The men corner Moondi again, repeatedly asking him if he plans to run away, to leave for the coast and work. He keeps saying no. Some of Tulutwo's clansmen appear too. They press in on both youths, whom everyone suspects to be in league. I am silent. Even Tulutwo is scared, and this surprises me because he is built like a boxer and the little likable fellow always acts so tough around the younger initiates. Finally, the men allow the two youths to go back briefly to village Nilangu, on condition that Oolerum, a young married man well trusted by all, accompanies them. They depart, and I am left still wondering about their initiation. Will they return?

An hour passes in relative peace and I breathe a sigh of relief. Doolu, Moondi's father, never budges. But otherwise I am left alone to have a cup of soup and write field notes. In walk Kanteilo and Weiyu: "Is Moondi going to run off?" More veiled exchanges like before. Kanteilo knows I am sympathetic both to Moondi *and* to him. The old man—to whom I owe so much for his social support, who was a great warrior and is still a great fox—plays on my sympathies, saying he is very ill (he has a large tropical sore). He is forever using this ploy to have his way.

Moondi suddenly reappears. Doolu rises. He stands 10 feet from his son but only half looks at him, saying "Moondi, what are you doing?" Quietly but firmly, "What about your initiation decorations? They are ready." Kanteilo keeps hammering away that Moondi's ritual sponsor, a Wantuki'u tribesman and Doolu's trading partner, has arrived. He was Moondi's first ritual sponsor years ago. Moondi, who barely knows him, does not feel close to him.

Kanteilo refers to his open tropical sore, baring his abdomen so we can see it, appealing to Moondi to listen to him. "I am old and sick," he says to a silent Moondi. When his father appeals again, Moondi angrily snaps back, *"Koonanu!* [Lies!] No." His face and voice are tense. The others then leave. Doolu stands alone and sad in the thankful darkness of the room. I feel awful. They have come close to cursing each other—a fatal turn in a father-son relationship that would never be forgotten, even if forgiven. Never once does Moondi look at his father, as is common in such arguments. He wanders off. His father leaves and I am alone.

Moondi returns shortly and for a moment we are in private; I ask why he came back if he does not want to be initiated. "I had no choice: Oolerum was with us." (He did bring my tennis shoes!) "So what now?" I ask. "I don't want to be made a bachelor yet. Very much not! I'm afraid of the great pain—I know what they'll do . . ." I sense that he fears another nose bleeding. I could only nod in agreement, adding that they will soon force him to decide.

How strikingly Moondi's feelings have changed back and forth over the past few days. A week ago he repeatedly said he disliked initiation because it would block his thinking: he never would get back to school, never learn, or never learn as fast again. He had seen this "blocking" occur in several other youths and wanted no part of it. He is too young to be married yet, he says. Later, he admitted something else: he didn't want to be shamed at school. "Why shamed?" I asked. Third-stage initiation "says" you are grown, that you have pubic hair, semen, and sexual urges (that is, have reached puberty) and that a female will be assigned in marriage for you, he argued. The schoolboys make fun of these things; they laugh at the initiated bachelors among them, who are in turn shamed. I believe him, for he has been in school and the Sambia have a terrible fear of being shamed. But now, right down to the wire, as it were, Moondi reveals his *fears* about initiation ordeals: beatings, nose bleeding, and who knows what else. Moondi later added a more personal fear: that he must now stop consuming men's semen and, through sex, give semen to younger boys. "When I think about that, I'm afraid, afraid to be a bachelor! What if I don't grow big quickly? I won't be able to eat more 'milk' [semen] later."[4] Here, Moondi referred to the fact that bachelors can never reverse sexual roles once initiated: They can only give, not receive, semen. Powerful fears these were. But the social pressures were more powerful.

Enter Kanteilo again, who plunges ahead: He says Moondi must be crazy *(abrumbru)* to be acting like this. What will Moondi do? Kanteilo lectures him: "Your body isn't the same as a white man's. Nor is your food . . . you've got to be initiated to stay as strong as your age-mates and marry." Here, Kanteilo hints that I have exercised a bad influence on Moondi through sharing my food and my Western ways. At one point Moondi scoffs that the old man's talk was all *koonanu* (a lie or a joke). *"Koonanu!* Boy, what do *you* know? Do you understand these matters?" The elder's voice rises and his chestnut-colored face turns red with anger. Weiyu, as if to calm him down, chimes in, agreeing with Kanteilo. They glance at one another, but Moondi keeps looking away.

Chemona comes by a bit later, word of the ruckus having spread quickly. He is Moondi's older friend. He says nothing after eyeing us except "Wait," in response to something from Doolu. Chemona consoles Moondi; they talk quietly. He persuades the youth to come and eat with him. A minute later I go to Chemona's hut, where they continue talking privately. Here Chemona gently coaxes Moondi, trying to make him give in. He refuses. We all eat Chemona's taro. Meanwhile, Oolerum comes by and joins in, and together they try again. Soon they break off in whispers among themselves. This is remarkable: Sambia never whisper in front of close company. Moondi stops them, afraid of their intrigues. Then a plan emerges, a bargain: Oolerum will "stand in" as a special ritual sponsor for Moondi, saying he won't let Moondi be really "killed" with pain. I take this to mean they will not let Moondi be nose-bled, although their meaning is only hinted. (Later, I discovered that this is indeed what they had agreed upon.) Their promise calms Moondi, who finally relents. He seems satisfied. They all leave for the dance ground.

---

[4]By his own reckoning, Moondi says he has slept promiscuously with more than two-score bachelors and men over the past seven years. He has had sex with over 20 of them at least twice. Besides Erujundei (a young man), Chemona has been Moondi's favorite bachelor, to whom he was attached for a few weeks four years ago. During that period they had fellatio (he served as Chemona's fellator) at least once a day. With Erujundei, however, he has continued to have homoerotic contacts sporadically over the past four years, the most recent having been 10 days ago, at the time of the cult house–raising ceremonies. (Unlike Chemona, who prefers smaller boys, Erujundei openly favors older boys who are masculine and pubescent.)

Moondi's decision has been made; there is no further personal drama for him. On the dance ground the men too do an about-face. No one reproaches or questions him; they are all smiles. His presence speaks for itself. After a moment he blends into the crowd and is absorbed by his age-mates.

THIRD-STAGE INITIATION

The third-stage initiates are led from the men's house to the cult house, where they are left in seclusion until dark. Moondi is with them. Now they fall under the burden of many ritual taboos. They cannot drink water or take food. It is forbidden to talk under threat of harsh punishment. Nor can they move about or sleep. In this motionless state, they can reflect on themselves and the momentous changes they are experiencing. Their ritual decorations, some originally selected by their parents years ago at first-stage initiation and other new decorations, are prepared and placed on them by their ritual guardians. An all-night songfest is held. Early in the morning ritual experts lead the youths to the forest for purification ceremonies using ritually sacred trees, such as the giant redwood (selected for its qualities of sturdiness and longevity). These rites are done to remove any feminine residues from youths and masculinize them. The sequence takes hours. Afterward, the bachelors remain under the seclusion taboos. Hungry, thirsty, tired from lack of sleep, and worn out from the long trek to the high forest, they return at nightfall for still more moonlight dancing. What an endurance test! They dine very late at night on cold taro.

In the morning the youths undergo more forest purification rites, followed by severe thrashings with cassowary quill bones. Both these rites strengthen and stimulate the growth and aggressive characteristics of youths. The most violent Sambia rite—the nose bleeding—follows this. These occur throughout the male life cycle, coordinated with initiation: at first-, third-, fifth-, and sixth-stage initiation rites; and always thereafter when a man's wife has her monthly period. (Because of its importance and the difficulty of describing all types of nose bleedings, we will return to a full discussion of this ritual behavior under first-stage initiation.) The nose bleedings, done violently and by surprise, reintroduce the ritual flutes to bachelors, who learned of them originally in their first-stage rites years ago. Then they are decorated for dancing again. Later, for the first time in days, they are allowed a night's sleep.

The final events of third-stage initiation lead the men back to the forest, to a special ceremony that identifies the bachelors with the strong, "masculine" black palm tree. This also reveals how much they share (as a male group) in the passions of secret collective rituals (Herdt 1981).

At the very last, their new warrior armbands are placed on their forearms; they are young men now, and the armband is the key gender sign of puberty in males. New shell nose plugs are also placed on them. The youths scatter to their respective hamlets, where they again reside in their clubhouses. Soon, though, they are called upon to leave with adult men for the high forest to hunt possum again—this time for feast gifts for the second-stage initiates, for whom they too will serve as initiators.

SECOND-STAGE INITIATION

Several weeks later, the old first-stage initiates are elevated to *imbutu* status in the second-stage rites. These are the simplest of all collective ceremonies, although they still stretch over several days and are colorful, with red pandanus fruit and red decorations being the focus of decoration. The initiates are collected as an age-set from all the neighboring hamlets and are placed in the cult house. Now the new third-stage bachelors are key actors in organizing the main events.

The second-stage boys are still very young: 11, 12, a few a bit older, the latter with peach-fuzz facial hair. These second-stage initiates are more confident than the younger boys at first-stage initiation, although they are not as hardened as the older third-stage youths. For one thing, they have never been on a war raid, and most of them have never fought in a real battle. When they dress up in the warrior garb befitting their status, however, they make a handsome and proud lot.

These second-stage initiates, too, assume heavy food and behavioral taboos. For some days they cannot eat, sleep, or drink; they must not speak at all, which is no different from the preceding initiation. The same taboos are applicable to them. These are taught in the initiations and enforced for the duration of their time in this ritual position. First-stage initiates, for instance, have many food taboos, which include all red and blue foods (identified with women), such as red pandanus fruit oil, red and blue yams, and many red-colored leaves. The feasting in second-stage rites ends these particular taboos. This is the trend throughout ritual life: Initiates begin with a very few acceptable foods and a great long list of food taboos. By final initiation few taboos remain, and by old age all the food taboos are gone because Sambia see the elderly as relatively genderless. Food is identified with sexual potency and gender, as is most everything in the Sambia world, so food intake is ritually restricted to ensure health, long life, and fertility.

The forest purificatory rites are colorful and dramatic in second-stage initiation. Tali and several ritual experts take boys out at dawn each morning to rub dew from the meadow grass on their faces, to "cleanse" and masculinize them. Following this are purifications using river stones, orange forest muds, wild taro plants, cabbage palm, young pandanus-nut trees, wild ginger, brown tree parasites, white-colored forest shrubs, and blond and blue tree grasses. An extremely painful and violent stinging-nettle rite is held. Boys are dressed up and dance before the crowd in moonlight festivities on several nights. They are distinguished by having cassowary quill bone nose plugs ceremonially placed in their noses. A day later, in secret, they are lectured on the importance of continuing to ingest semen. During boy-insemination teachings, elders tell them that their cassowary quill bone nose plugs will erotically arouse the bachelors, who will want to inseminate them in the mouth. So the quill bone is used explicitly as a symbol of penile erection. The importance of assisting in hunting and gardening is also constantly stressed. Certain myths surrounding the origins of foods, pandanus fruit in particular, and animals are told. After several more days, the boys are given a feast and allowed to sleep.

Figure 4.2 The intensity of ritual oratory; a war leader teaches first-stage initiation, 1975

The next day, boys have their final feast and are lectured again on the need to be warriors and hunters (see Figure 4.2). The elders implore them to ingest as much semen as possible, to grow strong. The boys have homoerotic contacts at night in the cult house. These will increase in the coming days before they are released to return to normal life in their own hamlets.

FIRST-STAGE INITIATION

The first initiation of Sambia boys is special in many ways, being the longest and most elaborate initiation ceremony, and the most important, because it opens the secret world of men to boys. The boys' separation from their parents is dramatic, as is their virgin exposure to boy-insemination. Nor must we forget how young the boys are, and what they endure, learn, and change into is remarkable for 7- to 10-year-olds. We will examine these events in detail; but still, many things must be omitted from this short account (See Table 4.2).

These last events started on July 27, 1975, and lasted for seven days. The new third- and second-stage initiates were crucial participants. Both Weiyu and Moondi served as initiators during this time. This particular initiation was done at Yulami hamlet, in the lower Sambia Valley. You know already the political changes this initiation represented: Two opposing phratries with a history of warfare came together for the first performance in modern times. The men were primed for staging impressive displays after the preceding weeks of higher-stage rites, each side determined to prove that its phratry was the stronger in the initiation cycle.

TABLE 4.2   SAMBIA FIRST-STAGE INITIATION SEQUENCE OF RITUALS

Separation of initiates, guardian takes authority

Day 1   Journey to sponsor hamlet

1. First ritual thrashing
2. Shaman's ceremonial purification (black palm tree)
3. Taro-feeding ceremony and nose piercing
4. **Moonlight ceremonies**
    Sugar cane rite
    Firewood ritual
    Frog-feeding ceremony

Day 2   Purification at dawn

5. Ritual seclusion
6. Moonlight ceremonies and dancing

Day 3   Purification at dawn

7. Public ritual thrashing ceremony
8. Possum-liver spitting ceremony
9. Ritual nose-bleeding ceremony
10. **Penis and flute ceremony**
    Body decoration
    Ritual parade to dance ground
11. Bachelor impersonation of female spirits

Day 4

12. Ceremonial songfest with hallucinogens
13. Iwouwi'u ceremony
14. Name-changing ceremony

Days 5–6

15. Sequence of horticultural ceremonies
16. Bullroarer ritual

Day 7

17. Ceremony ending taboo on drinking water

First Day of Initiation

We depart our village and arrive two hours later at the village nearest Yulami—Kanteilo, Weiyu, Tali, Moondi, and other men and initiates. Here several rituals will be done before moving on to the cult house at Yulami. We are greeted well, for this is a sister-hamlet of our phratry (the last one before crossing into Yulami territory). The first initiation events soon start. The new initiates, we learn, have been taken from their parents, who returned only yesterday from a month-long possum hunt. Three boys ran away and tried to escape into the forest. One has been found already and the others are being trailed. One resisted mightily but was captured and guarded in the men's house.

Figure 4.3 Ritual sponsors cover initiates on journey to forest ceremonies

Soon the secluded initiates are prepared for the short trip to the dance ground. Many men and boys walk ahead of us. We wait 10 minutes. The men standing around the men's house halfheartedly sing war songs. Tulutwo departs and returns; he has changed from Western-style trousers into a grass sporran and, as always, the transformation is startling. He jumps into the organization of things with such a grown-up expression on his face; how different compared to his fear at the time of Moondi's indecision!

The ritual sponsors emerge from the men's house with their wards riding on their backs, clinging to their shoulders. They cover the boys with their new bark capes so the mothers cannot see their faces. Then the pairs walk through the hamlet (see Figure 4.3). Women and children watch. As the novices are guided past their mothers' houses—leaving them behind forever—the women begin to wail sorrowfully. Weiyu, who is walking with me, remarks that the crying women are the boys' mothers. Off to one side I see a middle-aged woman with long tears on her cheeks. An even larger group of women stand in the brush bordering the hamlet, and three of them loudly bawl as they watch their sons leave.

As we walk up the hillside to the forest, a man shouts out over the crowd of males, but no one responds. He taunts the initiates, telling them to defecate carefully during the next thrashing ritual so their sponsors' backs will not be so messed up! The boys are scared out of their wits, he implies. Just beyond sight of the new initiates and hamlet, some men take out flutes and play them. Meanwhile, the initiates are halted and seated on the grass. The men, however, continue on the path around a bend where numerous men are already secretly preparing for the beating ritual. We are now about 15 minutes above the village. Foliage is cleared to camouflage pairs of men hiding on either side of the trail. Sticks are distributed to everyone for the thrashings. The men lay in wait for a signal to jump up and frighten the novices.

The boys are now lined up, and their ritual sponsors hoist them on their backs. They round the corner on the path. At a signal, all the hiding men jump up and form two lines, with a passageway between them. They thrash the ground with switches, hollering and hooting, grass and debris flying everywhere. The boys look terrified. Their sponsors charge through the lines, so they and the initiates are repeatedly thrashed. Most of the boys cry. Two of them are so afraid that they involuntarily defecate.

Meanwhile, a ritual platform is completed off to one side of the men in hiding. The platform, made of roughly hewn poles, has been constructed around a young black palm tree. It is 6 feet by 8 feet in size and stands 5 feet off the ground. Two senior shamans attach the red ceremonial headband associated with shamans to the topmost palm leaves.

Now the initiates are assembled for their first purificatory ritual. The initiates climb onto the platform. Each is carefully rubbed with the topmost palm leaves and cloth (see cover photograph). The leaves are twisted into each boy's hair. Men say the black palm is like the boy's age-mate. Because the initiate's skin flakes and sweat have been rubbed on the leaves, some of his body essence enters the fast-growing tree. Like the tree he, too, will grow quickly. The shaman touches each boy's head with the red cloth and then jerks it toward the sky, making the eerie shaman's whistle (this is done in healing ceremonies too). The boys are instructed to watch the cloth, which is believed to pull down the sun's power and vitality, gliding into the boy's body via the magical headband. Here we see the sun used directly to help develop *jerungdu* in boys. Then the boy's childhood nose plug, a tiny piece of bamboo, is taken from him, another symbol of childhood lost.

These old nose plugs are collected and placed in a branch of the palm tree. Both the leaf rubbing and placement of the old nose plug in the tree are believed to help fortify the initiates' souls for the ordeals lying ahead. Sambia take care lest boys' souls are too frightened and "escape" their bodies, leaving them vulnerable to illness or death.

The whole group of men and initiates now returns to the village. It is early afternoon, and the initiates are locked up in the village's men's house. They are guarded should any try to escape. Even when allowed periodically to go to the outhouse they are escorted. Meanwhile, my friends and I relax at the hut of a local man.

A few minutes later, Tulutwo gives us sugar cane. Kerumulyu, from a nearby hamlet, is with us. Last week his wife gave birth to her first child, and his sixth-stage initiation has made him an adult. Weiyu's younger clan brother (Tulutwo's own age-mate) sits beside Kerumulyu and jokes with him. The youth makes a pass at Kerumulyu's grass apron, jokingly attempting to grab his penis. Kerumulyu is momentarily embarrassed, but they both laugh as he protests. Such homoerotic joking among males is common during idle moments of initiation. Then others begin to speak of the coming events.

The septum-piercing ceremony follows shortly thereafter. This ceremony, with its special feast foods, is said to hasten the initiates' growth. The ceremony is mainly symbolic because most boys already have pierced noses. The ceremony draws attention to the nose and their new status, following the first purification. Food then prepares them for tonight's ordeals and moonlight dancing.

The initiates are led from the darkening seclusion of the men's house and placed in a semicircle facing the men on the village plaza. Women and children are chased away so as not to see what happens. The boys wait only moments and then eight colorfully decorated men (carrying long red leaves) in a line run into view. These dancers hurriedly pass along the line of initiates and pound their chests. This is also done on older second-stage initiates, who are lined up behind the novices. Then Tali proceeds to ceremonially strike each lad with a second ritual object, the *kwolyi-mutnyi*. This object is believed to have great secret power to strengthen and help boys grow, and to make the group and its gardens fertile. Another senior man produces a string bag full of mashed green leaves. The elders chewed this green mash, and each boy gets a pinch placed in his mouth, again to stimulate growth.

Now a new nose plug is fitted for every initiate. Two boys do not have pierced septums, which is unusual since boys and girls customarily have their septums pierced at around age 4 or 5. The senior man performs the operation on these two matter of factly, jabbing their noses with a cassowary bone needle. They cry. Another elder follows and spits yellow masticated root on the forehead and chest of each initiate, again to strengthen them.

Cooked taro is carried out in a raggedy bark cape. It is broken into pieces and distributed by three men, two of whom are shamans. A chunk of taro is momentarily held before a lad's face, then a spell is muttered while taro is pressed between the shaman's hands and into the lad's stomach. The spell appeals magically to the eagle and to the hard white sap of trees to strengthen the lad and dissolve his hunger; he must be strong now, as later, when he journeys on war raiding parties and food is short. (At third-stage initiation a similar ceremony is done, traditionally to anticipate real war raids.) The boys quickly wolf down the taro, their first food of the day and their last until the early morning hours. Another ritual fast now begins.

The party from our village walks the main trail to the cult house, an hour away. It is dusk when we arrive at Yulami, the site of the great cult house.

YULAMI HAMLET   The hamlet is crowded when we arrive. I follow the initiates, who are placed in a small house near the cult house on the dance ground above the hamlet. The cult house is off-limits to the boys until a ceremony is done a bit later. Numerous people from Nilangu and Pundei hamlets are staying in temporary grass huts on the edge of Yulami, and the friendly relationship between them is obvious. A few older families camp together, sharing food and conversing. But sexual segregation is prominent. Women take up residence with their children in two large houses. Nearby, the men and older initiates stay in another house, where I also bedded. This kind of solidarity between our people and distant kinsmen from the area persisted during the initiation. On the other hand, the inhabitants of Yulami village—former enemies—did not make us overly welcome, a fact my party repeatedly complained about. Fears of sorcery were common.

A large group of men and women assemble in and near the women's house, where there emerges a lively and friendly atmosphere. Older people noisily chat, smoke, and chew pandanus nuts around campfires. Children are running everywhere.

Back in the men's quarters, our elders and senior men sit in the house, telling stories and chewing betel. Off in the distance I can see the vacant dance ground. At dark, the elders begin needling the bachelors and older initiates (a common occurrence in the initiation), reminding them of their ceremonial and homoerotic responsibilities. The men's reprimands are at first humorous. "Why are the initiates not up at the dance ground with the new initiates?" Our boys, men assert in a friendly manner, are the age-mates of the new novices. They mean, of course, that second- and first-stage initiates are all fellators, who should be concerned with "growing big." Our second-stage initiates shrug and try to ignore them. Elders say they have "worked hard" recently to elevate the younger boys to second-stage initiate status. Moondi defends our boys, saying everyone feels reticent about being here in Yulami, which is a strange and hostile place. He also criticizes the hamlet for its tiny population, a fact that is both funny and worrisome (fears of sorcery?), it seems. But Kanteilo retorts that the second-stage initiates and Moondi too (who is now a third-stage bachelor) should not be "lazy" and hang around the elders here. Bluntly, they tell the initiates to go and ingest semen. Weiyu, sitting nearby, adds: "Yes, that's true, you don't want to fall 'sick' [from lack of semen]! Go on now." So the boys reluctantly leave for the dance ground.

Soon, the remaining young married men engage in their own verbal duelling, as is common between in-laws and male cross-cousins. Erunjun and Weiyu joke with men of Pundei hamlet, trying to extort pandanus nuts from them. Two of the men are their in-laws, and one of them is a cross-cousin. Weiyu chides them: "Come on! We gave you our 'sisters' quickly; they developed breasts quickly; now you should give us pandanus nut 'milk' just as quickly!" They all laugh at this; Weiyu is given more of the precious nuts.

MOONLIGHT RITUALS OF THE DANCE GROUND   On the first night of initiation, men perform glamorous public rituals. A great central bonfire lights the center of the dance ground. Its brilliance is compared to the moon's rings. The weather is beautiful. Senior men and older and newer initiates dance, while groups of older warriors sing choruses of war songs. Women and children build small campfires just beyond the dance ground, around its fence, to warm themselves through the long night. Women participate in the early dancing; later they perform their own Firewood Ritual. Here is a rare occasion in which women take a ceremonial role. What emerge in these opening rites are graphic demonstrations of the always-present antagonism between the sexes.

This mood of sexual polarity persists during the remaining days of the initiation. As "rituals of rebellion," these moonlight dance ground ceremonies are inflammatory and tense. Women are not only allowed but are expected to rhetorically chastise the initiates for their laziness and unmanly conduct. In no other context of social life can women collectively launch such attacks. As the night proceeds, women extend their harangues to the men as well. Likewise, elders, in their teachings to boys, seize upon the opportunity to criticize the women. Castigating the boys for their laziness, the elders continue by condemning them for the misuse of male ritual items, such as trees and cordylines. Again, they generalize their verbal attacks by holding the mothers responsible for the boys' sacrilege of male ritual and ritual items. Indeed, at one point they even accuse women of motivating their sons to make fun of the sacred rituals in this way. Women are assailed for ignoring their subsistence tasks too. Male speeches on this opening night, then, anticipate two themes underlying later ritual acts: the rebelliousness of insubordinate, uncooperative women who challenge men's control of persons, events, and resources; and the harmful essence of the depleting and polluting women. Here we see dramatically the bitter tug-of-war between men and women over the initiates, who are, this one last time, caught between the two worlds.

There is also another theme in the rhetoric: interphratry political rivalry. The men begin with the Sugar Cane Ritual. The ritual performers carry in a structure resembling a moving fence of sugar cane. The tops of the cane leaves are inter-twined to create a living wall. The initiates are first hit with the sugar cane and then surrounded by the performers. These men hold the sugar stalks between their legs, thrusting them up and down, bumping the butts into the ground as if riding them like broomsticks. As with carrying the bullroarer pole at other times, their action is blatantly phallic and aggressive. The ceremonial teaching follows. The elders first lecture the women, reprimanding them for ignoring the culti-vation of sugar cane. An elder of our phratry then says to the boys:

> This sugar cane is like the calves of your legs; you must put up supporting sticks when planting it. You may not eat this cane, for it is tabooed to you. This is true for the second-stage initiates too. If you eat it, you will be rubbish men. You can eat it later following third-stage initiation. This ritual is ours—not that of the Yulami peo-ple. You must plant the cane—so you can offer some to any male visitors. Do not be lazy. If your wife cuts down this cane, you should cut her with your knife as punish-ment! She must not think that you are afraid of her. She might want to take another man, so she will cut off the leaves of your cane. If she does so, you should take your axe and cut her, as a warning.

Here we see how ritual is used to define specific activities or foods (sugar cane) as being male. Women are told to leave cane alone. We see also that such items are sometimes used to teach about adultery. Elders' attitudes are to not "spare the rod" in dealing with such women. Such explicit socialization of sex attitudes strongly influences the boys.

Then the Cordylines Rite is begun. Another elder does the orating, but this one laments past warfare between the hamlets assembled here, long-standing rivals who had often fought before the Australians brought peace. In the late 1950s many men of the Yulami hamlet group died, and their deaths were attrib-uted to the sorcery of men in the Seboolu group. People say the sorcery was in retaliation for a fight over eel-trapping rights in the river. (It is known that many men died in the Seboolu hamlets during the same time period, possibly from an epidemic.) Several ceremonies are performed that exemplify this past warfare.

Next is the Firewood Ritual, which temporarily overturns the men's control. Unique to all Sambia initiations, women in this event are permitted to do a cer-emony face-to-face with the initiates. Perhaps this openness expresses the importance of the bond to their mothers, which ritual brings to an end.

Women begin gathering around the inner circle of men by the bonfire in preparation for the ceremony. The men make a larger circle enclosing the few women who are closer to the fire. These women carry smoke-blackened sticks of firewood, a sign of their female domestic role. They dance frantically round the fire, beating the ground with their sticks. The crowd's eyes are glued to the scene.

Now the men bring the novices into the women's circle. The women, some of them quite aged, start hitting the boys hard against their chests, stomachs, legs, and hips. The initiates bawl. The women, as serious as ever I have observed Sambia women, mercilessly castigate the boys. One initiate in particular is singled out by a bitter-faced, frowning woman. She instructs a man (his father?) to hit the boy, and he does. Two women lecture the novices, "You initiates must feel sorry for us . . . We have brought firewood for your dance ground fire . . . Later, when you are in the forest, bring firewood back for us." Somewhat later the male elders add: "You initiates must bring wood back to heat your wives' skins whenever returning from the forest. That is your manly duty, not the women's."

At last the boys are removed from the circle, crying and weary, leaving the women alone and now vulnerable around the dying bonfire. Instantly the men grimace and remark among themselves that the women went too far and said too much. Some younger men mock them: "We are no good; we are spineless for not collecting firewood, are we? That angers us." They challenge the women: "So it is only you women who collect wood! This firewood may be yours, but if we push you into the fire, it will burn you—even though you say you are its 'mother'!" But the women show no fear and even chide the men, replying: "Are you men eels [cold and slippery] that your skins will not be burnt too [if you try to corner us]?"

The women begin a terrible thrashing of the dying bonfire. Great bursts of embers fly into the air, creating a blazing orange fountain. The circling men surround and begin pushing the women into the fire. Edged closer into the fire, the women barely maintain their dancing movements. The men joke at how the women's grass skirts may catch fire. Finally, nearly forced into the hot coals, the women exit, which triggers a triumphant war cry from all the men who have succeeded in expelling their "opponents" from the dance ground. The men celebrate. They compete against one another by dancing, seeing who is able to bounce his grass sporran the highest. They seem unabashedly exhibitionist as the admiring crowds of spectators look on.

This ritual sequence, like others, reveals the tense and conflictual involvement of women in the male cult's public activities. By assuming their complementary role in performing the ritual, women indirectly reinforce the male position. The cooperation of men and women in the ceremony quickly deteriorates. Not content to criticize only the initiates, women direct their remarks to the men as a group, who respond to women as a group. The resulting exchanges, in heated words and scuffles, confirm the opposition between the sexes.

FROG-FEEDING CEREMONY   The dance ground quiets down in the early morning hours following the Firewood Ritual. Men and initiates continue to dance and sing, although much more subdued from weariness. The final nighttime event is the Frog-Feeding Ceremony.

This ceremony provides the initiate and his mother with their first and last opportunity to be reunited. For a few boys, a sort of "ritual mother" (the wives of the guardians usually) substitutes for their true mothers if they are deceased or sick. The setting is highly emotional in spite of the hour. The boys know that this is the last time to sit and eat and talk with their mothers for years to come.

The possessive way in which women remove the boys from the throng of men on the dance ground is striking. Again we see the competition between men and women, here focused on the struggle for temporary control of the lads.

For over an hour women attempt to extract their sons from the crowded dance ground. But the men dominate and hold back the boys. There are scuffles and even arguments. Several times men angrily curse the women, who move back only to approach again. Astonishingly, a few women actually charge into the dancing men to search for their sons. The atmosphere is tense enough for a brawl. An initiate is literally jerked from the dance ground by his mother and another woman. Several moments later, however, Tulutwo raids the women's group and retrieves his initiate—for he is the boy's sponsor—loudly protesting that the women cannot "have him yet."

By 4:00 a.m., women succeed in collecting their sons for the quiet, intimate food ceremonies. For the first time in hours the dancing stops. Each boy is led by his mother to a grassy spot outside the dance ground where she sits with her other children and female kin. Women say that the boys should eat frog until their stomachs are filled because thereafter this food is tabooed until they are married and have their own children. I see a woman place bark capes on the ground and then her own cape over them as a tablecloth. The smoked frog (stored in bamboo vessels) and some possum meat are laid out. I notice that nearly all the novices self-consciously cover their faces while eating these delicacies, continuously tugging at the head-cloak to hide their faces. This self-control is very unlike the uninitiated boys they used to be and rather like the initiated cult members they have become. Women make quiet comments to their sons. Initiates later tell me how their mothers said, "Now you must go to the men's house." Their mothers cry, saying how they will no longer be able to see them. The boys say that many of them cried too, so much so that some boys had no appetite to eat at all.

How do we explain the difference in the boys' behavior? Earlier that day elders had instructed them to hide their faces while interacting with their mothers. The boys recall that the black palm purificatory ceremony is done on their faces, making them its age-mate. Lest they forget, elders warn boys that they will not get to be handsome if women watch them eat. It is even hinted that watching them could somehow harm their mothers. Thus boys have already learned two important reasons for all later avoidance of women. It is apparent that the boys internalized this view and acted on it that night. The ritual resocialization already has shown its effects. The initiates remain with their mothers until sunrise, but they are not allowed to sleep.

Second Day of Initiation

The second day repeats many events of the first day.

Third Day of Initiation

Another purificatory ritual is performed at dawn. The flutes are blown and the initiates are taken back to the dance ground. Then the main public thrashing ceremony is held (see Figure 4.4).

Figure 4.4 Initiates carried by sponsors in thrashing ceremony

This ceremony occurs early in the morning. Unlike the earlier thrashing, this one is public and the initiates' mothers (or in a mother's absence, the guardians' wife) play a part in it. The ritual sponsors again carry initiates through lines of men who wield sticks with which to hit them. The boys' mothers take a complementary role to that of the guardian by attempting to shield their sons' naked buttocks. Pre-initiated boys have naked buttocks until first-stage initiation. This is associated with an immature state, and they are teased for it. Initiation garb includes a bark cape cover for the buttocks, worn for the rest of the boys' lives. Men say that women lay themselves open to thrashings too by going through the lines. The women risk this because "they feel sorry for boys." Yet, men also state that the women's "interference" angers them: "If you women hide the boys' arses, you must want to be hit too!" So the boys, their sponsors, and their mothers are simultaneously thrashed. There is an ordeal for the men too: Those who wish to join in the thrashing of boys must first submit to a private cassowary quill bone thrashing inside the cult house. Both these thrashings are very painful.

When I reach the dance ground with my party early that morning, we hear men singing war songs and the flutes playing inside the cult house. Outside there is a great throng of noisy, excited people on the dance ground. Inside and near the entrance to the cult house, warriors beat bamboo sticks against the phratry totemic bamboo posts that decorate the inner entrance.

We see the initiates lifted on the backs of their sponsors. They prepare for the scary trip between the parallel lines of men and initiates. Twenty-five men kneel in the dusty earth on either side of a pathway that bisects the dance ground. The men clamor for the thrashing to begin. Their thrashing raises so much dust that it is difficult to see to the farther side of the line. The boys' mothers are grouped at the end of the pathway, adding to the congestion of sponsors and initiates assembled there. The mothers hold green cordyline leaves in their hands. The boys are tied to their sponsors' backs with new bark capes, which are knotted. These pairs begin walking through the lines, the mother following closely behind, holding the leaves to shield the boy. Sometimes the mothers succeed in covering boys and sometimes not. The guardians move slowly through the lines, allowing the men many opportunities to swat and inflict blows on initiates. It is like a ritual whipping, and the men take delight in it. Most initiates cry. More startling is the treatment of the mothers, who are hit even harder by the men. The women are usually struck on their backs, their bark capes taking the brunt of the blows. But some are hit hard enough that they fall to the ground and are even hit while on the ground. I observe one third-stage initiate (about 15 years old) land a cruel blow on a woman who had fallen down. He cheers and laughs to call attention to his feat. The sponsors are barely hit at all. The mothers and boys take the heaviest blows, as we can see in their faces, for even the women look afraid when walking through the lines of warriors.

Toward the end of this event there occurs a particularly striking example of an initiate's fear and resistance. A boy refuses to be hoisted onto his sponsor's back (see Figure 4.5). He is older and bigger than his age-mates, and it takes three men to do the job. His mother approaches to take her spot, but he grabs hold of her bamboo necklace. She tries to pull away but he will not release her. Tears wash down his face as he repeatedly cries "No, no," and then "Mother,

Figure 4.5 Initiate holds onto mother before thrashing ceremony

mother." The poor woman's face is a mask of sad helplessness, and she is nearly in tears herself. The boy clings desperately and she struggles. At last the men direct the boy's guardian to go through the lines as the initiate holds fast to his mother. But now she is unable to cover him properly. The outcome is brutal for the boy: Although the sponsor hurries through the lines, the men severely swat the boy with blow after blow, as if to punish him for his fear.

A bit later as is customary, very small pre-initiate boys, some no older than three or four, are carried through the lines and more gently swatted. They are not being initiated but merely being tested for later. The father must decide to do this. Sometimes the mother will not agree and arguments break out. There are always a handful of men who insist upon having their tiny sons symbolically thrashed in this way. Why do they do so? They tell me it is to "strengthen and toughen" the small boys quickly. Besides this, it also communicates to tiny boys that eventually they too must be initiated.

POSSUM-LIVER SPITTING CEREMONY   Later that morning, inside the cult house, the next ceremonial event is organized. This is the possum-liver spitting ceremony, another act of masculine performance for initiates. The ceremony captures the interest of men who show no reluctance to cheer on their hamlet's initiates and cheer against those of others. The ceremony "demonstrates" which boys will become war leaders, virile hunters, and shamans. Like the thrashing ceremony, it is a test of manhood. Those who fail in the task are stigmatized as rubbish men. From the boys' performance in this feat, men tend to generalize about the future masculine prowess and strength of the lads in other facets of warriorhood life. Consequently, boys are placed in competition with each other, as age-mates and as up-and-coming "men." But they can only compete and succeed over peers, not their elders, who completely control the course of the events.

First a man scales the cult-house roof and makes a small hole in its grass thatching. More men enter the house as the initiates are lined up. The women outside are gone. Some minutes later, the roof "window" completed, we look up from inside to see a hole just large enough for the moon face of a shaman to peer in from on top of the outside roof. The man is a senior shaman, and once again we see how the boys must face toward the sky—they will spit toward the shaman—so the symbolism of the sun's power and the shaman's control of it come into play. The guardians lift each boy, in turn, toward the hole. A bit of raw possum liver (mixed with leaves) is placed on the tip of his tongue. The possum symbolizes masculinity and the hunt. Its liver contains the essence of possum strength, which enhances male purity. The boy's goal is to try and spit this up through the roof opening and smack the shaman's face. All of the new and second-stage initiates have a turn at it. The bachelor third-stage initiates do not take part in the competition, for such would be inconsistent with their dominant position over the younger boys. The crowd of men loudly responds to each boy's attempt. Those who fail are dismissed instantly. The successful ones find praise, and their success is met with finger snapping, the sign of masculine bravado. Men refer to them as war leaders, as boys with *jerungdu*. Although some 50 boys take part, only a half dozen succeed in accomplishing the goal. What matters is that here again we see but one of many ritual examples of training for warrior aggressiveness.

Of the remaining days of first-stage initiation, two key rituals stand out: the nose bleeding and the flute ceremony. They both occur later this day, and I will now discuss these in detail. Remember that other events and smaller ceremonies occur too, although to study ritual and gender we will have to largely ignore them.

THE NOSE BLEEDINGS   The nose bleeding *(chemboo-loruptu: chembootu,* "nose"; *loropina,* a verb meaning "to cleanse and expand")* act is considered the single most painful ritual by initiates and men alike. Their feeling is understandable. Physically, nose bleeding is a penetrating trauma of the nasal membranes. The psychological effect of nose bleeding is enhanced by secrecy. So when men perform it on boys—and do it forcibly by surprise at that—this bleeding is like a violent assault whose effects are probably close to producing real trauma in initiates. Boys often refer back to the nose bleeding with expressions such as "I feared they were going to kill me." The ritual symbols and personal meaning of collective nose bleeding are highly focused on the actual blood flow. The assembled initiators always concentrate on a generous but controlled blood flow, the sight of which is greeted triumphantly with a unified ritual/war chant. The ritual bleeding amounts to a forcible penetration of the boy's body boundaries. For, aside from its surprise and dramatic context, the psychological impact of nose bleeding is greater when we realize how much Sambia emphasize the nose as a part of their self-image. Only the genitals are of more importance in anatomy. Yet the nose is second to none in notions of beauty and in the image of masculine gender, as we saw with the nose-plug symbols. The nose also conveys symbolism of the penis, as we saw in reference to nose plugs in general and the cassowary quill bone plug during second-stage initiation in particular.

Nose bleeding is hidden from all women and children, for men are somewhat ashamed that they do it. Bleeding is also done in later initiations, but this information is hidden from younger initiates until they are older and experience the final initiations. Sambia recognize two different procedures for nose bleeding that are associated with different phratries. Traditionally, the magical knowledge of these different practices was hidden from men of opposing phratries in the Sambia Valley. This is because the magic is incorporeal property: ritual customs or trademarks of the groups. (We saw in Chapter 2 how theft of ritual could lead to war.) Following the Australian peace, the opposing sides revealed some of their magic to the other side. The most common nose-bleeding technique consists simply of thrusting sharp cane grasses into the nose until blood flows. This is always used in first-stage initiation. The other technique, forcing extremely salty water down the nose, is also painful, but there is less severe penetration since no hard projectile is involved. A beastly saline solution is made from soaking water in native vegetal salt, which is then sponged into the nostrils as the face is held upwards. Blood instantly flows following this action. This technique is used mainly in fifth- and sixth-stage initiations.

All the Sambia groups in which I observed nose bleeding used the cane-grass technique in the first- and third-stage collective initiations. The practice is regarded as more dangerous than the water technique, mainly because men feel there is always a chance the cane grass might break off in the nose, risking death. After third-stage initiation, the choice of which bloodletting technique to use is made by elders on the basis of the phratry of the hamlet performing the rites. Among the individual men doing private nose bleeding on themselves when their wives have menstrual periods, personal needs, not public glory, are involved; no one else sees them do the solitary ritual. But in public the cane-grass technique is riskier and more daring, so it is seen as the more masculine form. The men's experience seems pinpointed on the need of a hard projectile actually penetrating the nostrils to achieve the painful, inward-to-outward effect of blood release. Elders see the penetrating thrust of cane grass as necessary in accomplishing the act of nose bleeding in first-stage initiation, which in turn is crucial for boys' gender change.

There is another general reason why nose bleeding is felt to be dangerous. Sambia believe that all blood loss from cuts or wounds is dangerous. Left unchecked, these injuries rob one of circulatory blood and even of life itself. Large cuts are handled immediately; even with minor scrapes, men are anxious to stop blood loss. (The single greatest expense in my fieldwork medical budget was for bandages; people constantly asked for them.) Blood is vital stuff. Like ourselves, Sambia view blood loss as a critical symptom of life-risk and a key indicator for later recovery. Birth giving and menstrual bleeding also carry medical risks but of a different sort, because the female body is believed "naturally" to control blood flow. In other words, nose bleeding is done even though it is painful and the blood loss is disliked; men are that desperate to remove female contaminants from the body and blood to reinforce warrior aggressiveness.

Keep in mind that the initiates have already been through three days of ordeals. They have had no sleep, have taken in little food and water, and are becoming hyperactive and afraid of the constant surprises and tricks of the elders. This very morning the initiates' mothers are told sarcastically that their sons will be killed in order to be reborn as "men." So women again begin ceremonial wailing. Later we will see how the men's play on words about "killing boys" is dramatically used against women. The boys too are threateningly warned to "watch out" because of something that lies in store. The mysterious power of the flutes—heard, yet still not seen—comes into play again, heightening the boys' growing fear of the elders' power over the spirits and themselves.

In mid-morning the boys are taken far above the cult house into the forest. (The men are very careful about concealing nose bleeding from women.) Since dawn the men have worked to make an elaborate ritual setting near a small creek. After waiting some time in tense anticipation, the boys are led by their guardians up to the ritual site. The boys at first confront a massive vibrating wall of thick green foliage, a fence of young sapling tightly woven together. Pieces of the shaman's red headband are tied up in branches of the green mass. Inside and unseen to the boys, a chorus of bachelors shake the foliage while making an eerie sputtering sound associated with ritual ordeals. The effect is calculated to be bizarre; when one approaches from a distance, it appears as if blood were

Figure 4.6 Sponsor carries initiate through nose-bleeding passageway

dripping from the branches. The initiates are pushed into this "bloody" chaos, tied to the backs of their ritual sponsors so they cannot escape. They enter through a small opening at its center. Many scream, some squirm and struggle to escape, but all are thrust into this green barricade and through a muddy, narrow inner chamber that leads only one way—into an even narrower, cage-like, 20-foot-long passageway of naked saplings tied together as a fence on both sides (see Figure 4.6). Here it is impossible to escape. (The passage space is barely wide enough for me to squeeze through, and I am rather thin.) Lined up on the outsides of the fence-passageway are many warriors holding wild ginger stalks, which are believed to grow quickly. As the sponsor–initiate pairs push through the fenced enclosure, they are pounded on both sides of their legs and backs. Here again the pounding is believed to help the boys grow strong. Most of the boys cry; indeed, by the time they exit into the forest clearing, many look terrified. Several boys cry out for their mothers as the all-male audience looks on.

Now the initiates are grouped around the pool of a small brook flowing down from a thicket. A huge crowd of men assembles, fencing in the boys. The nose bleeders themselves take center stage. Several are wearing upturned pig's-tusk nose plugs (worn with the tusk points turned up only during war and these rites). The men are serious; even as their tense bodies strain forward in anticipation of bleeding the boys, some of them actually grimace (see Figure 4.7). A "strong" man—an aggressive war leader—steps forward and silently plunges cane grasses up his own nose; in full view of the shocked initiates, blood streams down his face. He betrays not the slightest emotion. He bends over into the water to let blood. Somewhere, still out of sight, the flutes hauntingly serenade his feat. The crowd of men responds with a loud war cry, a signal that they want more. Only now do the boys grow truly alarmed, realizing what is to happen.

Figure 4.7 Men prepare to nose-bleed initiate

The first boy is quickly grabbed. He struggles and shouts but is held down by three men. Before we can catch our breath, the initiator, Karavundun, rolls cane grasses, pushes the initiate's head back, and shoves the grasses repeatedly into the boy's nose (see Figure 4.8). Tears and blood flow as the boy is held and then relaxed forward over the water. Next one and then another boy is grasped and bled. One lad tries futilely to run away. Seemingly as a punishment, he is bled harder and longer than the others. The next initiate resists fiercely, so four men lift him off the ground and, there suspended, he is forcibly nose-bled. After each boy is penetrated until blood flows profusely, the men raise the ritual/war chant time and again. The smell of blood and fear sours the air. The act is almost mechanical for the initiators, who are the boys' clansmen, cross-cousins, and matrilateral kin. The guardians passively assist by holding the boys. The initiates' fathers stay removed.

Many of the previous first-stage initiates, from an initiation held several months earlier, are nose-bled again. They stand in the wings of the group. Some resist; others do not. They are not as frightened as the new initiates. I am stunned; the emotions are so heavy, the scene nearly overwhelming.

The reactions of the boys intensify. Many struggle and are forcibly bled. The men show little pity for the lads, and those who resist are even more severely bled by prolonging the action and thereby brutalizing it. All of the initiates are bled. Afterwards, they remain standing over the stream to let the blood flow. The water ensures that women cannot discover any signs of blood, and it also allows the boys to wash themselves off. Then sponsors dab the boys' noses with ferns, wiping the face clean of any remaining traces of blood. An elder carefully collects the leaves, but we are not told why.

Figure 4.8 An initiate is nose-bled

Following the bleeding, the boys are lined up by the stream for the ritual teaching. The men's speeches describe the nose bleeding as punishment for the boys' insubordination toward their fathers and elders. Women's pollution is also mentioned. Merumie, a respected fight leader and shaman, does the ritual teaching. He begins by telling the initiates about the norm for male hospitality:

> If a man visiting your hamlet comes and asks you for water, you must offer him some. You must not hide your water vessels. He ought to be given water; if there is none, you must go and fetch some, even if it is dark and raining.

The boys are told always to obey their elders' instructions and fetch water when asked to do so. Next Merumie reprimands the boys, saying that as children they made "bad talk" and sassed older ritual initiates. He says that if the boys defy their elders' orders to fetch water or betel nut, they will be nose-bled again as punishment. For this childish insolence, Merumie says, "We now pay you back." The boys are told they must "change their ways."

Last, Merumie lectures the boys on their mothers' harmful effects and the value of letting blood:

> You [initiates] have been with your mothers . . . they have said "bad words" to you; their talk has entered your noses and prevented you from growing big. Your skins are no good. Now you can grow and look nice.

A teaching about warrior aggressiveness was also performed until the first-stage initiation in 1973, at which time it was abandoned. Traditionally, elders stressed that nose bleeding could help boys become more fearless during warfare. They were told to be strong and fearless on the battlefield. Having been nose-bled themselves, they must never fear the sign of their age-mates' or brothers' spilled blood on the battlefield. In fact, elders stressed, the sight of their people's blood was a challenge to seek revenge against the enemies responsible for this loss of blood on their own side. Here we see the fear of nose bleeding converted into the opposite: a stimulus to aggressive warriorhood.[5]

STINGING-NETTLES RITUAL   The Stinging-Nettles Ritual is performed two hours later. The boys are taken to a deeper part of the forest. There is no ritual teaching here. The men say simply that this act "opens the skin" by "burning off" the fine body hair of the boy's childhood skin, making way for the growth of a new masculine skin. Fresh nettles are rubbed all over the body, including the face and genitals. This is a tremendously painful act, and it is hard for me to see this done to the boys right after the nose bleeding. It seems so brutal, and at one point I look away. The boys must feel somewhat like they have gone through an electric shock treatment. Many scream and struggle. Afterward they look dazed. This occurs immediately before the ceremonial body decoration and the penis and flute ceremony. So the nettles' rubbing has the effect of making novices even more frightened of the men and what is to follow next. In this physical ordeal we see once more the accumulating effect of fear changing the boys' basic consciousness. The flute ceremony is the key and final activity we will examine in this regard.

THE FLUTE CEREMONY

We will now study ritual behavior focused on the secret flutes. This activity occurs in two primary contexts: the penis and flute ceremony (hereafter referred to as the flute ceremony); and the new initiates' first entrance into the cult house, an event that leads to sexual encounters with the bachelors the very same evening. The meaning of the flutes—as ritual symbols and as gender signs— stems from their verbal and nonverbal uses. So we will see the meaning of the flutes from the naturalistic behavior of the ceremonies, as well as from what people spontaneously say about them (see Figure 4.9).

Sambia have several types of ritual flutes, but they lump them together under the term *namboolu aambelu* ("frog female"). Some initiates associate this name with the fact that the flute sounds like a certain kind of frog-croaking heard in the deep forest. Remember too that only women hunt frogs, that their mothers fed the boys frog two days ago, and that the forest edge land is the dwelling place of the female spirits. Each flute is made from freshly cut bamboo left open at one end. The hollow tubes vary in length from 1 to 3 feet; they also vary according to their thickness and color. Two types of flutes are blown vertically from the mouth (like a jug pipe); another type is blown horizontally to the mouth through a blowhole. Bachelors or adult men always blow flutes in pairs. The flutes are said to be hostile to women and children. They are also felt to be "married" to the initiates, as we will see.

---

[5]The best and most sensitive account of nose bleedings in New Guinea is in K. E. Read's marvelous book, *The High Valley* (1965), Chapter 3.

Figure 4.9 An elder begins the flute teaching (note the small and large flutes)

As the flute ceremony nears, I sit with the men in my party, who casually recline on the grass watching the ceremonial decoration (see Figure 4.10). Some pranks occur. A married man nearby pretends to copulate with an old tree trunk. He acts as if the tree is a new initiate-fellator, contorting his grinning face as if to express the breathless rapture of sexual pleasure. The men around roar with laughter at this clowning. He repeats his show three times. More laughter. Lewd jokes are cracked. We watch the guardians prepare their wards by dressing them in ceremonial decorations (see Figure 4.11). A man nearby jokes that the sponsors are starting to act "strange," for, as they attach the boys' new grass aprons, our men say, the sponsors' penises are erecting! A second time they suggest that the sponsors' penises are erect. This bawdy insinuation provokes huge guffaws of laughter. Some men joke about others sitting nearby on the grass; they must "smell" the new grass aprons of the boys for they are "smiling." Later they will "coax the lads into sucking them," they say, which provokes more laughter.

This lewd joking amazes me as much as the homoerotic horseplay I described earlier, because Sambia never joke like this! Something is very different here—the ritual and bacchanalian atmosphere. I glance over to the initiates, who look puzzled, and grow scared.

Then comes the flute ceremony itself. The atmosphere suddenly and completely changes. It begins in military silence as the initiates are lined up, decked out in their stunning new attire. They must await the surprises in store for them.

Figure 4.10 Elders and men look on as jokes are made about body decoration

Figure 4.11 A ritual sponsor prepares his ward for body decoration and the flute ceremony

Way off in the distance we hear flutes. They slowly move closer. Two groups, each composed of four bachelors playing flutes, arrive from the dark forest. They slowly circle the boys. There is total silence but for their music. The boys look terrified; this is the first time they have seen the flutes. The flute players are paired; one man plays a short flute, another a longer flute,

Figure 4.12 An older initiate shows how to suck the flute

their musical chords harmonizing. They play for about five minutes; otherwise there is dead silence. During this period, Karavundun (the same man who bled their noses earlier) picks up a long bamboo containing a narrower flute within it. He passes down the line of novices, attempting to insert the tip of the smaller one (contained inside the larger) into their mouths (see Figures 4.12 and 4.13). About half the boys refuse to suck the flute. Karavundun does not press them. Nor is there an angry scene such as I saw at a different initiation flute ceremony, when Moondi's bachelor-friend, Erujundei, threatened uncooperative boys with a machete. When an initiate refuses to suck, Karavundun simply smiles. He even jokes about the stubbornness of those who react with displeasure. Some men nearby openly snigger at the uncooperative and surly boys.

On the other hand, those initiates who take to the act, "correctly" sucking the flute, are lauded, the surrounding spectators nodding their heads in approval.

Then—in visible anger at the defiant boys—Kokwai, a bachelor and my friend, unexpectedly enters the scene and vigorously hits the novices with a long flute. An elder shouts, "Hit them hard. It is not like you were fighting them to draw blood!"

And then the instructing elder Merumei repeatedly intimidates the boys by drawing attention to the large assembled crowd of men: "You uninitiated boys like to make jokes . . . Go on now, make jokes for the crowd here, we want to hear them!" He commands the boys: "You boys—open your mouths for the flute! They will place it inside . . . to try it on you. All of you, look at the large group of men . . . this large group . . . You initiates put it [the flute] inside your mouths, try it!"

The flutes are thus used for teaching the mechanics of fellatio. In their first references to it, elders use themselves as authorities to verify their words. Two

Figure 4.13 A new initiate is tested to suck the flute

groups of well-known elders lecture. Damei and Mugindanbu remain at one
end of the long line of initiates, while Merurnei is at the other end. Kanteilo is
nearby.

The elders condemn the boys for their childish mimicking of the flute
sounds. As they do so, the flute players again strike the boys' chests with the
butts of the flutes. Mugindanbu says: "When you were uninitiated, you all
played a game of imitating this sound 'Um-huh, um-huh.' Now tell us, does this
sound come from your mouths?"

Damei adds, "You boys think fit to imitate the flute sounds, [so] now make
this sound, show us how you produce it. Why should we elders *show you*
how to make it!" Mugindanbu butts in and points to Damei, our great older
war leader:

> All of you boys look at this elder. What do you think he has done? Heard the law this
> moment and grown to be big? All of them [the men] "sucked" the penis . . . and grew
> big. All of them can inseminate you, all of you can suck penises. If you suck them,
> you will grow bigger quickly.

The boys are sworn to secrecy concerning the rituals and then told of the
fatal consequences of breaking this taboo:

> For if you do [reveal the secrets], they will kill and throw your body into the river.
> Sambia boys, you will be thrown away into the Sambia River. Moonagu [phratry]
> boys, you will be killed and your bodies thrown into the lower Sambia River. The

big men will not help you, they will not jail us either; they will help us hide it
[the murder]. This custom belongs to the Baruya and other tribes, [to] all men
everywhere. . . . The sun itself brought this custom, which we hold! If you speak
out, the stone axe and the stone club will kill you . . . When you were children you
saw the bodies of initiates. They are like the nice *inumdu* [shrub], green, smooth,
and young. They are handsome. Those initiates suck the penises of men, and they
grow big and have nice skins too. If you do not, you will not grow quickly or be
handsome. You must all ingest semen.

The elder Damei praises initiates of an earlier first-stage initiation two
months ago. He reveals how the elders were pleased with those boys for their
acceptance of homoerotic activities. He thus urges the boys to follow the example of their peers over at the Yellow River Valley:

There we performed the rites . . . Our initiates "slept with" [sucked] the men. They
drank the men's semen quickly. The bachelors were pleased with the boys . . . They
felt "sweet" [erotically satisfied]. The Yellow Valley initiation was truly good . . . !
This flute we will "try out" [penetrate the mouth] on all of you. Later the men will
want to copulate with you . . . They will do the same thing.

Damei and Kanteilo then spontaneously represent themselves as authorities, tes-
tifying and sanctifying the "truth" of the penis teaching. They relate that only by
ingesting semen can the lads grow truly masculine:

Do you boys see us? We have white hair. We would not trick you. You must all sleep
with the men. When you were smaller you erected the poles for banana trees and did
other things. Now we have initiated you; you must work harder. When you climb
trees, your bones will ache. For that reason you must drink semen. Suppose you do
not drink semen, you will not be able to climb trees to hunt possum; you will not be
able to scale the top of the pandanus trees to gather nuts. You must drink semen . . .
it can strengthen your bones!

In the next ritual teaching, semen is likened to mother's milk. Boys are
taught that they must continually consume it to grow:

Now we teach you our customary story . . . And soon you must ingest semen in
the cult house. Now there are many men here; you must sleep with them. Soon
they will return to their homes. Now they are here, and you ought to drink their
semen. In your own hamlets, there are only a few men. When you do sleep with
men, you should not be afraid of sucking their penises. You will soon enjoy them . . .
If you try it [semen], it is just like the milk of your mother's breast. You can
swallow it all the time and grow quickly. If you do not start to drink it now, you
will not ingest much of it. Only occasionally . . . And later when you are grown
you will stop. If you only drink a little semen now, you will not like the penis
much. So you must start now and swallow semen. When you are bigger your own
penis will become bigger, and you will not want to sleep with older men. You will
then want to inseminate younger boys yourself. So you should sleep with the
men now.

Another man shouts that unless the boys drink semen, they will fail to blow the flutes properly: "If you do not think of this [fellatio], you will not play the flutes well. A boy who does not sleep with men plays the flute badly, for his mouth is blocked up . . . If you sleep with men you shall play the flute well." (Tali, our ritual expert, says this is a double entendre: first, that boys who do not suck the penis cannot properly blow the flutes; and second, that this is because without fellatio their throats stay "blocked up" with the contaminated food of their mothers, like little boys, not warriors.)

In the final sequence, the elder Mugindanbu dramatically cuts the boys' old pubic aprons with a machete. The limp pubic coverings then become the focus of a castration threat aimed at the boys as a warning against adultery. The flutes are played again for several minutes. Merumei then lectures and shouts to the boys:

> When you are grown, the attractive wife of another man cannot sexually excite you. You can touch your own wife, that is all right. The flute will kill you, for, if you steal a woman, her sexual moans will cry out like the flute, and her man will kill you. If you touch another man's wife you will die quickly . . . They will kill you. We are testing you now for the time later when you might think to steal another man's wife. Then, we would not just cut your grass skirt. If your penis rises then and you want to steal a woman, we will cut it off!

The elder cuts the old pubic covering midway between the abdomen and the genitals. "No one will help you, we will cut off your penis and kill you." By this final act, therefore, not only is homosexual fellatio praised, but premarital heterosexual activities are tabooed and condemned. Now the boys know the secret of the flutes.

Following the flute ceremony, which lasts an hour, the boys are carefully lined up for a final inspection before their ceremonial parade back to the cult house. They have been on the move and constantly frightened all day. The large group of initiates files down the hillside to the dance ground, preceded by adult men who form garrisons around the area, separating the boys from the crowds of women and children who have assembled for one last view of them.

A great spectacle this is. For several minutes, led by a renowned shaman, the initiates are paraded around the decorated dance ground (see Figure 4.14). He then conducts them inside the new cult house for the first time. (Until now, they have slept in a shabby lean-to, next to the cult house.) From now on the boys will sleep in the cult house until the initiations are over. This public display is the last occasion on which women can study the boys for years to come. This is a time of honor: The boy is dressed as a novice warrior. He is proud. This is his payoff for all the pain and ordeals. Mothers try to guess which boy is their son. Yet the tranquility is short-lived.

The moment the boys are out of sight, dramatic events unfold. The bloodied fern leaves (collected from the nose-bleeding ritual) are retrieved by Moondamei from his string bag. He unveils them surprisingly before the women. The men then bark out angry accusations that the women are "bad mothers" of the

Figure 4.14 Ceremonial procession of decorated initiates on dance-ground

boys. Moondamei holds up a handful of the leaves, silently flaunting them (see Figure 4.15). He says the men had to "kill" the boys to make them into men. Suddenly, without warning, two men run over to a woman seated on the edge of the dance ground. She is one of the boys' mothers. They grab hold of her and violently force some of the bloodied leaves down her throat. She is cursed and castigated and pushed away. They frantically criticize the other women too for "saying bad things" to their sons, thus stunting their growth. I was astonished; the woman's treatment was ghastly and shocking (see Figure 4.16). The abused mother sits downcast on the ground, looking humiliated and sad. Her women friends are furious and rise to assault the male attackers.

Meanwhile, another younger man hysterically charges into a group of women. He holds more bloody leaves, and with bow and arrows in hand he curses the women and chases them. He seems to be completely beside himself. Everything is chaotic and the language so blurred that it is hard for me to follow his words. I ask Weiyu (who is also watching him) what the young man is screaming. Weiyu says: "You women say bad things to our sons. You yell at them. Now we have killed them. You can eat their 'blood' because it belongs to you, you caused it. Only you can claim this bad blood!" Weiyu adds, "The big men are cursing the women so that they will not say bad things to their younger sons later." The angry women search for the two men who assaulted the mother. They want revenge. The elders try to placate them. This fails. Finally the men pick up sticks and threaten them, a show of force, which works; the women recede. The rebellion fails.

Figure 4.15 The war leader, Moondamei, reveals the bloodied leaves

Figure 4.16 Women and girls look on in horror as a mother is assaulted with bloodied leaves

This drama continues for a few minutes more; the other women are chased away as the degraded mother sits alone, speechless. This was the most remarkable and graphic example of sexual antagonism in the initiation. Why were the younger men so hysterical? It seems that the blood and the sight of women here can create violent reactions in them. Something in their gender identity is touchy, like an unhealed wound.

During the shouting outside, another cassowary quill bone ceremony is performed upon the initiates inside the cult house. Their ornamentation is quickly removed. They are stung much harder this time, and as they cry, the men raise war cries to drown out the crying and thus prevent the women from overhearing.

A while later something striking occurs. It is dusk again, and the women and children are gone. The boys are led outside and fed. Then they are led back to the cult house. As they enter the area they hear the flutes being played within. The boys are taunted. "You can't go inside the cult house," the men say. They shout: "It's the menstrual hut of women! . . . Women are giving birth to babies . . . The babies [the flutes] are crying!" Then another man says: "Look! An *aatmog-wambu* [female hamlet spirit] is in the ritual house!" The boys are afraid. They are led into the cult sanctuary just the same, and soon something even more remarkable happens.

The boys are seated on the earthen floor of the cult house. After going through days of initiation—especially this particularly long and trying day—they look worn out. The elders are gone, leaving the bachelors in charge. A fire has been built and a smattering of men sits idly around the hearth.

Several shrouded figures unexpectedly tramp inside, playing flutes. There are two groups of four flute players each, as there were in the earlier flute ceremony. The actors are disguised. They wear raggedy old bark capes. There is silence again except for the flutes. A man says to the boys, "An old woman spirit has come . . . She is cold, she wants to come sit by the fire." The flute players then squat to the floor, their bodies obscured by capes and shadows.

They are youths impersonating female hamlet spirits. A young man says, "She is an *aatmogwambu;* she has come to cry for you . . . Go away! Not good that she swallows her spit looking at you. [A common metaphor for erotic desire.] You must help straighten her out. [Another common metaphor, this for sucking the bachelor's penis until ejaculation, which "slackens" the penis.] If you feel sorry for her, you must help her out." The innuendos are unmistakable: Boys should serve as fellators to the bachelors.

The other bachelors then joke squeamishly among themselves about this "play." The flute players hobble around behind the tense boys, playing their flutes beneath their capes. The boys are again struck on their chests with the flutes and are told not to reveal the flutes' secrets. The bachelors unmask themselves. The boys are hit one last time on the heads with the flutes, which are then thrown into the hearth fire. The lads are made to stand near the fire, warming themselves and "strengthening" their bodies from the magical heat. The formal ceremony is over, to be followed by homoerotic play.

Several of the bachelors, including those who had cloaked themselves, come alive. It is nightfall; by custom what begins are the first erotic encounters that result in private fellatio between themselves and the boys. The bachelors begin with outlandish and unprecedented erotic exhibitionism, as is also customary: They lift up their buttock covers, exposing their naked buttocks to the boys while engaging in childish games that imitate—and thereby humiliate—the uninitiated boys the initiates previously were. Yet the initiates must honor ceremonial silence, the breaking of which causes them to be soundly thrashed. The bachelors dare them to laugh. This exhibitionism and reversal of roles are telltale signs of the special ritual circumstances: that the boys are still in a liminal state of being.

What soon follows, at first initiated by a few of the more aggressive boys, is the initially awkward, soon-to-be frantic, and then steadily erotic horseplay inside the house. This leads to private homoerotic intercourse outside on the darkened dance ground area. Not all the initiates and bachelors join in this, but most take part. It goes on all night long. And the next night too. And before the conclusion of the initiation five days later, all but a handful of the new initiates serve as fellators, not once but several times more.

How do we explain the sudden change in the boys' mood? There is nothing mysterious in it. They have been tied down for days. No chance to run about, laugh, have fun. Be themselves. This is the first night of release from the terrible tension and fear. They go wild with relief. And some of their wildness is channeled into homosexual activities. In this way they can also "get back" at the bachelors for the the hazing, ordeals, and whippings. Already, then, we see a blending of being desired as a sexual object, being enabled to sexually interact with others, and the aggression expected of the adult warrior.

THE SEXUAL TRANSITION—THE BOYS' INITIATION

How do boys experience the Flute Ceremony? Let us refer to their own words to understand. What follows are examples of what they told me in interviews later. From the boys' remarks we learn that they perceive different values associated with the flutes and homosexuality. Their values are in conflict because they are still in transition between the female and male worldviews. Boys begin with responses to the penis teaching. They feel shame about it. They refer back to their earlier socialization. Kambo (a 12-year-old) says: "I thought, not good that they [elders] are lying or just playing a trick. The penis is not for handling; if you hold it you'll become lazy [our parents told us]. And because of it in the culthouse I felt, it's [penis] not for sucking." Childhood experience is the cause of this shame about fellatio; children are taught to not play with their own genitals. They must forget this and learn something new. Kambo's remark pertains as well to the sexual naiveté of children and to the boys' prior lack of knowledge about their fathers' homosexual activities.

Another new learning concerns the perceived nutritive value of semen. The boys are told that semen will make them grow strong. The source of this idea is the men's ritual teaching that semen is mother's breast milk. Do the boys understand and accept this belief? They seem to adopt it quickly in their own subjective orientations toward fellatio, as we can infer from things they say.

Moondi talked to me about the matter. Here is a typical example of his semen beliefs resulting from the Flute Ceremony:

> The juice of the pandanus nuts . . . It's the same as the water of a man, the same as a man's juice [semen]. And I like to consume a lot of it [because] it can give *me* more water . . . For the milk of women is also the same as the milk of men. Hers [breast milk] is for when she has a baby—it's for the baby who drinks it.

The association between semen and breast milk is widely recognized. Here is Gaimbako, Moondi's age-mate: "Semen is the same kind as that [breast milk] of women . . . It's the *very same* kind as theirs . . . The same as pandanus nuts too . . . But when milk [semen] falls into my mouth [during fellatio], I think it's like the milk of women." Thus boys' semen beliefs motivate their homosexual activity.

There is another shame-laden side to the teaching too. This is a powerful reactive attitude: Boys feel they are "sucking a penis" like their own. Kambo felt this way immediately on hearing the penis teaching of the flute: "I was afraid of [their] penis! It's the same as mine—why should I suck it? It's the same kind, [our penes are] only one kind. We're men, not *different* kinds!" What is Kambo saying? He is first shocked by the idea of fellatio—it is so new. But he is also complaining that fellatio is not right since it is sexual activity between the same sex. He suggests, then, that males are of one kind, as distinct from females. This reveals his childhood view that only men and women should have sex together. He senses the power play in the homoerotic dyad; remember the coercive nature of the Flute Ceremony. The men's hostile jokes made during the preceding body decoration convey clearly to boys that they are to be the men's sexual outlets. Initiates are sexually subordinate, a fact expressed by the saying that the boys are "married" to the flutes, which symbolize the bachelors' penes. Boys suck the small flute, which represents the mature glans penis, further symbolizing their passive role. Reference to flute marriage makes boys sense that they are being compared to women and to wives. As age-mates they are equivalent only to other immature initiates. Sucking a man's penis directly expresses their inferior position. Eventually, then, they aspire to get semen to be strong like bachelors so they will be independent agents.

Nearly all initiates perform their first act of fellatio during the initiation. Their experiences are very important for subsequent masculine development. Moondi has said:

> I was wondering what they [elders] were going to do to us. And . . . I felt afraid. What will they do? But they inserted the bamboo in and out of the mouth; and I thought, what are they doing? Then, after they tried out our mouths, I began to understand . . . that they were talking about the penis. Oh, that little bamboo is the penis of the men! My whole body was afraid, completely afraid . . . And I felt heavy, I wanted to cry. Then my thoughts went back to how I used to think it was

the *aatmwogwambu* [flute spirit], and then I knew that the men did it [made the sounds]. And . . . I felt a little better, because before (I feared that the *aatmwogwambu* would get me. But now I saw that they [the men] did it. They told us the penis story . . . Then I thought a lot, very quickly. I was afraid—not good that the men shoot me [penetrate my mouth] and break my neck. Ay! Why should they put that [penis] inside our mouths! It's not a good thing. They all hide it [the penis] inside their sporrans, and it's got lots of hair too. "You must listen well," they said. "You all won't grow up by yourselves; if you sleep with the men you'll become a strong man." They said that; I was afraid . . . And then they told us clearly: Semen is inside—and when you hold a man's penis, you must put it inside your mouth—he can give you semen . . . It's the same as your mother's breast milk. "This is no lie," the men said. "You can't go tell the children, your sisters." And then [later] I tried it [fellatio], and I thought: "Oh, they told us about breast milk [Moondi means semen]—it [semen] is in there."

What becomes of these feelings in later months and years? Many things could be added. For instance, despite great social pressures, some boys show low interest and seldom participate in fellatio, while others feverishly join in. But those are the extremes; the great majority of Sambia boys regularly engage in fellatio for years as regulated by taboo. I mentioned earlier that males cannot have sex with any kinsmen. This taboo is the ideal. In fact, however, male cross-cousins and distant kin do have fellatio sometimes, although it is kept quiet. Boys who are considered especially attractive are pursued in this way, even though they are kin. This suggests that sexual excitement is a factor in men's homosexuality too, not just the ideal belief that it "makes boys grow." Homosexual practices are a touchy subject among males for many reasons. They begin in a ceremony, it is true, but their occurrence and meaning fan out to embrace a totally secret way of life. What matters is that boys too become just as involved in this hidden tradition. We should expect them to acquire intense feelings about bachelors, fellatio, and semen, as indeed they do.

Here is an eloquent example. One day, while I was talking idly with Kambo, he mentioned singing to himself as he walked in the forest. I asked him what he sang about. From this simple question he surprised me by saying:

> When I think of men's name-songs, then I sing them: that of a bachelor who is sweet on me; a man of another line or my own. When I sing the song of a creek in the forest I am happy about that place . . . Or some man who sleeps with me—when he goes elsewhere, I sing his song. I think of that man who gave me a lot of semen; later, I must sleep with him. I feel like this: he gave me a lot of water [semen] . . . Later, I will have a lot of water like him.

Not only do we see pinpointed here the male belief that semen accumulates and makes boys strong. Even a simple activity like singing can trigger a mood of reflecting on past male associations and prolonged homoerotic contacts. Kambo shows us his wish: that he too will acquire abundant manliness, like the admired friend of whom he sings.

The men's flutes come to symbolize a whole lifetime of experiences like these. Initiation thus creates a line of development that has definite effects on a boy's sense of himself and his maleness, his gender identity.

This leads us to the bachelors' impersonation of the female hamlet spirits. What does this symbolic learning mean? What about the bachelors' motives? Why do only certain bachelors volunteer for this impersonation? Gaimbako recalled that the bachelors presented themselves as "wailing old women spirits." He noted that the men told "stories" about the "milk" of the flutes.

"This flute isn't crying out for just anything—it wants the milk [semen] of men. You must all drink the milk of men." The significance of the flutes is clearly complex.

Transitional objects are things that a person symbolically treats as halfway between himself and another person. Dolls treasured by children and used as comforters, but which do not have the full value of a person, are transitional objects. Such objects help children make the transition from infancy and dependence to self-reliance. They are the next best thing to the parent when a child is lost or frightened. Eventually, children outgrow them and become independent without the object. As adults, they may even repress memories of the object.

The Sambia flutes are such a transitional object for the boys in initiation. They provide a means of linking boys with substitutes for their mother: a penis for a breast, semen for milk. The flute spirit is a transparently disguised symbol for mother herself. The wailing old hamlet spirit does what mother did when the boy was taken for initiation: cry for him. Only the spirit is powerful, and will protect and nourish the boy, whereas mother was powerless to help him. So the spirit offers a new kind of powerful protection to be desired. There are actually three transitional objects in initiation:

1. The boy's ritual guardian, who removes him from and replaces his mother, protecting and comforting him during initiation
2. The flute spirit, which is a symbolic female but imparts male essence
3. The bachelors, who are first disguised as the spirit and who later act as inseminators to provide the breast milk substitute

These are elements of what we could call the shared *fantasy system* of the men's cult. This fantasy system has several functions. It motivates boys to engage in homoerotic activity; the image of mother and her milk rationalizes fellatio.

After ritual brainwashing, they change their beliefs about the flutes. The flutes as transitional objects help motivate them to internalize the men's secret beliefs. The fantasy system creates a double identification: The boy identifies with the guardian as a nurturant man and with the spirit figure as a powerful, fictional female creature—a phallic female, we could say, having attributes of both males and females. This final symbolic learning suggests that boys' core identity contains both feminine and masculine elements that are difficult for them to consciously accept or act out. The fantasy of the flutes provides a symbol that can unconsciously express this core need for the males as a group.

In their identity formation, boys reach for a compromise solution. They reconcile their own promiscuous and homoerotic role as semen recipients with their independence and growing sense of masculine power. Interestingly enough, they often relate their feelings of having lost mother to their secret homosexual lifestyle. Note this vivid line of thought in a final comment by Moondi regarding the changes in him following initiation:

> I felt sorry. I thought, why should I lose my mother? I thought a lot about Momma and Papa . . . I was sorry for [them] . . . "I was sorry when I was still a first-stage initiate. I wanted to remain an uninitiated boy with her [mother]. Later, later, I was a second-stage initiate. I slept around—I didn't worry much. I thought, "Oh, it's nothing." After I was initiated I stopped worrying about Momma and Papa. When I was still an initiate, I thought: What will I do if my parents die? Who'll give me food and things? Now that I'm a second-stage initiate I sleep with all of the men, I don't worry. It's nothing: I've lost my Momma and Papa now.

Moondi obviously is rationalizing his detachment from his mother and father. He seems to have reached a compromise with himself. He longed for his mother and resented initiation, but he soon recognized that he was powerless to prevent it. Initiation brought homosexual relationships, and these somehow lessened his need and worrying about his parents. This has changed Moondi's concerns about homosexuality. He says that fellatio is "nothing"—neither unusual nor scary—a feeling that expresses his recognition and acceptance of having forever lost the world of childhood.

The secret of the flute is that in its core it is female and that it symbolizes, for the men, a set of transitional fantasy objects kept secret from the women because they create in men their masculinity. Women are naturally fertile and reproductive. Men are not. Yet the men are ashamed of this idea. It is a fantasy, not a fact, for it is a gender belief of the men's world. Men dread that women will learn that they were once passive insertees of older men. They fear this because they feel women would mock them if they knew the secret. Women would want to be "on top" sometimes too. They cannot allow that to happen. This is why the men keep their rituals hidden; they shield a secret identity. For they seem to feel—as their fantasy system expresses unconsciously—that women really are more powerful than they. The men do not see that what they fear in the secret part of themselves is their feminine side.

THE REMAINING FESTIVITIES

Later that night the elders return to the cult house. A songfest and more teaching occur, while sexual play continues outside. The next morning at dawn the all-night songfest breaks. All the initiates are involved in this. They are then taken to the forest for the usual purification ceremonies on trees, accompanied by the flute players.

Later that morning the initiates and elders are enclosed in the cult house. No one may leave or enter. First a shamanic healing ceremony takes place. During this, men ingest hallucinogenic leaves and tree fruit. The hallucinogens serve two ends: to alter the actors' perceptual awareness and to enhance the boys' suggestibility to being taught ritual lore and the shaman's role. Elders recognize how boys have been subjected to difficult ordeals over the past days. The shaman's healing is a response to their concern. The men believe ritual anxieties can provoke further weakness in the soul at this point, making boys vulnerable to sorcery, sickness, and soul theft by ghosts. The shaman's exorcisms allay lingering anxieties on the part of boys and their kin. Shamans also prophesy. They predict which of the novices may become shamans or fight leaders and, in a morbid vein not unlike the enigmatic role of shamans, they also predict who among the boys may prematurely die.

What ritual instruction do the boys receive? Elders concentrate on teaching food taboos and masculine rules. The men detail the extensive and onerous food taboos believed vital to a boy's growth. The trancelike state induced by sleeplessness and the hallucinogens, men say, is particularly appropriate for learning these taboos and hunting magic. The trance state seems to tap into a deeper level of learning than ever before. Sometimes when shamans are initiated, their apprentices compete for power in these trance ceremonies. Mythology is taught pertaining to the origin of sweet potato and the bamboo knife. Again, the urgency of ingesting semen, hiding homosexuality, and avoiding women is built into the whole experience. These activities continue until mid-afternoon. Meanwhile, other men outside prepare for the *Iwouwi'u* Ritual, while women collect food for the name-changing ceremony that follows it.

Of all the rituals performed by the Yulami people, the *Iwouwi'u* was the most striking in this initiation. The context of the performance was highly emotional and dramatic for two historical reasons. First, the ritual represented the most fearful supernatural power associated with the Yulami groups. It had been traditionally performed in secret, and men of the Upper Sambia Valley had never before observed it. Our men, for instance, said that the sorcery power of the ritual enabled the Yulami to kill them, and they truly were afraid. Second, the ritual performance conjured up a dreadful history of warfare, sorcery accusations, and death, all of which directly concerned the participants. Men say that this turmoil began generations ago. We saw in Chapter 2 how legends tell of the immigration of the Seboolu phratry into the valley. The Seboolu subsequently raided and killed the Yulami people, the original inhabitants. A combined war party of the Seboolu and Sambia phratries attacked the Yulami. They fled south, seeking shelter with the Moonagu phratry group, later settling in their present locale. In the last generation fighting broke out between a Seboolu hamlet and Yulami over wife stealing. The adulterous Seboolu men died in the following months, their deaths attributed to sorcery by the Yulami men.

An ironic outcome of this tragic history was that sons of three of the sorcery victims were new initiates at Yulami. Because this was the first initiation ever performed jointly by the former enemy groups, a Yulami elder angrily warned the Seboolu men: "If your sons steal our women, they await the same fate as their fathers" (see Figure 4.17). The Seboolu elder Meinji, who lectured the boys, agreed. He related how he felt sad for the deceased men and for their brothers and age-mates who had adopted the boys and upon whom the economic burden of their support had fallen all these years (see Figure 4.18). Adultery, bloodshed, sorcery, and revenge are still powerful forces in Sambia society.

Figure 4.17 An elder warns boys against adultery in the Iwouwi'u *ritual*

Figure 4.18 A Yulami village elder argues over Iwouwi'u *ceremonies*

An hour later, women burdened with gifts of sugar cane and banana begin assembling on the dance ground (see Figure 4.19). They are preparing for the Name-Changing Ceremony, wherein the initiates publicly lose their childhood names and receive new adult names bestowed by their parents. The boy's mother not only has a say in the selection of the new name but here she is the first

Figure 4.19 Mothers bear food gifts for the name-change ceremony

person to publicly say it. Adults henceforth refer to the boys by their new names. The boys themselves are tabooed from using these names with each other, and they may not use each other's childhood names. While they live in the cult house, they use only personal pronouns in speaking to each other. This reinforces their status as liminal people. After initiation, when boys reside in the forest rat house, with the help of the bachelors they devise age-mate nicknames for one another. Subsequently, they refer to and address age-mates by their nicknames; even when their older peers may use these nicknames. (Women never do.) They retain the age-mate names in interaction with one another until third-stage initiation. This name change recognizes the personal change in boys. They must forget the past; their childhood names are tabooed because they remind boys of early memories. Their new adult names symbolize their new adult identity. After the food gifts are offered, the men worry about women's contamination. Elders carry fire over the whole dance ground to purify it of women's pollution.

Over the next three days, further rituals bring the initiation to its conclusion. On the fifth day of events (July 31) there is a full day of ceremonial activities, opened by agriculturally oriented rituals. These stress the economic responsibilities of initiates. In the afternoon elaborate *Wolendiku* ceremonies take place, teaching about fire making and hunting. This series of rites and teachings ends with the Bullroarer Ritual. Here the men teach the secret of the bullroarer, a sound instrument also played at ceremonies, matching what boys learn of the flutes. Then the entire ritual group returns to the dance-ground, where the adult men engage each other in the most violent thrashing of the whole initiation. They compete with each other in a final masculine test of strength. Here the boys see the full force of adult aggression in ritual. On the

Figure 4.20 The Yulami graduates pose as an age-set

sixth day there are two key rituals at night. They also stress the economic duties of initiates, convey stories, and provide lighter drama. The seventh and final day (August 2) concludes the initiation with a Water Ritual, ending the taboo on drinking water.

The initiates as an age-set are taken the next day to the forest, where they will live in the special lodge called the Rat House. Here they hunt forest rats and possum. They are removed from all contacts with women for weeks. Bachelors dominate them, socially and sexually, throughout this period. They are trained to follow all orders by their seniors and are hazed, shamed, and physically punished if they disobey orders. Socialization centers on the hunt, avoiding women, and serving as sexual partners for the bachelors. When the boys return to their own hamlet clubhouse, they are monitored for months to ensure that ritual norms are not violated. Elders, fathers, and bachelors are their main monitors. But age-mates, too, carefully watch each other's behavior, and they shame their mates or sometimes report to bachelors if they suspect violations of taboos. Boys are once again evaluated against the abstract images of the rubbish man or war leader. Those who are active, strong, assertive, brave, and successful in hunting and other male tasks are praised, while boys who fail or cry are mocked, shamed, and stigmatized (see Figure 4.20).

THE WAR RAID

Until the early 1960s, an intertribal war raid followed the collective initiations. The new third-stage initiates were expected to participate, and, indeed, Sambia say that such raids were often launched at this time in order for the bachelors to prove themselves. We have seen that third-stage initiation is a puberty rite establishing the social and biological maturity of a youth. The ritual system expresses concerns that bachelors achieve manliness in physique and interpersonal aggressiveness. They must demonstrate, that is, their *jerungdu,* their prowess. Their masculinity is conditional—and requires proof of their fitness and achievements, in two contexts. First, in the ritual initiatory cycle, the youth is advanced to third-stage warrior status and he then assists in the first-stage initiation that follows immediately. His elders individually select him as the dominant homoerotic partner for a boy initiate. Their sexual intercourse marks the bachelor's social/erotic change from being a fellator (insertee) to a fellated (insertor). Because of his insemination, the small initiate can now be ritually incorporated into the men's secret society, and the youth is thereby ritually perceived to be biologically mature, the inseminator. The fellatio act also changes the character of their social behavior toward each other too; it confirms that the bachelor is dominant in all encounters: social, ritual, and erotic.

War raids provided a military counterpart to this process of masculinization for the bachelor. The youth went on a raid not only to acquire hard experience on intertribal raids. It had a more specific function. The raid tested his *jerungdu* in the ultimate way: by killing another human being. That act of homicide constituted a final, incorporative rite of passage, needed to confirm his warrior manliness in the real world. Cold-blooded killing was an ideal; only a few ever actually accomplished it. But the best among them did, those who were to become war leaders. The others, whatever else holds true of them, knew that they were lesser men. And it is undeniably clear that, like the Papuan tribes of the Trans-Fly river (Williams 1936), Frederick Hendrick Island (Serpenti 1965), Southwest New Guinea (Van Baal 1966), and other peoples, Sambia believed that the highest expression of masculine prowess was this war raid and its glory.

Two other ideals concerned the war raid. If he were man enough, the new warrior could attempt to capture a woman, steal a wife from the enemy tribe. The tale recounted in Chapter 2 illustrates precisely this possibility. Furthermore, youths were taught that if they did cut down an enemy war leader, they must not kill him immediately, for his body would still yield something precious. Once the warrior had fallen, his semen could be procured either by masturbating him or awaiting his body's spasmodic ejaculation. That last burst of strength was felt to contain his greatest *jerungdu,*the physical power and life force that had made him a war leader. The ingestion of this would transfer such powers to the youth. This was, ideally, the only appropriate occasion in which bachelors could temporarily reverse roles to fellate again.

The youths returning home from these raids were real heroes in the old days. The very fact that they were manly enough to brave strange and distant places with the seasoned war leaders proved their aggressive potential. So here another psychological effect came into play. A bachelor who could kill in war was someone to respect and fear. The younger initiates would do so. And eventually the women would too, for they wanted a war leader, not a rubbish man, as a husband—or so the men believed. That men had killed or were capable of killing could never be forgotten by their wives, who, like it or not, were the only soft spots in the men's lives.

FINAL INITIATIONS: MARRIAGE AND FATHERHOOD

Collective cooperation between hamlets ends with the third-stage initiation. All further masculinity and ritual treatment is the responsibility of the bachelor's village. The young warrior-bachelor must undergo three additional initiations leading to fatherhood and full manhood. Achievements of the highest order they are, Sambia reckon, for even the culture-hero Numboolyu had to surmount many difficulties to attain them, myth says. Involved too in these transitions are great psychosexual changes in the young men.

Youths remain residents in the clubhouse until their late teens or early twenties, following marriage and menarche in their wives. During this period they are exclusively homoerotic in their relationships. Once initiated, at ages 7 to 10, no heterosexual activity is permitted and initiates may serve only as passive fellators who ingest semen from the bachelors. No other sexual activity (including masturbation by oneself, mutual masturbation, or anal sex) is allowed, and research indicates that none is practiced (Herdt and Stoller 1990). After the third stage, then, youths switch from the passive to active sexual role with boys, inseminating them. This transition is fraught with anxiety. Elders recognize this, and they counsel youths to "go easy" in their sexual contacts. Thus the situation remains until marriage.

It may be difficult to imagine the tremendous power Sambia associate with sexual arousal because our society is much less restrictive than theirs. Just looking at a prospective sexual partner is for the Sambia teenager loaded with potential for arousal, fantasy, shame, and—in the wrong circumstances—social disapproval, scandal, or even physical punishment. Their sexual behavior is extremely structured. Until adolescence, all heterosexuality is ruled out.

It is the ritual cult that applies an absolute brake on the manifest development of heterosexuality. Three mechanisms do the work: institutionalized homosexual practices, female-avoidance taboos (especially regarding menstrual pollution), and fears of semen depletion. Not all heterosexuality is eliminated, only its overt expression. Boys may have fantasies about girls but cannot express them until later. Remember that even though heterosexual contact is suppressed, boys are encouraged by their fathers and elders to acquire semen so that they, too, can achieve marriage and fatherhood. The *gender function* of the secret cult is not to destroy heterosexuality, for this would be suicidal for the society. Rather, ritual creates a fierce, powerful warrior's masculinity, which is associated with a very highly structured heterosexuality. The men desire and dislike, even fear, intercourse with women. But here let us consider the three mechanisms suppressing heterosexuality: boy-insemination, female avoidance, and semen-depletion fears.

Third-stage initiation or "social puberty" brings a new period of sexual freedom to Sambia youths. For the first time in years they are no longer under the thumb of the older bachelors who sexually dominated them. Now the tables are turned. The younger boys are in the subordinate fellator role. Whereas before the youths had no sexual outlet available to them, not even masturbation, now they are free as bachelors to inseminate the initiates. This proves to them and to their age-mates that they are strong and have *jerungdu,* because their bodies are sexually mature and have semen to "feed" to younger boys. They feel more masculine than at any previous time in their lives. So the bachelors go through a phase of intense sexual activity, a period of vigorous homoerotic activity and contacts, having one relationship after another with boys. Their sexual behavior is promiscuous, for the initiates are concerned mostly with taking in semen, while the bachelors mainly desire sexual release through domination of younger boys. Occasionally a youth and a boy will pair off for a few days or even weeks. But these infatuations seldom last long, both parties fearing that others will stigmatize them as "unmanly." The norm is for intense, promiscuous activity that usually subsides to less frequent but still steady boy-inseminating.

Eventually Sambia adolescent boys become more interested in females. They cannot express this interest directly, although they are ambivalently motivated to "steal a woman" and risk the consequences. Through whispering risqué jokes and gossip about girls and women they find attractive, the age-mates begin to challenge the absolute power of their elders to control sexual access to women. This is their "locker-room" talk. It peaks in intensity at marriage. (Yet all Sambia men in later life enjoy talking and joking about women, as this provides an outlet for otherwise pent-up feelings.) Teenage boys also begin having daydreams about sexual encounters with women. This is very private talk; they share these daydreams only with their most intimate male friends, if at all, as they fear being shamed or punished. These conscious thoughts are also reflected in their night dreams. At this point adolescents report that their wet dreams shift from homoerotic to heterosexual images. In a sense, these are the youths' first heterosexual *experiences,* so they react with anxiety when they awaken from a wet dream, fearing a spirit woman (the flute spirit) may have stolen some of their semen. These fears pass soon enough, however, to be replaced by more powerful concerns about interacting with and marrying real women.

No interaction is permitted with women until a bachelor has his fourth-stage initiation ceremony. This also functions as the formal marriage rite. Usually several youths simultaneously undergo this ceremony, together with their brides from other villages. It is an exciting, power-filled time of new social recognition for the young men and women, for they are undergoing such profound changes in their lives, the transition from being adolescents to becoming adults. And of course they have their first sexual intimacy with the opposite sex to look forward to—remarkable and dangerous thoughts about a total stranger! Perhaps the young man's fears are eased by having such clear-cut roles to play in the ceremony itself, which dramatically represents the unequal social positions of Sambia man and woman, husband and wife, from the very start. The ceremony is called *nuposha,* as we have seen—a name that also means "newlywed."

The name *nuposha* refers to all the brides lying flat on their faces hugging the earth in the dusty soil of the hamlet plaza, completely covered by their new bark capes. They are still and lifeless, corpses arranged for public review. There, in the groom's hamlet, the marriage bargain is formally sealed for life. The elders and the grooms have returned after weeks of possum hunting. A long rope, hung between tall poles staked across the plaza in front of the clubhouse, has suspended from it a string of packages of smoked possum, ear-

Figure 4.21 Nuposha (4th stage) initiates fully decorated and assembled

marked in payment of each bride. Everyone knows the youths caught the meat with their bare hands, which falls into the waiting and almost greedy hands of the bride's kinswomen. The youths stand stiff and alert, in full warrior garb, overlooking their brides and the crowds, peering stone-faced into the sky as they have been directed to do (see Figure 4.21). This is, after all, their first public appearance before women since they were children. They must be careful not to contaminate themselves by looking directly into women's faces or to betray their inner panic (*kowuptu*) and awkwardness at this drastic and long-anticipated moment. All the pomp and ceremony disguise this feeling, which is applauded by the onlookers, for Sambia dearly love such picturesque displays. Then a great celebratory feast follows. The newlyweds do not, however, join in; the meat is forbidden to them, and taboos still keep them apart. This is the context in which custom begins to break down the great distance dividing the newlyweds.

For bride and groom alike, the marital contract has this rigid and stony-hearted foundation. The marriage begins in a mood of festive conformity to predetermined roles. Like clay figurines, carefully molded and colorfully glazed, the newlyweds are thrown into a staged drama not of their own design. The couple begins to interact slowly and cautiously, usually in semipublic situations with their parents present. The effects of these social and erotic encounters are important for the next stage in the couple's developing relationship.

Sexuality is part of a general pattern, not isolated from everything else. Newlywed men continue sexual relations with initiates at their discretion until they become fathers. Since they cannot have genital-to-genital sex with their premenarchal brides, initiates provide an easy and "safe" sexual outlet. But now that they are married and nearly adult, warfare and hunting activities occupy more of the newlyweds' time. They also begin clearing forest land, and with their wives' help they prepare it for gardens. Newlywed men are safe from female pollution by still living in the clubhouse, which makes it easy for them to have sex with boys after everyone else is asleep.

In order for young men to begin sexual intercourse with their brides, they must learn two sets of ritual techniques: purifications to eliminate the chance of menstrual pollution, and semen-replacement techniques to help them against the fear of loss of their semen. These are the two other mechanisms beyond homo-erotic activity that regulate the development of full heterosexuality. Menstrual pollution is dealt with by nose bleeding. Monthly nose bleeding in secret to elim-inate this contamination begins when the youth's wife has her first period. In this way, too, we see how the final initiations and ritual changes in gender are fully complementary and interlocking for the bride and groom. Before this, however, the semen-replenishment technique must be taught, so we will look at it first.

In the fourth- and then the fifth-stage ceremonies, men learn increasingly better ways to replace their semen with white tree sap. Since semen contains strength, all sexual intercourse depletes men and deprives them of *jerungdu*. Heterosexual intercourse is felt by men to be especially draining. Depletion by boys is not feared as much, which may attest to how much more comfortable homoerotic contacts are, and how much more power is perceived to be contained in female sexual contacts. So men are taught to ingest tree saps called *iaamoon-alyu,* "tree mother's milk," which replaces the semen lost through heterosexual intercourse. The sap is privately collected from the trees or directly drunk from the trunk. How ironic that the tree sap is symbolized as "milky mother's sap." Like the homoerotic fellatio teachings in earlier initiations, men seem to model both the semen and its substitutes on mother's milk, even though semen is thought to be a vital male essence! This seems to be another expression of men's envy of women. This ritual teaching paves the way for the youths to have sex-ual intercourse with their wives.

The customary first sexual intercourse between spouses is fellatio, mirroring the relationships between younger and older males. This is very difficult and sen-sitive for the couple, and one or both newlyweds may avoid this for months. For instance, Tali has always complained how he had to "chase his wife" for years before he could inseminate her. He says she would avoid it because she was afraid of him and because she had not yet had formal teaching from female elders about sex with men. My female informants say that it is not until their menarche ceremony—held at the same time as the men's fifth-stage initiation—that women are instructed in sexual practices. They then learn of heterosexual fellatio and semen ingestion in the functioning of their marriages. This does not mean they agree with the men completely about the meaning of sexual intercourse, only that the rituals are performed according to custom and have their personal impact at this time.

Initial heterosexual intercourse is both hard and exciting for the men too. Heterosexual fellatio is difficult for the men to begin. After all, they have had sex with only boys for years. Not all men can overcome their fear, as I note. What helps the young men is this: Newlywed brides dress in bark capes and wear cas-sowary quill bone nose plugs such that, to a remarkable degree, they resemble young boy initiates facially (especially in dim light). Their breasts are also covered. This reminds youths of their long-standing and comfortable homosexual activities. The brides' similarity to boys and the fellatio thus help to provide an erotic bridge between the homosexual and heterosexual lifestyles. Thus it continues until the birth of a child. (George Devereux told me that our distant cultural ancestors, the Spartans of Greece, hit upon the very same solution—dressing new brides as boys—to get men through their former exclusive homoerotic attachments.) The young men feel that this boy-like appearance in their wives makes the women more attractive. Here we have a clear example of how sexual intercourse is contextualized and made specific to the images and pressures of society.

The woman's first menses changes their sexual relationship. She goes into ritual seclusion in the menstrual hut. Her husband has his fifth-stage initiation, and he learns purificatory techniques that ward off his wife's terribly feared pollution. The main ritual practice is private nose bleeding. Again, unlike previous ritual nose bleedings, this one is taught to the young men to be done in private, after each one of their wives' regular menstrual periods. These periodic nose bleedings seem oddly enough to be based on the *havalt-nuntu* competitive value between age-mates. It seems like the young men must bleed themselves to "keep up" with the physical activity of their wives.

What matters is that learning this practice enables a man to have genital sex with his wife for the first time. Men believe that vaginal intercourse can pollute their bodies with menstrual/womb blood. By inserting their penises into their wives' vaginas, blood may penetrate into their urethra. It will then accumulate and "block up" their bodies, weakening them, bringing illness and death. Nose bleeding is their only remedy or preventive measure. Sex and menstruation thus go hand in hand for the Sambia couple.

Genital-to-genital intercourse is harder for Sambia couples to begin. They are adults, and yet they come from such different emotional backgrounds. Sex begins only in the forest, far away from public view, for Sambia are very prudish. After a few months, people (especially parents and in-laws) will begin exerting pressure on the couple to go alone to the garden or collect forest foods, to encourage them to begin genital sex. The community expects the couple to produce children, which are crucial to village survival. It is at this time that newlywed couples are vulnerable to terrible jealousy, arguments, and wife beating. The men are very insecure of their position in the marriage, and the women are able to do only so much in allaying their husbands' fears and anxieties about menstrual pollution and semen depletion. Usually with time, and with children, these problems subside and the couple settles down.

This is the period of bisexuality for Sambia men. The men may still desire sex with boys, who are "safer" and easier to have than women, but they can have genital sex with their wives too. The men must keep knowledge of their sexual activities hidden both from women (as usual) and also from boys, for they do not want boys to know that they may be contaminated by a penis that has entered the pollution-ridden vagina of a woman. The initiates themselves express concern over this, but there is little they can do except to figure out through the grapevine which men have sex with their wives. So we may say that young men are truly behaviorally bisexual. They enjoy sexual contacts with women and boys, but in both contexts they are dominant, "on top."

Men play down women's sexuality. Though the women are not controllable and are adults, men try to treat them as immature children. Indeed this may be one key to understanding why Sambia men think of their appropriate marital partner as being younger and less experienced than them—sometimes as much as 5 to 10 years younger in age. In addition, men generally deny that women have orgasms. They say orgasm is something only men have; they cannot imagine that women experience this. Moreover, the preferred sexual technique of men is the "missionary position." Most men also say that they experience ejaculation inside their wives very quickly, within minutes. They fear their wives' bodies and therefore the shorter their contact, the less chance of pollution or depletion. Of course this must affect and limit their wives' enjoyment of the contact too. In both denying women's orgasms and by being "on top," we see the men's need to affirm control of sex through their behavioral and ritual patterns.

The men may continue to have homoerotic contacts with boys until their wives have a baby. Then the ideal norm is for them to stop. Indeed, most men feel that homoerotic activity after fatherhood is immature and unimportant—even beneath them. Strong social pressures are exerted on them to change their behavior, and so they usually conform. But there is no question that some men look back longingly to the time when they could have easy and unbridled sex with boys prior to their becoming fathers. They are becoming authorities in their community, so to continue homosexuality is to violate norms and undermine the whole social order. Moreover, it is felt by the secret society that the younger initiates are the "sexual property" of bachelors, not married men who have wives as sexual outlets that the bachelors lack. This is the meaning of the ritual teaching that the flutes are "married" to the initiates. Besides, most men prefer women erotically after marriage.

Are there Sambia men who fail to achieve these sexual transitions and move onto marriage and sex with women? Research has revealed only a rare number of such men in the valley. Kalutwo, a conservative, somewhat gruff man in his late 30s, is such a person. He has been technically married four times (twice to the same woman, a widow) under pressure from the men. But he dislikes women sexually and prefers boys for his sexual outlet. In his younger years this aroused little attention. Many Sambia men have troubled marriages and fear women. Kalutwo, however, is an extreme case. Each time the elders gave him a wife he would avoid her, and especially intimacy with her. Each woman in turn left him or was taken by another man. He has told me he has had sex (oral sex) only once with a woman (his second wife) and that she initiated it. As he has aged, the men have joked about him, mocked him for his marital failures. He himself has grown sadder and more dejected. He is stigmatized as a rubbish man, as one who has failed to make the transition into full adult marriage and fatherhood. For the Sambia, a man is not truly mature or respected until he is a family man. Kalutwo's problem is not so much that he continues having sex with boys. Several other men in the valley do this, but they are married and have children, so they are respected. No, Kalutwo is stigmatized because he *prefers* boys over women, so he has not conformed to the ideal manly social role. Kalutwos are rare; I know of only two other men in the valley who have the same sexual history and homoerotic adult preference.

Sambia consider Kalutwo to be a "odd" but they do not reject him. No other form of sexual variation occurs, however. For instance, it is forbidden to reverse sexual roles among males; no Sambia man could suck an initiate's penis. To do so would be truly shocking for it would prematurely rob the boy of his sperm, leading him to early death. This would be a moral outrage. Only two reports of such (hearsay only) are known to me. The best known of these was by a local man who is classified as being "permanently insane" in the valley. Thus Sambia do not polarize homosexuality and heterosexuality as we do; they allow more flexibility in this area. But they do have taboos and limits and a moral sense of what must never be.

When a man's wife has her first child, this signals his final or sixth-stage initiation. His wife goes into seclusion for many days. He learns all the final ritual techniques to maintain his gender: more purification, more nose bleeding, and more semen replenishment from tree sap. This final initiation marks the attainment of full manhood: fatherhood. It brings to a close an entire era of his life. He moves on now to becoming a parent, a socializer of his own sons. It seems understandable that for him to do this job in an effective way he should stop having fellatio with younger boys. It is fitting and timely, then, that during this last initiation a young man has revealed to him the most secret and important of all Sambia stories: their myth of male parthenogenesis. It is a story that explains the origins of the men's secret society and of boy-inseminating rituals.

The hero of the myth of parthenogenesis is none other than Numboolyu, the ancestor and culture-hero. It tells how once upon a time there were only two people, Numboolyu and Chemchi (Chemchi is the secret name for menstrual blood). They were age-mates. Both were of ambiguous biological sex, having small penises and feminine breasts. They were, in short, like hermaphrodites. Numboolyu was the bigger and older of the two. He initiated fellatio with Chemchi, copulating with Chemchi's mouth, for this, the myth says, was the only available orifice. As he did so, Numboolyu's breasts slackened and his penis grew bigger. Chemchi, however, grew bigger breasts and a smaller penis. The myth then alters their sexes, so Numboolyu is fully masculinized, while Chemchi is now referred to as "she," the feminized one. She becomes pregnant and Numboolyu cuts open her genital area, creating her vagina and permitting delivery of her first baby. Now they are married and Numboolyu may copulate with her vagina. Eventually she has another boy child. (Chemchi is the mother-ancestress and is also associated with creation stories.) The story might have ended happily ever after here, except that their sons grow up. And when the first reaches puberty, Numboolyu is presented with a crisis.

The firstborn son comes to Numboolyu one day complaining that his own penis is erect and he has no sexual outlet. What should he do? He wants a sexual partner like his father's wife, but none is available. For a few moments the father contemplates allowing his son to have sex with Chemchi, only to reject the idea because this would make himself jealous and would lead to fight-ing. Therefore, Numboolyu teaches his older son to have homosexual fellatio with the boy's younger brother, who has not yet reached puberty. This solves the problem of providing the first son's sexual outlet, while masculinizing the younger boy too. Numboolyu has them hide this from their mother (though the myth is silent about why they must keep it secret). In this way, the elders tell the young fathers, male and female were created out of an amorphous male being, womanhood was established, and homoerotic fellatio became institutionalized in society.

This Oedipal drama is a surprising climax to the whole initiation cycle. Why do the elders wait so long to reveal the myth? It seems that they would want to allay boys' concerns earlier than at marriage. But the myth is a tale of con-frontation between father and son who would compete in a drama of attachment over the same woman. Can it be that the initiations have been concerned with incestuous feelings all along? That ritual boy-inseminating is a cultural mecha-nism to prevent incest and patricide?

In the initiations the men pound in the idea that, because the boys have been too much with their mothers, masculinity is endangered. Men also know intu-itively that they must powerfully and rapidly make up for having been aloof and distant fathers. So in the initiations, the men are suddenly and overwhelmingly present. From then on boys can live only in a male world, isolated, on pain of sickness and death, from females. Cut off from their mothers, the boys are harangued, beaten, radically resocialized, and threatened with terrible physical dangers, including death. The rituals demonstrate absolutely the fathers' power to punish. Whatever incestuous yearnings the boys may have had for their moth-ers are completely thwarted and repressed. Yet in the same ceremonies, the boys are also enticed with the promise of growing to be one of the men, of becoming a husband, a father, a warrior, a hero, and even in time an honored ancestor.

It seems that the myth reflects some deep self-doubt Sambia males have about being fully masculine. It shows that maleness emerges out of ambiguity, even femaleness. But this cannot be revealed to boys too soon as it might frighten them, and raise doubts and fears of being feminized in the homoerotic fellator role. So the story is hidden until they are grown, married, and can iden-tify as fathers with the happy outcome of being successful like the ancestor.

Stripped of its tremendous drama, does this scenario of power relations not also describe the culminating stage of Oedipal conflict for boys in our own, manifestly blander world: that the child shall forgo present desire, a task made bearable by the promise that lies in identifying with adult men?

Sambia reveal both the early childhood (pre-Oedipal) and pubescent (Oedipal) aspects of the development of masculinity. For the childhood stage, there is the close attachment to their mothers. This involves the boys in their mothers' world and creates a roadblock to the expectation of social manhood. They must separate psychologically from mother. Initiation does this. Then the boy can advance to adolescent Oedipal matters: to desire to *have* a woman like his mother, rather than *being* like his mother. And, with that accomplishment, he earns the right, pictured in the myth (Oedipal conflict), of identification with a desired, feared, admired father. Homoerotic relationships between younger and older males are the royal road to this gender achievement. However, it takes a long time to make it.

The promise at the center of that identification become explicit in the progression of initiations made known to the boy. In time he is fit for marriage, sets up a separate household, and reaches full adult status as a father and warrior, perhaps even becoming a war leader—the highest status one can achieve. Then he becomes an initiator like his own father was. It is his right and responsibility to fill his father's shoes. This means giving up sexual contacts with boys. But what he gains in social recognition and self-esteem more than offsets this giving up of a transitional sexual pattern he has outgrown.

5/The Magical Age of 10, or Why Sambia Initiate Boys So Young*

For 30 years a question has puzzled me: Why do the Sambia feel the urgent need to initiate boys *before age 10?* Why so early? Is it just chance or cultural coincidence? Not according to the Sambia. They feel that the development of a child's desires and sexual behavior are governed not by the intrinsic elements we would label "sexual orientation" but rather by cultural and material forces. Indeed, Sambia lack a construct of "sexual orientation." They assume, instead, that it is possible through social control of children, including punishing them for sexual play, and through ritual imitation that creates powerful taboos of avoidance and gender segregation, that they can regulate the expression of attractions, desires, and sexual behavior. Sambia implicitly believe in a plasticity of sexuality in the human condition; and indeed, their concept of conditional masculinity reveals that they believe in the plasticity of gender as well. Through ritual the men teach boys how to inhibit and control, how to direct their sexuality into homoerotic relationships, and how to redirect their mental energy years later into sexual relations with women. Thus, the effort of ritual initiation is to discipline the context of how attractions occur and desires are expressed to change the outcome of sexual and gender development. While a good deal of this claim has been substantiated in the previous chapters, the question remains: Why age 10?

By the age of 10 young people typically recognize their attractions to others, especially peers, among the Sambia, and indeed, perhaps all human groups. Something changes in them around this time that allows these desires and attractions to become stable and memorable characteristics of their ongoing interaction with others, as well as part of their self-concept. Prior studies published on the United States, the Sambia, and other societies in Melanesia suggest that this developmental period results from powerful internal changes associated with *adrenarche,* a hormonal process that is the first stage of "puberty," or what I call "adrenal puberty," beginning at ages 6–8. Gradually the process builds up so that

*Herdt, G. "Why the Sambia initiate boys before age 10," in Bancroft, J., editor, *The Role of Theory in Sex Research,* p. 82–109. Copyright © 2000, Bloomington: Indiana University Press.

by age 9.5–10 on average for boys and girls, whether gay or straight, a sense of stable attraction emerges on the stage of everyday life. Typically this is around 4th grade in the United States. Within a year or two, the second stage of puberty, "gonadal puberty," takes hold and is often associated with the expression or inhibition of sexual attractions. So striking are the subjective changes that accompany this entry into the gender and sexual arena of early adolescence that I like to refer to it as the "magical age" of 10 (Herdt and McClintock 2000). It was the Sambia who actually encouraged me in this discovery, as I shall explain.

The Sambia express an intense belief that a boy must be initiated before he is "too old" or "too big" for the rite of passage to have its necessary and desired effect. That effect, in brief, is to (1) separate the boy from his mother; (2) "defeminize" him through ritual practices such as blood-letting; (3) "masculinize" him through other ritual practices, especially insemination of the boy's body; (4) socialize him into the role of being a warrior/hunter in preparation for warfare and the perceived dangers of marriage; and (5) forever anchor his subjectivity and desires, including his homoerotic desires, in a secret utopian world regulated by the men's house. In fact, Sambia date the absolute threshold of this necessary and desired change at no later than age 10—otherwise, they say, it will not take hold.

As we have seen, elders teach the dangers of ignoring this "taboo"—warning against failure of the boy's biological male development and the social failure that breaking taboo would mean to him and to society. But they are never clear what the failure to initiate by age 10 would do to the boy's sexual development. Are they worried that boys will not marry women or produce children? Or the opposite: that they will be unable to regulate the boys' sexual desires and thus prevent their premarital relationships with girls and women, which would disrupt the so-carefully balanced marriage system? Perhaps elders fear boys' resistance to initiation would increase until the lads would be too big to force them into the men's house. And again, if the boys remain with their mothers and the women, would the boys be too "soft" and fearful to act as fierce warriors, thus risking the community defense? All of these fears seem plausible and are in keeping with cultural beliefs and social practices.

The Sambia are like many other traditional peoples, including the Ancient Greeks, who reason that the physical body is the vessel for all maturation and social recognition in the person (Lloyd, 1979). By altering a boy's routines and habits, the physical boundaries of his body, what goes in and comes out, and the sexual definition of these entities as well, Sambia attempt to change the interior of the novice (Turner 1964, 1978)—his subjectivity—by altering his body or skin surface, which in Melanesia is a common metaphor for the self (Strathern 1979). To understand why age 10 is critical to the Sambia folk theory of sexual development requires an excursion into three different areas: the Sambia and their place in New Guinea anthropology; sexual identity development in self-identified gay and lesbian teenagers (aged 14 to 20) and their parents, studied in Chicago (Herdt 1992; Herdt and Boxer 1993, 1995; Herdt and Koff 2000); and the physiological and psychosexual significance of adrenarche and menarche, which suggests that between the ages of 6 and 10 the awareness of sexual attraction grows and culminates in the first remembered attraction in child development (McClintock and Herdt 1996).

Figure 5.1 Three initiates at age 10

WHEN IT BEGINS

In Sambia initiation the effect of the rites, typically begun for an age cohort from a group of villages of many boys around age 7 or 8, is to wean the boy from his mother, her body, and cultural world, and to move the boy physically into the men's world. In fact, the Sambia pinpointed this cut-off point at between the ages of 7 and 10 years old; individual boys' ages average approximately 8.5 years. Sambia are emphatic that the boy must never be more than 10.[1]

The developmental change at issue for the Sambia is restricted to males. Females, as far as we know, do not engage in homoerotic relations in a customary fashion nor is there a female cult, which parallels that of the men (Gillison 1993). If the existence of such an ancient ritual practice can be demarcated in the

---

[1] A caution regarding the estimation of absolute chronological ages among the Sambia, a people who lack a written language and records: While it is difficult to make age estimates for any individual among the Sambia, their propensity to think in terms of age cohorts for birth, ritual initiation, and major life events, such as menarche, is of great help in placing individuals in absolute chronological sequences within their small communities. As I have noted before in my work, the ability to place individuals in relation to major social and historical events in the region has enabled me, over a period of more than 20 years of fieldwork, to calculate close age approximations (Herdt 1987a). Within the past 15 years, the presence of a mission station within the Sambia valley and the existence of government birth records have provided different cross-checks for my own guesses, which have usually been borne out by the other records. Finally, in guessing the age of a particular person the tendency to estimate more or less inclines structurally to the entire cohort, evening out random error. The research literature in New Guinea as a whole has tended for many decades to use age markers, which are in keeping with the same age norms claimed for the Sambia (see Read 1954). I therefore remain convinced that while these figures are based upon estimates, they are relatively accurate for population aggregates.

development of the child at age 10, then we obviously must pay attention to the significance of the age marker for generations; gender differences in development are critical here. The fact that females do not have a comparable age marker in the Melanesian practice suggests that while the age of 10 has potential significance for the development of all sexuality and gender, the social stress on transforming the physical body of the boy, and thus his desires and behaviors, may be so large as to require gross change, while in females the stress may be less great and therefore less urgent to change (Herdt 1987a, 1990).

"Puberty" ("gonadal puberty," which follows adrenal puberty) or the onset of secondary "sex characteristics" in adolescence was unusually late in pre-colonial Melanesia (until the 1970s) in the Highlands of New Guinea. Boys did not achieve these sex characteristics until the ages of 14 years and up, while girls reached menarche as late as 19.2 years (Malcolm 1968). This fact makes the importance of age 10 as affirmed by these New Guinea cultures all the more remarkable. Clearly, these tribal peoples are recognizing a change in the child's phenomenology, in his total being—physical and mental—that differs from the subsequent gonadal puberty. It may be the case that due to the lateness of gonadal puberty, the prior period of adrenarche is also "late" in blooming, which might tend to extend the age norms later than those in western populations (McClintock and Herdt 1996). If so, that suggestion would provide an intriguing perspective for rethinking what we know from Melanesia. The evidence from Melanesia, nevertheless, suggests the age of 10 has special significance for traditional peoples such as the Sambia. It is at that ritual age, or very shortly before or after, that initiation as a psychosocial intervention is imposed by the society as a means to manipulate the psychosexual changes associated with this developmental pathway (Herdt 1989). In these societies, in short, where the polarity of the sexes is huge and the expectations of masculine development are so great, an abrupt and dramatic change is imposed upon the developing boy—typically by age 10, or perhaps a bit later, at 12. This leads us back to the psychobiological developmental literature to rethink the meanings of this age threshold.

HORMONES AND SEXUAL ATTRACTION

Let us consider the interaction between hormones and the development of sexual attraction in order to rethink what might be critical about the age of 10. This exercise is in part an attempt to reconsider the overall role of puberty in the gender and sexual development. Another goal is to think further about the role of hypothetical intrinsic mechanisms, especially the connection between desire and intrinsic sexual orientation, in the cultural regimes of child development cross-culturally in societies like those of the Sambia.

A note about the concept of "attraction." For a child, attraction is not the same thing as for an adult. A child's more diffuse properties, such as liking, friendship, admiration, and emotional closeness, have meanings different than for an adult who is aroused. A child may experience these intimate feelings but have no genital arousal. (Genital arousal begins early in life, as many parents know.) And of course the content of such experiences varies by culture, just as the subjectivities of desire and attraction are dependent upon the meanings and practices employed by parents and others in social life to shape these things for the child. Attraction for the 10-year-old may start out as friendship and move into more explicit sexual expression as maturation advances and the individual transitions into adolescent sexuality and gender roles.

Today, thanks to new and important studies of sexual development and maturation in the United States, we are more knowledgeable about the relationship between sexual attraction and pubertal processes in general. We no longer need to accept the claim that sexuality begins in adolescence. It was of course Freud (1905/1962) who most famously proposed that sexuality began in infancy. The difficulty with Freud's formulation, however, was that he reduced nearly all motivation to sex, and he relied upon observations of adults, not children. As is well known, many of Freud's more popular ideas were readily accepted into American culture, but not his suggestions about childhood sexuality. Childhood remains the last frontier and taboo—an icon of cultural innocence in America.

The relationship between adrenarche and puberty in samples of American men and women has recently been the focus of a major critique (McClintock and Herdt 1996). While many previous studies of hormones and the development of gender identity and sexual orientation have appeared in recent years (Byne and Parsons 1993; Meyer-Bahlburg 1997), such studies have tended to deal far more with sexual differentiation and gender atypicality rather than with the emergence of sexual desire or attraction. It is particularly striking that, with the exception of Robert Stoller's (1985) earlier work on hostility and sexual excitement, and Daryl Bem's (1996) later work on the development of arousability and sexual attraction, little attention has been devoted to the age- and gender-specific mechanisms surrounding the subjectivities of erotic attraction. As Meyer-Bahlburg (1984) has noted, the literature is largely concerned with but one element of this huge developmental area: namely, the brain and genital differentiation of the child, with special consequences when the boy's gender behavior is atypical or feminized (Green 1987). These studies tend to take sexual orientation as a given, treating culture as an obstacle to sexual expression, or ignoring social regulations the expression of sexuality, thus ignoring the effect of sexual orientation on the emergence of sexual attraction. Another powerful failing of the older research literature is the general tendency to treat sexual attraction as synonymous with puberty after the age of 11 or 12. Clearly, something prior to gonadal puberty is transforming the child's body and psyche in the direction of sexual attraction and eventual arousal.

What might be the precursor of this phase of sexual development? Adrenarche is a good candidate for the primary (if not the sole) source of the first erotic attraction. First, the adrenals release hormones that are known to be relevant to sexual attraction in adults. (The adrenal glands are small, pyramidal glands located above the kidneys that produce hormones responsible for metabolism and the regulation of salt and hormones.) Second, there is no difference in the ages at which girls and boys develop. Third, the same hormones continue to rise in concentration during gonadarche. If the gonads provide the bulk of the biological priming for sexual attraction and development of sexuality, then it intuitively follows that the same hormones at earlier ages have a similar effect. Fourth, dehydroepiandrosterone (DHEA), the primary sex hormone released by the adrenals, is only two metabolic hops away from testosterone and three hops away from estradiol—the major adult sex hormones.

The research literature provides a new picture of these processes, however, in samples of heterosexuals and homosexuals in the United States (McClintock and Herdt 1996). Separate studies of gay-identified males conducted by different investigators from different disciplines in different parts of the U.S. have pinpointed age 10 as definitive of the onset of first attraction to the same sex. This remembered developmental age is all the more remarkable in that it seems impervious to cultural and historical change. That is, one study has a mean age of 37 years (Hamer, Hu, Magnuson, Hu and Pattitucci 1993), while the other has a mean age of 17.9 years (Herdt and Boxer 1993). The difference of approximately one generation suggests that the developmental onset of first awareness or first attraction to the same sex may be independent of social/historical age-cohort differences or simple social learning. In fact, one might have predicted that the sexual revolution in the 1960s, and the AIDS epidemic in the 1980s and 1990s, would have altered the age of first attraction in the older generation (Gagnon 1990). Not so! What is even more remarkable is that the age of 9.5 to 10 years is the time when first sexual attraction occurs for heterosexuals as well as homosexuals—a fascinating correspondence of development that is not apparently modified by sexual orientation. A comparable age (10.4 years) has recently been found by Bailey and Oberschneider (1997) in a smaller sample of gay men. These studies thus imply that sexual orientation is independent from the mechanisms governing the onset and manifestation of erotic desire and attraction.

Boys in these studies experienced first-remembered attraction at a slightly younger age than did the girls; this difference may itself be significant for understanding subtle but still very powerful micromechanisms of the cultural environment that influence the emergence of attraction (Herdt and Boxer 1993: Chapter 5). In fact, sexual attraction before gonadal puberty, erotic fantasy, sexual desire, and perhaps generalized arousability linked to gender differences (Bem 1996) all suggest that these elements are not dependent upon the biosocial concomitants of the pubertal process in any simple sense. It should be pointed out that the precise identification of pubertal onset in all of these males has not been established (McClintock and Herdt 1996). Erotic and social precocity may, however, be linked to the observation of early attraction, although precocity as a distinctive feature of sexual identity development in gay men has long been questioned or denied (Meyer-Bahlburg 1984). Indeed, there are plenty of reasons to believe that—in developmental and cultural terms—the age of 9.5 to 10 years is a time of critical transition in cognitive, emotional, and social adjustment. It is just that our culture lacks a specific ritual or social marker to signify this critical transition.

As McClintock and Herdt argued in 1996, androgens have developmental effects in adults in a variety of areas, such as aggression, emotions, and sexual development. This is certainly consistent with the important theory of psychologist Daryl Bem (1996), who argues that biosocial variables do not "code" for sexual orientation as such but rather for the childhood temperaments that influence preference for gender-typical or gender-atypical preferential practices. For example, a child who is aggressive in temperament may favor gender-typical "masculine" roles and practices more than one who is not (this is true for both male *and* female children!). Such effects have not been demonstrated in children but are presumed to be causative of the same microareas in their developmental systems.

Hormonal growth has been regarded as a key effect of sexual development in a continuous sequence from childhood through adulthood, with gonadarche the apex. Here, *gonadarche* means menarche in girls and spermarche in boys. Previous sexual developmental research has attributed changes in adolescent behavior to changes in hormone levels accompanied by gonadarche only. If gonadarche were responsible for these first sexual attractions, however, then the mean age should be later—around age 12 for girls and age 13 for boys. Clearly, as studies have shown repeatedly, gonadarche happens earlier for girls than for boys, and so it follows that girls ought to express their attractions earlier.

Herdt and Boxer (1993) studied a group of self-identified gay and lesbian teenagers (ages 14 to 20, with a mean age of 17.9 years) from a broad cross-section of Chicago. This cohort revealed a sequence of ages of first same-sex attraction, first same-sex fantasy, and first same-sex behavior; the mean age for same-sex attraction was around age 10 for both males and females, but sexual behavior began a bit earlier for boys than for girls. Girls, in particular, inhibited the expression of their sexual attractions until later than boys, and their life stories and sexual histories typically suggested that social pressure on gender roles from parents, older siblings, and peers was the primary reason. However, by the time both genders had reached age 16, the gender difference had leveled out. In short, culture influences the expression of desires and attractions and may inhibit one gender more than the other in sexual expression, perhaps even the formation of sexual desires.

The developing hormones of a child between the ages of 5 and 12 are critical for understanding both the physical bodies and the psychological (interpersonal and intrapsychic) development of preadolescents (Money and Ehrhardt 1972). Hormone levels are fairly predictable across the population. The hormone levels remain low until the maturation of the adrenal glands at ages 6 to 8. Then they begin to climb, in an exponential manner, until reaching adult levels. They begin to plateau after this in both boys and girls. The hormones released during preadolescence are androgens (typically identified as "male" sex hormones). Around ages 6 to 8, adrenal glands begin to develop in both males and females. The adrenal glands (specifically the adrenal cortex) begin to secrete low levels of androgens (typically identified as "male" sex hormones), primarily of DHEA. The specific androgen released by the adrenal glands is in the same metabolic pathways as testosterone and estrogen. There is no sex difference in the rate, onset, or hormone levels until gonadarche. Adult levels of DHEA are reached by age 12 for girls and age 13 for boys The levels of these hormones begin to steadily climb upward and increase significantly around age 10. While these levels are low compared to normal adult levels, they are many (10 to 20) times what typical children aged 1 to 4 experience. The hormone levels required for an organizational (long-term, permanent) effect are unknown, but the levels experienced between ages 6 and 10 are within activational (short-term, temporary) range (McClintock and Herdt 1996; Herdt and McClintock, 2000).

Given the strong possibility that the current popular model of puberty and development is incorrect, we must rethink puberty and test the new models in a wide range of fields. Adrenarche clearly increases androgens to significant levels, and if those hormones are responsible for the effects seen in sexual attraction, then they also may influence a wide range of other behaviors, including aggression, cognition, perception, attention, arousal, emotions, and, of course, the development of sexual identity and attraction. Even if the hormones released from the adrenal glands are not responsible for the changes in sexual attraction, the concept of "puberty" must now be greatly enlarged and unpacked. The current work suggests that there are two separate maturational processes occurring: adrenarche and gonadarche. Social research that uses "puberty" as a stage in development needs to break down the relevant developmental and social behaviors into the two different stages of pubertal formation and maturation, with the start of adrenal puberty in normal individuals occurring at around ages 6 to 8, and the end of gonadal puberty being completed at ages 15 to 17. In between, the age threshold of 10 may mark the average onset of sexual attraction in human populations.

If the onset of sexual attraction is indeed strongly motivated internally by these hormonal developments, and especially the adrenal puberty that seems to reach its peak before the adolescent years, then it is no surprise that nonwestern peoples such as the Sambia have hit upon customs that institutionalize significant life course changes around age 10.

In this view, over generations, the Sambia may have inferred that the microevents and processes, which lead to sexual arousal, attraction, and behavior development in the boy, require *formal recognition and social control* before gonadal puberty. Their effort to impose separation from the mother and siblings and to impose gender segregation, followed by powerful identity changes in the boy through forcible ritual initiations, thus prepare for and anticipate the changes that will occur before age 10. By placing the child in a new context for learning and perceiving, the Sambia have actively engaged the internal and cultural processes of sex and gender development in the direction of their society's social order.

DEVELOPMENT OF SEXUAL ATTRACTION IN SAMBIA

Explanations of Sambia sexual culture have been used both to defend and attack "social constructionism" and to defend and attack "essentialism" in theories of sexual development. I mean by these paradigms approximately what Carole Vance (1991) has shrewdly denoted in her remark that an "essence" is what that culture defines as above and beyond what can be modified or changed. Thus, anthropologists, sociologists, historians, and other social theorists have argued that the ritual character of Sambia sexuality may represent a universal potential of bisexuality or homosexuality.

These universalizing views of Sambia sexuality by developmentalists assume the existence of "sexual orientation" as a predictable universal. John Money (1987) has claimed that the Sambia system can inhibit the formation and development of particular sexual habits, such as masturbation or childhood sex play, and stimulate the practice of other habits, such as boy-insemination rituals. But these developments are in line with what he sees to be an intrinsic model of sex-role learning in the direction of masculinity. According to Money's conception of sexual culture, then, sexual development is characterized by significant *continuity* in gendered objects and sexual desires, with a strong inference that what was desired in childhood (as Freud might have said) would be expressed in adulthood. Sure, there might be interruptions along the way, or lateral movements within the same "dimension" of sexuality (as Alfred Kinsey might have said), even with plenty of interruption. Nevertheless, in the end, there would be little change in the main line of sexual orientation, and thus, of sexual development. For these theorists, it is unnatural to think that desires that were "hardwired" by sexual orientation would exist without the possibility of expression in the social commerce of local sexual cultures.

Where I differ is in accepting the force of microevents and micro learning as sociocultural influences affecting the outcomes of childhood sexual desires. Sambia parents sense that, if left to his own designs, the boy would fail to make the required successful transition into the warrior role. He would then fail to achieve adult reproductive competence. The role requires a kind of social and political ability to manipulate sexual transitions that would not be expected of a boy growing up in a close attachment to his mother. Furthermore, and here I side with psychologist Daryl Bem (1996), I believe that the boy and girl in this developmental regime may inhibit expression of their strongest desires and emotions to conform to social norms, thus reducing the sense of difference, of being exotic compared to the other, to register desire toward others. It is not the creation of sexual desire itself that may suffer in this case (as claimed by Freud's universal Oedipal complex) but rather the ability of the culture to socially regulate this desire as the boy turns age 7 or 8. Without a major intervention, the boy's micro learning may not produce the kind of idealized, even essentialized, masculine attachments and warriorhood behaviors that the culture desires. To influence his desires, his father and the men remove him from his mother's world and place him in a homosocial environment. To be doubly certain of his conformity to the masculine role, they make the boy the object of sexual desire by older boys, a "pull" away from his childhood phenomenology. By doing this under the influence of the adrenarche, they may be able to influence and alter the boy's subjectivities, to be attracted to male things and to the romanticized figure of the Great Man. Thus a boy is initiated into sexual life and has awakened, for the first time, erotic awareness—which will fold into development the desire to be a hunter/warrior, the supreme achievement of the men's house.

Others suggest that the ability of Sambia men to halt their inseminations and move on to heterosexual contacts (reviewed by Connell and Dowsett 1993; Greenberg 1995; Vance 1991; and others, noted in Herdt and Boxer 1995) attests to the fluidity and the adaptable nature of sexuality in human beings. However, there is a tendency in these discussions to conflate the construction of sexual behavior with the development of sexual attraction, so that attraction and behavior are treated as synonymous. It will now be obvious why that cannot be true and, in fact, as attraction precedes sexual expression and is often impeded by cultural pressures to conform to gender roles, we must be careful to recognize the difference.

I believe that for the typical Sambia boy and girl growing up in traditional village social life, the development of sexual attraction remained socially suppressed, and psychologically repressed, until at least middle childhood, if not in fact until initiation, which for the age cohort of boys in a village is in the age range of 7 to 10. In growing up, boys and girls sometimes engaged in exploratory sex play and, occasionally, sexual intercourse, although these behaviors were seriously sanctioned by their parents and were generally hidden (Herdt and Stoller 1990). As Penjukwi's case study reveals (Chapter 3), girls experienced attractions toward boys and even dared the taboo of childhood sex play, but the risk of punishment was great. Moreover, there are many stories of sexual coercion and rape among Sambia women, and it is obvious that sexual coercion was common in the context of boy-insemination. In my interviews with many individual boys, adolescents, and young and middle-aged men, ranging from about 5 years of age to about 70 years of age (Herdt and Stoller 1990), sexual repression was a fundamental theme of their life stories. The evidence for repression also comes from the longings of men about their feelings about their mothers and fathers, as well as their playmates (Herdt 1992). The effect of this repressive developmental regime was the delay of conscious and explicit awareness of sexual desires and attractions until after first-stage initiation. In Chapter 6 we will study how mechanisms of power and secrecy perpetuated this system of sexual repression.

Take note of one piece of the phenomenology of insemination in Sambia development: The fellator in sexual interactions is the psychologically active person, as George Devereux, the anthropologist–classicist, suggested long ago. The phenomenology of the experience is real in the folklore of the men's house, where boys will spend long periods comparing the differences in taste, viscosity, and volume of the seminal flows of bachelors (once I referred to this banter as the semonology of the Sambia; Herdt 1981). The person who is sucking, whether the boy or a woman, is psychologically engaged in the task of arousing, avoiding gagging, and swallowing. Sambia ensure continuity in sexual subjectivity and behavior by requiring the young bride to dress with some warrior garb and fellate her new husband—a "bridge" and sexual transition from one phase of sexual development to the next. From the cultural perspective the equation of semen with mother's milk blurs the boundary of what boys "get" from mother and what they "get" from bachelors. From the bachelor's perspective, the sexual experience of orally inseminating a boy or a young woman is not greatly different. Sambia boys focus on the swallowing—that is key to their masculinizing. Some boys report being aroused as they are doing the sucking—especially the older second-stage initiates that may actually be undergoing gonadal puberty. However, they do not express their own erections and, as far as is known, do not masturbate. Many Sambia initiates do report wet dreams, however, and these dreams have a cultural pattern: They first remember night dreams in which they are "playing" with younger initiates and inseminating them, and later they graduate to dreams in which they are flirting with women and copulating with them. Sambia boys experience a gap between their sexual development (gonadal puberty) and their cultural roles, which does not allow them to express their attractions until the rituals have elevated them to the next stage. No wonder it is a difficult and frustrating transition for them!

Do these changes in sexual desire and behavior occur only in this sequence, and can they be expected to result in transformations both in the material and the subjective being of the Sambia male (Herdt 1999)? As I have shown before, the early developmental changes before age 10, while difficult to document before initiation at age 7, can be demonstrated after the boy enters the men's house. There, boys begin to think about their material bodies, develop plans to "capture" semen and "grow" themselves, and often engage privately in risqué commentaries with their age mates regarding the virtues and values of being inseminated by particular men (Herdt 1981; Herdt 1987a; Herdt and Stoller 1990). Likewise, as the boys achieve gonadal puberty, they begin to experience nocturnal emissions and start to fantasize about inseminating younger boys. Typically these youths begin enthusiastic careers as the dominant fellateds. They do not typically require masturbation or mechanical stimulation to be aroused but are fully able and eager to inseminate the boys they select for intercourse at this time. The exceptions to these normative trends, as I have shown before, tend to augment the strong change in desire toward the male body, even to the point of having exclusive interest in sex with boys rather than moving on to sex with women later on (Herdt and Stoller 1990).

SEXUAL LIFEWAYS, NOT SEXUAL ORIENTATIONS

The emphasis the Sambia place upon the physical and mental being of the boy raises the question of their own view and perceptions of these events. In an earlier time in theory, it was common to imagine that all or virtually all of this subjective reality conformed to "the unconscious" (Freud 1905/1962) or to the universals of cognition present in human nature (Piaget 1971). A construct of sexual nature that emerges from such a universalizing paradigm is inevitably insensitive to the cultural environment and predisposes us to cardboard biology.

"Sexual orientation" is the offspring of such a universalizing theory. As an ideal type, it still has conceptual value when it is understood to refer to a theory of innate development. But as an empirical pattern of reality, in the simple sense of absolute attractions to a sex object, and the scripts implied by such attractions, it is not discriminating enough. Many prior studies derive their impetus largely from the concept of sexual orientation (reviewed in Bem 1996; see also Gorman 1994) and an understanding of the importance of the earliest development of sex, romance, and attraction that begins in childhood and culminates around age 10. My view is that the concept of "sexual orientation" has utility when restricted to simple dichotomous variables, such as male or female sex object (Adkins-Regan 1984; Bell, Weinberg, and Hammersmith 1981; Kinsey, Pomeroy, and Martin 1948; Money and Ehrhardt 1972; Pattatucci and Hamer 1995; Storms 1981). However, the construct covers greatly disparate areas of human development for which the sources of development differ, and these areas should not be conflated. "Homosexual" and "heterosexual," in this model, are so general as to make meaning and predictability very difficult in human development. A case study from a nonwestern culture helps us to rethink just why this claim might be so. The onset of sexual attraction at age 10 is uniquely suited for the task.

A theory of sexual development that does not rely upon the conceptual crutch of innate "sexual orientation" needs to rethink "desire" as a heuristic concept for the operation of intimate sexual relationships and cultural institutions. Desire in this developmental cultural model is closer to what anthropologists have called "values," with the additions of the agentic dimension of personal intentionality and the directionality of cultural cognitions (Shweder 1989). Desires thus include what the actor likes and wants from another person, the general disposition to desire and want to possess a sexual "object" or a culturally valued social role (to be a husband, to be a chief) or a goal in life (to be virtuous, to achieve power and influence, and so on). It never has been explained how cultures manage to manufacture desires, like a factory produces paper clips, in the service of simple social learning and social constructionist theories.

How do sexual cultures manage to "stimulate" or "produce" desires? They do so in part by how they constantly teach what is "socially valued" and what a person needs to grow up and have the status and symbolic capitol of personhood. This sense of desire is broader than Freud's (1905/1962) aim/instinct complex that was focused more on erotic drives than on direct fantasy. Current research on human development suggests that desires can be modified, if not in fact learned; and sexual desires, when bundled together, more nearly resemble a sexual lifeway, capable of social modification and, under the right circumstances, social manipulation. Sexual lifeways are cultural models of sexuality and human nature that develop into a level of subjective "realness" unquestioned by the person and a part of their society, their ontological reality. The formation of sexual lifeways is highly dependent upon developmental and cultural processes that stipulate preferred sexual subjectivities and approved or tabooed sexual objects.

The fit between the desires of the person and the demands made by Sambia society is registered in the timeworn patterns of their sexual culture. Historically and in material terms, their sexual culture was heavily overdetermined by warfare, emphasized warrior roles for men, and the marriage trade that brought the women of hostile villages into intimate relations with men. The long-term solution to the contradictions and human weakness in such institutions was the initiation of boys before age 10; in other words, before the sexual attractions of boys could be rooted in the world of women rather than in the men's disciplinary regime of secrecy and warriorhood.

The Sambia were not unique in the creation of such a sexual culture. American anthropologist Bruce Knauft (1999) has made a similar case for the Gebusi people:

> In early adolescence (ages 11–14) boys extend their affection to older unrelated males in the community by establishing homosexual relationships with them—i.e., being their fellators. Rather than being based on subordination or domination, these relations tend to be coquettishly initiated by the young adolescents themselves. The ideological reason for insemination is to 'grow' the boys into men, but homosexuality appears for all practical intents and purposes to be grounded in personal affection rather than obligation.

As I have described in previous chapters, the early development of boys and girls took place almost exclusively in the women's world. Through the ritual initiations, boys were forced to *unlearn* what they had known since birth and relearn new concepts and roles that supported their adulthood and elected them in the eyes of the men's cult to a superior station in life. I once called this *developmental discontinuity*—boys have to unlearn emotions and cognitions (Herdt 1990). I still think that is an accurate description of the situation; however, it does not address the development of attraction.

Thus, to reiterate: In the Sambia boy's sexual development, he begins life in the shadows of his mother's female-centered heterosocial environment. His father is somewhere around but not available to him continually and often is emotionally unavailable. A boy is not regarded as an agent in his culture and is regarded as morally inoffensive and without agency. The culture is gender segregated, and ritual secrecy divides the society into two parts. This division of developmental subjective being thus pervades the emergence of gender, especially through ritual secret practices, and introduces the boy into alternative systems of desires and meanings otherwise never learned in growing up with women and children. By accepting his position as an object of ritual treatment, the Sambia boy's social rank is elevated. By then learning the position of being an object of erotic desire by the adolescent bachelors, the boy gains agency, in that he can begin to refuse, to say "yes or no," to their sexual advances. With each of these micromoments, the boy's sexuality is changed and his desires are enhanced, in the sense that he is moving willy-nilly into the masculine life way of his culture. In time, his inseminations enable his growth and manliness, according to the cultural ontology. His learning of the sexual behaviors that come with this territory equips him to become more agentic and eventually to succeed those who formerly dominated him. Meanwhile, he is learning to take himself as a subject; when this process is complete, his transformation suggests that he has learned the desire to inseminate a younger boy. His sexual agency is not complete, but he is sufficiently differentiated from the women and the women's world that preceded this transition that he can experience them again as totally exotic and dangerous, and thus eligible as sexual objects.

Exotic becomes erotic, as Bem (1996) notes: What is exotic to one person (a girl to a boy, for example) becomes exciting, and eventually sexual. But if a culture wants to ensure the optimal result for its own preferred form of sexual attraction, it should do so before age 10 and use its full power to channel the developmental subjectivities that make a desire worth desiring and then expressing in sexual behavior.

A NOTE ON THE ANCIENT GREEKS

The Sambia have a system of boy-inseminating that bears comparison to the ancient Greeks, in spite of some of the great differences in these societies. As I have long suggested, one can compare the Greeks of the Homeric period with the Sambia in New Guinea; even though these cultures are very different in many social and political characteristics, they share a social and mythological devotion to warfare (Herdt 1984, 1997). If we make the change in scale, the Ancient Greeks can be compared to the Sambia, and indeed the military character of many pre-colonial Melanesian cultures, as has been noted by classicists in recent years (reviewed in Herdt 1993). The dynamics of ritual insemination in both cultural traditions may have been quite similar. The men did not have social and emotional relations with women. The sons were involved in close social and intimate relations with their mothers, and their political relationships to their fathers were thus complicated. Such a cultural world created a kind of sexual life way that did not fit into the men's social needs and public practices—not without dramatic ritual and, as it turns out, sexual changes in the younger boys. Indeed, the early Greeks' problem of their budding boys was not only what to do with them but how to bring them into their rightful places as noble warriors and free citizens (Halperin 1990). Here the Greek emphasis on social citizenship in the later Socratic period becomes helpful in its stipulations about what was allowed and what was taboo in sexual and intimate relations (Williams 1998).

Take note of a striking age similarity that unites the pattern of male sexual development between the Sambia and the Greeks. Here there is a singularly important age parallelism with regard to the commencement of initiation. The Sambia commence initiation beginning at age 7 (up to age 10); the ancient Spartans also commenced initiation at 7 years of age. In both cases the boys were separated from their mothers and taken into the men's house or men's camp; they lived for the duration, until well into adulthood, in the gender-segregated quarters of the warriors.

However, the respective ages of the onset of sexual interaction were very different, and in one important respect, exactly the opposite! The Sambia begin their sexual careers immediately upon initiation at age 7, and they continue to be the recipients of semen until they achieve physical and social puberty, at approximately ages 13 to 15. The Spartans, however, did not commence sexual interaction until they achieved gonadal puberty, which is believed to have been about age 14 (Williams 1998). Only after they began to have post-pubertal adolescent traits (especially the presence of some beard on their faces) did they become the object of sexual attraction for Spartan men. In fact, the classical scholar Craig Williams (personal communication) describes how the attractiveness of the Spartan youth peaked when he achieved a prominent beard, at about age 18. That is about when a Sambia youth also has a noticeable beard. But in terms of homoerotic attraction, the Sambia have precisely the opposite sexual desire. The boy is sexually attractive and desirable as an object *only up to gonadal puberty,* at age 14 and up. When a Sambia youth clearly shows physical manliness—and the facial beard is a peak—he is no longer regarded as an object of desire by older males. In fact, Sambia males find the post-pubertal boy to be sexually unattractive and a culturally inappropriate object of insemination. True, a few men continue to inseminate boys and in this way are bisexual, but they must hide what they do from the other men and be discrete; otherwise they risk a loss of masculine respect. Hence, puberty can be perceived either as the beginning or the end of regard for the child as a sexual object.

But the hormonal process sets the stage and gives a context for the sexual attraction. It is culture, not the hormones, that determines the next steps for sexual development and its outcome. Society does that, and so do you.

6/Sex/Gender, Power, and Social Inequality

How are social inequalities created and what role do sexuality and gender play in the process? Social inequalities are the forms of indignity, social stigma, discrimination, and violence that create human suffering and destroy human potential. The emergence of a new paradigm of anthropology that looks deeply at social oppression and sexuality as the precursor or result of inequality is critical to social research in the 21st century (Teunis and Herdt 2006). While many differences separate the Sambia from late modern societies such as the United States, I believe that the Sambia provide some critical lessons for all students of the human condition, due to their unique sexual culture.

Among the Sambia, the men's secret society and its initiation system created and reproduced power relationships from sexual and gender meanings and practices. Social inequality, the explicit definition of categories of people as being "higher" and "lower," "pure" and "impure," "strong" and "weak," was the result. Women experienced many social inequalities in the pre-colonial society. Within the men's secret society, a hierarchical ladder of higher and lower status surrounded the initiations, with elders and war leaders at the top of the totem pole, and first-stage initiates at the bottom. Sexual and gender objectification played upon these inequalities. Sexual exchange and gender roles were also instrumental mechanisms in reproducing the structure of power relations through social relationships, as well as through culture, that is, the meanings and beliefs of everyday life and the self. This chapter studies these social inequalities in the context of war, marriage, sexual antagonism, secrecy, and the harsh realities of the ritual initiation system of the Sambia. We will also study how social change has disrupted the male power system and introduced new categories, social practices and meanings of gender and sexuality, which have changed the balance of power.

As long as war prevailed, the structure of power relationships remained intact and resisted change, both internal and external, to Sambia society. We saw how some boys traditionally resisted initiation sufficiently to run away into the forest (Chapter 4). As the conclusion to Chapter 2 reveals, the pacification of the

Figure 6.1   Four adult men flute-players, Sambia Valley 1993

Sambia in the early 1960s began irrevocably to alter male identity and culture—and to erode male power and hegemony. Change began to overtake a variety of arenas of social life, leaving the ritual initiation system intact until the 1980s. Sexuality and gender roles began to change dramatically, as the CD-ROM accompanying this case study reveals. Before we examine the impact of these changes, however, we first need to understand the traditional system of hierarchy and the social inequalities that it perpetuated.

Like most warrior societies, and certainly many in Papua New Guinea (Schwartz 1973; Meggitt 1977; reviewed in Knauft 1999: Chapter 3), Sambia adaptation to the conditions of perpetual warfare exacted a heavy toll in social suffering. What did this include for the Sambia? The threat of daily violence and mayhem; political fear and assassination; family conflict, including tension and hostility between the parents, as well as wife-beating; the coercion of initiation; socioeconomic exploitation by men of women; sexual violence and rape; sexual shame and suicide, with female suicide outnumbering male suicide by four to one; female infanticide; sexual antagonism and mistrust at the village level; and pollution ideologies that promoted misogyny at a general level. There is no simple "transition" in Melanesia from such dreadful realities to contemporary "civil" and humanistic Western values (Knauft 1999: 180), and the Sambia are a case in point (Herdt and Stolpe, 2005).

The offspring of Sambia couples were caught in a drama of conflicting roles: the sons having divided loyalties between mothers and fathers and his warrior-comrades; the daughters experiencing even closer attachments to their mothers, and the political contract of being "married off" via the exchange system to sons in other villages. The close identification between mothers and children was powerful in bonding boys to a longing for mother and a nostalgia for childhood prior to initiation that we observed in Chapter 4. On another level of social life, however, these complex familial relationships, so divided by the politics of marriage and the marriage of politics, gave rise to lifelong rivalries across villages, genders, and generations.

But how did these childhood factors link up to sexuality? The maternal relationships are the deepest and most profound of all bonds for many Sambia individuals, deeper than the competitive age-mate relations; unconditional and innocent compared to the politically arranged marriages. While early bonding/ relational factors cannot explain the development of sexual orientation, they certainly influence independence, resilience, the development of attraction and desires in the child, the comparison between the intimacies of mother and intimate sexual partners, and the role that these developmental subjectivities play in shaping individuals. One of the basic points of departure in this analysis is to look at who and what is regarded as "sexual" and "attractive" and "beautiful" in Sambia sexual culture. This is where "desire" begins in the social development of the child.

MEN ARE THE SEXUAL OBJECTS

Why are men the sexy and desired objects of Sambia popular culture (Herdt 1999)? It took me some years to ask this question—why, I am not sure, because long ago (Schieffelin 1976) it was reported that at least in some Melanesian societies men groom to beautify themselves as if they are on display in a beauty pageant.

How strange to the American mind to think of men as sex objects, at least until recently. After all, beauty pageants are still all about women, since traditional heterosexist society depicts women as the poster objects of sex appeal, and the desired sexy objects to be "consumed" and "used," like a Playboy magazine. Recently this image has changed, as mainstream underwear companies began to use the image of scantily clad attractive male bodies—once reserved only for female objectification—to market and sell products in magazines, on billboards, and on the web. Sure, Americans objectify male film stars and celebrities today, even treating them as sexual objects, for which they are handsomely paid; but their money and fame give them extraordinary power with which to manipulate others too. Commercializing sexuality in this way is a complement with a cruel edge, because it is the body, not the whole person, that is being used as a commodity to desire, and to sell products. Thus, to be sexually objectified means in one way that men are treated as objects. It certainly goes against our traditional gender norms to think of men this way, which suggests of course that our own norms are changing rapidly.

The Sambia are different, because males, especially bachelors and young men, are sexualized as the high point of what was admired and desired. Knowledge of this sexual objectification is actually encoded into Sambia ritual, myth, and the broader cultural system. And Sambia are not alone. As Maurice Godelier (1986) has remarked for the neighboring Baruya culture, the idealized and preferred sexual object and object of beauty and attraction is not the female but the male in many Melanesian cultures. Not only is the male the most sexy and ornamented person but to desire him is normal and natural—for both genders. For the Sambia, the admired and idealized image of the Great Man, a warrior-hunter—strong, potent, and powerfully sexual—who can take many wives and kill many men—is prominent in the men's house folklore. It is a kind of glamour that is prestigious, intentional, and performative: if you can do it, you get rewarded with sex and power. To bluff, to intimidate, to aggress, and to attract, are all linked.

Typically, Americans think about "sex objects" and being sexy as being susceptible to victimization, even abuse, because of the exploitation inherent in such sexualization. The sexual script underlying this imagery is that to be sexual is to be powerless. Concomitantly, another script, the heterosexist one, led men to feel that they were the more powerful and socially superior, and therefore they got to "define" who or what was sexy. Male "consumption" of the sexual object was referred to as, "that's just what men are," "that's male nature," and "that's natural masculinity." But all of these sexual scripts could and often did lead to abuse. The parallel script of the sex object was a role that was also felt to be powerless, weaker, a victim. These sexual scripts were present in Sambia society but not in the way that you might think.

There is a sexual paradox in Sambia society. The men have the *jerungdu,* the semen; they are the warriors; they hold the power; and they are the stakeholders in a patriarchal society where descent and property flow down the male line. And yet in Sambia sexual scripts, males are the sexual objects. How is it possible, in such a highly male-dominated, patriarchal culture, that men would be sexually objectified and treated as the sexy, poster objects? Why would they want to be the desired sexual objects? Is it possible that desire plays a different role and sexual objectification has a different developmental outcome than in the United States? If the answer is "yes," we begin to understand how sexuality and gender can construct society and influence power in very different ways than we typically imagine.

The sexual objectification of Sambia males arises from two fundamental sources: (1) boys, not women, are the ones lacking a voice in their society, being more marginal,[1] women being a lot more powerful than men grant them; and (2) men's power, that is, masculinity is conditional, and highly permeable, beginning with the awkward and very cumbersome creation of a secret form of masculinity through insemination in a boy's development. It is this permeability of male power that ritual secrecy protects. What is hidden from public discourse is the secret ritual understanding that, to become powerful and masculine, an adult man has to be inseminated by many men as he grows up. "Desire" in this sexual culture is thus the product of and is dependent upon ritual, secrecy, and the cultural control of masculinity in the men's house. Similarly, anthropologist Gillian Gillison (1993: 354) has suggested of the Gimi people: "Men design flutes—and, by analogy, their whole society—not to valorize female fertility but to cure the fatal consequences of men's own desires."

---

[1]The "subaltern," in post-colonial studies, while not comparable here due to the character of precolonial Sambia society, nonetheless conveys a sense of the oppressed without a possible voice.

Among the Sambia, being sexy and sexually objectified are not the antithesis or the negation of masculinity but rather the means to overcome the powerlessness of being boys to become gloriously masculine. To understand how the whole system works we first need to see who is higher and who is lower in Sambia society.

CATEGORIES OF HIERARCHY

Through the ritual system of male and female initiations and the secret society, Sambia created and reproduced across generations a hierarchical set of categories of people. Ritual ultimately anchors this sexual classification. These were ranked social and religious status positions, involving differential roles, rights, and duties. Through this system of markers, Sambia discriminated the most basic or essential forms of contrast in their nature, culture, and thought, and reproduced social inequality.

At the most basic level of cultural contrast, these categories distinguish all males from all females, and all people as semen donors (inserters) or semen recipients (receptors). There are four marked categories of ritual-based male personhood: (1) All first-stage and second-stage initiates are categorized as *kuwatni' u,* or "initiate," the lowest of all initiated male status positions, and the semen recipients, with little agency. All older males exercise political and sexual control over them. Within the age-mate group, though, initiates are both peers and competitors. (2) Third-stage initiates are classed as bachelor-youths, *aatmwonungenyu* (literally "male bamboo," a euphemism for the mature penis), prototypic bachelors who are sexually mature inserters nearly eligible for marriage. Fourth-stage initiates are "in-between men," Sambia say, for they are married but not yet living with their wives; they still reside in the clubhouse and engage in boy-inseminating. So they are referred to as *nuposha* (named after the marriage ceremony), their ritual status title. They are closest to what we would call "bisexuals" in the United States. (3) However, these males are typically lumped together with fifth-stage and sixth-stage initiates as *aatmwol chenchorai,* or "newlywed," a higher status because it means that they have wives. (4) The high-ranking category is *aatmwunu* or "adult," a term of respect for men who have fathered (preferably two or more) children and who exercise legal and moral authority over all younger initiates, women, and children. *Aatmwunu* with multiple wives have the highest status of all.

There are three categories of status among women: *tai,* or female child; *taiketnyi,* a woman who has experienced her first menstruation; and *aatmwunu,* a woman who has married and preferably has two or more children. Female elders, women in their 30s and up and women shamans, are the highest ranking of all Sambia females.

Situationally, married women and female elders are higher ranking and usually will command respect from all children and *kuwatni' u.* All other categories of males rank above females in all situations, and even initiates on occasion will balk at the directives of female elders. Each of these categories is easily recognizable by distinctive ritual and gender signs. Gender signs are emblems or body decorations that denote power and ranked status. The Sambia typically employ

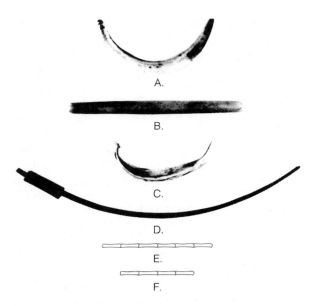

Figure 6.2 Noseplugs

body decorations, such as noseplugs, which differentiate males into higher or lower types of social status, and by degrees of biological development (see Figure 6.2). Small children do not wear noseplugs, but in late childhood, the nasal septum in boys and girls may be pierced to anticipate initiation. After initiation, however, all males wear the noseplugs of their ritual status as an insignia of their status. In the youngest initiate category, small sugar cane stems are used (see Figure 6.2, types E and F). This is the sign of lowest masculine development. Next are second-stage initiates, who wear cassowary quill bones, noseplug type D. (Nubile women also wear quill bone noseplugs) Third-stage initiates can wear type C noseplugs. Category 3 men, newlyweds and young men, may wear type B. But only fully initiated older men and elders can wear type A, *sogamdu*—the famous pig's tusk-tie hallmark of proud and aggressive Great Man. (see Mon in Figure 2.1) Normally the tusks are worn with the points down. But in initiation and in warfare, they are pointed up, "like an erect penis," men say. The link between these body icons and the phallus is therefore obvious— revealing the deeper misogyny of the Sambia.

RITUAL SECRECY

Institutionalized secrecy associated with sex segregation creates social inequalities in New Guinea cultures like that of Sambia. Because sexuality and gender roles are so strongly related to secret ritual initiation, the mechanism of secrecy itself plays a huge role not only in daily hamlet life but in the larger definition of social reality (Herdt 2003). Secrecy divides the genders via gender-role segregation. Since ritual knowledge is so important in Sambia culture, and because this information is gained only by age-graded entry into the men's or women's secret ceremonies, secret knowledge is a key cultural barrier that always separates the sexes. Secrecy is essential to the very operation of Sambia society, and one marvels at the incredible lengths to which it has been carried here. To illustrate: Many things have secret names, the list of which in plants, animals, and folklore numbers in the hundreds. Since secrecy creates unequal power, it creates distrust between the sexes.

Inside the hamlet, people operate and behave in three types of social situations: public, secret, and private. The secret life is established by ritual, whereas the private is defined by each person. These situations occur in various institutional settings basic to Sambia society. Social action in each situation corresponds to one of three different types of talk: public talk (*iyun-gacheru yungalu*, lit. "free talk"), secret talk (*ioolu yungalu*, lit. "hidden talk"), and private talk (no marked category). Public discourse defines daily village gab and rhetoric. It is associated with domestic situations in women's houses, casual gatherings on the plaza of a hamlet, work teams, and formal public meetings. Local meetings shape how Sambia now use the pidgin concepts *tok publik* (public talk) and *tok hait* (secret talk), because all ritual is *tok hait*. Warfare and village disputes are public talk. Gender integrated audiences of men, women, and children define the public situation—public affairs—whereas gender segregation immediately invokes secret language.

For the Sambia and many other New Guinea men's societies, a paradoxical theme emerges: In public affairs the men profess their superiority to enemies and women, while in secret they confess their inferiority and dread of woman as Other (Herdt 1982a). Ritual rebirth and ritual regeneration are the concepts used to express what happens to initiates. Ritual secrecy is the means of creating alternative cultural reality in the men's house; ultimately expressing an idealizing, if not "utopian," desire of the men for trust in their comrades—a call to a purer, cleaner, orthodox, and resplendent masculinity, removed from the pollution and instabilities of the world.

Ironically, men never fully trust the transmission of ritual secrecy to their sons. Many accounts of initiation focus on the anxieties of the boys in their fear of being conscripted. These boys' fears and anxieties are real, but from the perspective of the reproduction of the men's ritual society and secrecy, it is the profound mistrust and anxiety in being able to trust the boys that is perhaps a far greater threat to the clubhouse. What do the men have to fear? Betrayal of the secrets to the women—which would be a great humiliation and a devastation. Why would the boy-initiate do such a thing to his own father and brothers? After all, does he not admire and respect them, and want to be like them? Will their legacy not be his, their land his, and his wife bestowed by them? All of this is true, but we are not dealing only with rationality. Social mistrust and paranoia, and the dread of being responsible for the death and destruction, are the ultimate conditions of masculinity. This is what secrecy protects.

Through the collective action of ritual secrecy, social inequalities were reproduced on several levels. Military plans against other villages and tribes, even neighbors, could be made in the men's house and kept hidden from women and children. Women's loyalties were especially suspect when they came from hostile villages. Women could be punished for the suspected transmission of military information to enemy groups, including being raped or killed by their own men. Boys as well were carefully monitored for any sign of backsliding in passing men's secrets to mother or the women. The Burayu punishment for the betrayal of ritual secrets was so terrible that the men will kill a boy if necessary without possibility of blood revenge or retribution to his kin (Godelier 1989).

To sum up: three great ritual secrets condition the power and masculinity of Sambia males: the practice of nose-bleeding, which forces initiates to nose-bleed in order to remove female pollution and toughen their masculinity; oral insemination by an older male that is supposed to produce strength and masculinity, as well as virtue and good health; and the final revelation of the origin myth, which tells that once upon a time men were hermaphroditic. This hidden knowledge and practice entirely belies the public male mythology of male superiority and domination. The men themselves are profoundly concerned that the women might learn of this knowledge and practice, and would make the men feel deeply shamed and humiliated. This thought is such a source of distress and subjective vulnerability to all initiated Sambia males that it can only be whispered in the men's cult house (Herdt 1981).

MARRIAGE AND SOCIAL INEQUALITY

Social inequality is created through contractual marriage. At a very general level, the difference in ages is critical, and highly revealing. Sambia reckon the appropriate age in marriage to be between an older male and younger female, typically with a five-year age difference, but paradoxically, Sambia define the meaning of the male/female couple as being "of like kind," that is, in their meaning, "equal in age." This age difference, as I have noted before, applies to older and younger male homoerotic partners too (Herdt 1997). It is as if the Sambia man feels comfortable sexually only with a partner who is younger in age and typically physically much smaller.

At a symbolic and structural level, Sambia connect marriage of bodies to the flow of semen and blood across the genders and the generations. In simple terms, delayed exchange of women between clans creates temporary imbalances with expectations and demands offset with gifts and promises. The Sambia configure the marriage as the means by which one clan-hamlet has taken a woman as womb, or "garden," from another village, and the offspring of the new union must return to the donor village in the following generation to create a balance. The residents of Sambia Valley hamlets intermarried in this way, creating shifting, unstable alliances and provoking mistrust at all levels of social arrangements, interjecting suspicion and often paranoia into the spouses' sexual relationship, living arrangement, child care, and other related daily interests.

On the symbolic level these arranged marriages resulted in transfer of blood and semen across generations. Blood and semen flowed in opposite directions across generations. Blood was the arranged marriage of a woman to her brother's group, while semen was the fluid inserted into her brother in order to make him grow big and strong, and hence, consummate the marriage. Moreover, blood and semen produce offshoots in the breast milk that comes with them. Thus, blood goes one way, and semen the other in marriage and boy-insemination practices.

However, to counter-balance this situation, the man who had taken a wife could be expected in return to give his semen to a boy. So, while the man was the recipient of a womb-vagina, he acted as the donor of semen both to the woman and to her younger brother. She was expected to produce a baby; her brother was expected to produce the masculinity of physical growth and manliness embodied in the glans penis. The glans penis, in the third-stage initiation, which celebrates social puberty, was likened to a ritual rebirth, the growth and enlargement of the glans being its symbolic culmination. These marital relationships were unstable because they could never be purely hierarchical or purely egalitarian. By contrast, gender relations were expected to be stable and hierarchical, while peer relations were expected to be competitive and egalitarian. In fact, boy-insemination was a primary means of ensuring stability in the men's house.

How do men and women employ these beliefs? Sambia men and women have a tendency to objectify the organ or orifice of sexuality in their speech. Thus, men talk about their wives as "my Woman," "my garden," or "my work," and women talk about their husbands as "my Man," "my arrow," or explicitly as "my penis." Women and boys also talk about the semen of husbands and bachelors as "my water," that is, the semen that they claim by virtue of a sexual exchange with the man in question. In such ways the Sambia do objectify or, to use a Marxist term, they *fetishize* the penis, vagina, semen, and so on as commodities to value in production.

How does such fetishism work? The use of semen is the key to this process. Sambia cultural tradition values semen as if it has the value of a commodity, such as gold; the value placed on semen in this culture tends toward fetishism. I mean by *the fetishistic* the collective sense of a religious attachment that goes beyond Freud's (1905/1962) classical sense of a private, sexual symptom formation in which the individual derives pleasure from an obsessional-compulsive fixation to an object or body part that unconsciously represents a whole person (Stoller 1979). Sambia believe—along with a large number of other Melanesian tribes—that semen is not a "natural" male body product but must rather be introduced externally (as if it were a sex hormone necessary to androgenize the incompetent body, in western discourse) in order to institutionalize ideas of semen transfer, semen depletion, and semen replenishment. This means that as the boy is initiated and comes to share in the belief regarding the power of semen, he acquires a most powerful desire—the desire for semen. This desire, introduced by initiation rituals, is the basis for the development of a physical body that was phenomenological totally absent in the boy's prior experience. I believe that this serves as the context for the development of his sexual attractions as well. Now to follow through these cultural beliefs we will see how they structure diverse forms of sexual relationships that ultimately reproduce sexual inequality.

CULTURAL FORMS OF SEXUAL RELATIONSHIPS

Sexuality is referred to through the verb *duvuno,* "pushing or penetrating" the vagina of a woman or the mouth of a boy or a woman. All sexual intercourse among the Sambia is conceptualized as either work (*wumdu*) or play (*chemonyi*). It is *wumdu* to engage in successive vaginal relations for many months to produce a child but *chemonyi* to orally inseminate an initiate a couple of times before moving on to another boy. Systematically, Sambia have five distinct sexual meanings that structure their sexual behavior, each having to do with the exchange of semen (Herdt 1984). As we have seen in the previous chapters, these cultural forms of sexuality pertain to distinct and overlapping domains of life. Through these forms, social hierarchy and social inequality are created and reproduced.

Procreation (*wumdu*) is genital-to-genital intercourse between men and women aimed to create babies. *Wumdu,* the general verb for "work," draws explicitly upon the imagery of planting a garden. The basic form of daily work in pre-colonial life was gardening; a man clears the land, a woman tills and plants, and food is produced. To "work" is to "garden," which is essential for life. Procreative intercourse in cultural belief is therefore instrumental to the creation of life, with semen from the husband and womb blood from the wife commingling in the woman to create a fetus. Pleasure and fun are incidental. *Wumdu* privileges sexual relations between men and women as culturally significant in many ways. And in order to achieve full personhood by producing children, *wumdu* is required of all adults. A man without a wife is without gardens to produce, and a woman without a husband is like a fallow garden. In fact, Sambia do not imagine a category of adults who are not married to the opposite sex; that is, adult "bachelors" and "spinsters" do not exist for them.

Note that in belief, sexuality is always a relationship, of penetrating, of work. The Sambia do not have a freestanding category noun *sex* in their language and thought that would allow them to say, "I want sex"; instead, they have to say, "I want to penetrate you." In short, masturbation for the Sambia (solo self-arousal to orgasm) as a category of sexuality does not exist. This absence makes it much easier to control and regulate sexuality through social relations. In fact, Sambia imagine that sexual relations require another person's body as the semen recipient or donor. This means that sexual pleasure is strictly controlled by the power hierarchy.

Erotic play (*chemonyi*) is for pleasure and fun on the part of the socially higher male who is penetrating. Semen is expended and orgasm (*imbimboogu*) achieved, typically through oral intercourse, that is, boy-insemination. I say "typically" because Sambia sometimes compare the play of boy-insemination with only one other kind of sexual relations with women, oral or vaginal sex with a barren woman, whose inability to reproduce precludes sex with her being categorized as "work" or procreation. While both the older and younger males refer to the process as "play" and boys will invite a bachelor "to play" sexually with them, in fact it is the bachelor who experiences genital pleasure. The younger boy is forbidden to reverse roles and is discouraged from thinking about his own body, other than his mouth. Men say that boy's mouths have a kind of "sexual heat" they associate with the pleasure, and by comparison, they claim that boy-fellators' sexual heat is greater than that of their wives'.

By contrast, however, many men suggest that they enjoy *wumdu* with women more than *chemonyi* with boys when they have the choice. What is the basis for their personal feelings here? Two factors stand out: Procreative sexual relationships are more prestigious, and the vagina is said to be "hotter" and sexually more arousing than a boy's mouth. Hierarchically, procreative sexuality privileges marriage and male control of women as scarce resources.

Growth is a third cultural form that pertains to how semen is used to "feed" and "nurture" the recipient. The literal expression is *pinu pungooglumonjapi*, where *pinu* is an alternative form of pushing to *duvuno,* and *monjapi' u* is the common verb for breastfeeding. Of course, both women as newlyweds as well as initiates fellate older men, and in these contexts, semen exchange for growth applies. However, it is far more common for Sambia men to think of oral sex as for "growth," and in this sense, to commonly restrict this sexual form to boy-insemination. In fact, semen as nourishment for growth is male *monjapi' u*—the first form of sexual intercourse that boys experience in growing up. Oral insemination "feeds" semen in the belief system to grow a boy's body, making him bigger, growing him faster, and contributing to his eventual reproductive competence. Take note that Sambia boys will smear small amounts of semen on their faces at the end of a sexual interaction with a bachelor, in the belief that their face will become handsome and manly, that is, more sexy.

Men also believe that women's bodies require oral sexual insemination to create the breast milk needed to nurse babies, and this is their primary justification for heterosexual oral sex. Women traditionally may have accepted this belief, but today they are skeptical about it, and some reject it outright. As you will see from the CD-ROM accompanying this case study, even older and more traditional women express doubt and put up a lot of resistance to this sexual act. Here is one of the principle forms of resistance women had to the sexual culture of the men. As implied by the film, Sambia married women find performing fellatio on their husbands to be rather mechanical and one-sided. They implicitly experienced no pleasure themselves—clearly a gendered view of the system.

Strength (*jerungdu*)—such a pervasive concept—here applies to the ways in which semen exchange and insemination may strengthen the body of the recipient. First in the body of the inseminated initiate, the semen strengthens and toughens the skull and skin, and eventually contributes to the appearance of virility. A strong body, a forceful personality, fierce hunting and warring skills, and of course the availability of large seminal flows during sexual intercourse are all perceived outcomes of sexual strength. In the woman's womb, her husband's semen strengthens the fetus, especially the teeth and bones, and contributes to the strength of the mother's milk to masculinize the male offspring. Other products, especially pandanus nuts and cassowary, can supplement semen in human-strengthening processes.

Take note, once more, that the logical consequence of this belief is the concomitant effect of ejaculating and "losing" strength. Men must meter out their inseminations for fear that their semen will "dry up" and they will die. Fully initiated men know to replace the semen "lost" through inseminating boys or women by drinking ritually special white tree saps that can "replace" their seminal fluid. You will see examples of this milk-sap drinking in the CD-ROM, and you can also see and listen to Weiyu talk about this process.

Spirituality (*koogu*, "spirit") is the final category of beliefs that influence how and why people engage in sexual relationships. Like many other peoples, Sambia connect their bodies to their souls, and they implicitly believe that the loss of semen, as well as blood, can affect the spirit. Concomitantly, they believe that through the semen of a father, the offspring will inherit characteristics of the soul or spirit, most notably the spirit familiars (*numelyu*) and totems of their clan. For example, the clan that adopted me in Nilanga hamlet has as its primary totem the Harpy Eagle, which is a significant spirit familiar for clansmen. This metaphysical connection appears in dreams and healing ceremonies, and helps guide and protect the health of the person. Take note that girls inherit the familiar of their mothers through the mother's blood, especially her menstrual blood, one arena in which there is resistance to the hegemony of semen beliefs. Spirit familiars contribute to longevity, prowess in hunting and war, sexual strength, and the survival of the soul after death as an ancestral spirit.

There is a collective sense of spiritual sexuality for Sambia men, and it is called *kwol-aalyu-waku*. Objectively it is a secret name that refers to masculine decorations and ritual paraphernalia, especially medicine bundles. *Kwolaalyu-waku* also refers to a kind of imaginal, a collective pool of semen of all Sambia males who have ever lived that circulates through the bodies of boys and men. By being inseminated and exchanging semen across groups and generations, this pool is perpetuated, and it protects the health of individual men. The regulatory function of this pool is also a means of binding males in solidarity against women and making them dependent upon the rituals of boy insemination to attain spiritual well being.

In the 1990s a new form of sexual behavior was introduced, "luv" marriage, which emphasizes romance and intimate voluntary union between a man and a woman. It was a radical idea, and it caught on primarily through missionized Sambia. However, in a very short time, young Sambia were repudiating the norms of arranged marriage and embracing not only a new form of marriage but also a fundamentally distinct set of values that makes this heterosexual union more socially equal.

WOMEN'S POWER AND SEXUAL AGENCY

Sambia women were socially and sexually oppressed in a variety of ways, as we have seen, and yet they enjoyed a measure of power, particularly in domestic life, totally at odds with what the men acknowledged. We need to understand the bases both of their power and oppression in Sambia society. Within their own house, surrounded by children, and with the presence of father and brothers nearby, a woman's power was much enlarged, and while vulnerable, these social resources and support were hugely important in her status and social standing. However, younger women, newlyweds, those without children, and barren women were far more vulnerable to accusations of sorcery, disloyalty, and accusations of extramarital relationships, and punishment and beatings were common among them. In other words, the structural situation of women was more marginal politically and more vulnerable to the whims of men and war and sexual violence.

First, however, a word about sexual violence and rape. As I have noted in my earlier writings (Herdt and Stoller 1990), wife beating and sexual abuse of women was for me the most difficult of all the issues I had to live with among the Sambia. In reality, while the threat against initiates to keep secrecy sounded deadly and boys were hazed and punished in a variety of ways, in my experience they were not beaten. Women were, and the sound of a woman's body actually being repeatedly struck with a wood plank in the village was not rare and was dreadful to hear amid the moans and pleas for help. Sexual coercion was very common, inside and outside of marriage. Female suicide from sexual shaming was also frequent enough to be a worry to men. Typically this was a threat carried out by a woman who argued over her husband having an affair with another woman or wanting to take another wife. Rape was not common within the Sambia Valley, and it was dealt with in severe ways, ultimately sufficient to ensure that it was rare. But outside of her own village, a woman was considered "fair game" under certain conditions. And women typically were blamed for sexual innuendos that led to compromising situations; much as victims of "date rape" in the contemporary United States are blamed, rather than the rapists. These are the structural conditions that perpetuated social inequality between the sexes.

Traditionally women had at their disposal several tools to employ and threaten against mistreatment by a husband. For example, a woman could "forget to prepare [a husband's] food, refusing to make love, shouting and commenting on her husband . . . using sorcery or semen sorcery, and pollution poison in the food" (Godelier 1986: 150). As a woman matured and grew confident, she could also openly criticize him and even castigate him loudly in public, although she risked a beating for doing so. Young men are famous for their quick jealousy among the Sambia, and they can become vindictive of a wrong move on the part of their consort. Couples normatively had sex every few days or as infrequently as once every two or three weeks, depending on age, length of marriage, and other factors. However, the postpartum taboo forbids sexual intercourse for some two years following birth. Again traditionally, no public contact between the sexes was permitted in public, and holding hands, not to mention kissing, were shocking ideas to the Sambia—taboos that are changing radically, as we shall see in Chapter 7.

Second, through domestic living and the creation of a family, a woman would undergo two initiations, as we have seen, each providing her with ritual knowledge and power. The succession of births, the exposure to gardening magic, and the assistance of other women in childbirth and at times of distress, created a woman's social reputation. A "good woman"—wife and mother who shared food, was amicable, dutiful, and adhered to the ritual taboos, especially menstrual taboos—brought a higher level of agency for women. At middle age, as you will see such women in the CD-ROM accompanying this case study, women are self-confident, they have a voice in things, and they are no longer intimidated by the men. In fact, the case study of women shamans reveals one source of very real spiritual power available in pre-colonial times.

Figure 6.3 Women shamans

It was through women shamans that traditional Sambia culture observed the emergence of larger social purpose and agency among these special women (see Figure 6.3). How very curious that a male-dominated society with a phallic cult should have in its midst women shamans. This is especially peculiar when we recall the great popularity of the shamans and the heroic hope they provide.

Sambia recognize different sex-linked cultural patterns that characterize a shaman's calling. For men shamans, on the one hand, childhood experiences such as visions and dreams of spirits are later channeled into the ritual cult ceremonies. In the ceremonies, the signs of a calling are publicly reinforced and accepted. We have seen that women, however, are not abruptly separated from their mothers or childhood routines. So the dreams and childhood experiences of women shamans, foretelling their calling, are recognized in mystical situations that lead to possession and trance. In both cases, the young shamans are then apprenticed to older ones, men for boys, women for girls, who teach them how to heal. This leads to important sex-linked differences in Sambia shamanism. First, male shamans used to outnumber female shamans by a four-to-one margin (which has now evened up due to culture change). Second, the traditional cultural emphasis on the shaman's role highlights the masculine functions. Men shamans did magic ceremonies before and after warfare in past times. More social pressures are thus exerted on male shamans. The discontinuity and emotional upheaval of male cult initiations, with intense stresses resulting from psychosexual and aggressive demands, are hard on boys. After childhood there is no structural outlet for them to satisfy underlying needs, such as nurturance, in everyday life. These observations tend to confirm that there is no role except that of the shaman for the sensitive boy. And indeed, men shamans are the most nurturant and sensitive of Sambia men. Women shamans are sensitive too, but they tend to be the most aggressive and flamboyant of women. For them, the shaman's role also provides an alternative outlet, only the reverse to that of the men—they can be more assertive.

There is a well-known story among Sambia that portrays the strong and heroic qualities of the woman shaman. The infant son of a war leader was found missing one afternoon. A search party could not locate the child, and the parents blamed themselves for having selfishly left him in the care of his elder brother (implying, that is, a wish for the solitude of their garden to have sexual intercourse). As darkness fell the parents became distraught and began wailing for the child. They feared he had been abducted by ghosts. Kaiyunango, the woman shaman, was overcome with sorrow at the sight of the war leader and his wife shamelessly bawling and muddying themselves, starting the pitiful bereavement of Sambia funerals. A storm broke, yet Kaiyunango persuaded some girls to accompany her beyond the hamlet to search again for the child. Soon afterward, however, the girls became frightened at a noise near a gravesite and they fled to the hamlet. They thought the noise was a ghost, but Kaiyunango was not scared. Alone but undaunted, she searched for the child for she had seen in a trance that he had been stolen by ghosts who intended to eat him. She called the child's name into the rain and gloomy fog, finally discovering him crying and soiled and bewildered. There, she claims, a great black ghost suddenly appeared before her. The ghost struck and pursued her, finally ripping off her bark cape. She escaped, nearly naked, and returned to the hamlet with the child, where she was greeted in triumph for her courage. This tale was told to me years after the events by the war leader himself and other villagers. It offers an important moral: Though female, Kaiyunango's powers as a shaman gave her extraordinary strength to brave ghosts in a dreadful storm and accomplish a heroic deed at which even a war leader had failed.

Only grudgingly or in despair do men privately allow their dependence upon women's contributions. My friend Weiyu once gave voice to men's silent appreciation of the burden of women. At the back of my house one afternoon we stood talking, looking out into a bitterly cold and rainy last light of dusk. Women appeared from a garden, and we watched them as they filed past. They were returning from their daily chores, rain-soaked and burdened with food, firewood, and babies. They looked so wretched. Weiyu shook his head and then added spontaneously: "Sorry. Women . . . women are just like our mothers." I asked him how that could be and he said, "If only we did not copulate with them, they would truly be like our mothers. They provide us with our food, everything . . ." His voice trailed off, his sentence incomplete. This moody comment, triggered by the hard sight of the women and conveyed to me in tones of quiet sadness, unveiled a sense of longing and guilt normally disguised by men's bravado.

BOYS' SEXUAL AGENCY AND SOCIAL OPPRESSION

Of all the categories of the marginal and the socially oppressed in Sambia culture, initiated boys were the most troublesome and, here I will claim, those with the least amount of power. They were totally lacking in a voice in Sambia society until they graduated into third-stage bachelors. They were sexually objectified and subject to coercion with almost no recourse while they lived in the men's house. Sexual objectification was greatest when the boy's body is most like a pre-pubertal girl's and most unlike an adult man's. Stated differently, the more like a man a boy looked and acted, the greater his agency and the less desirable he was as a homoerotic object. He was, however, but a pawn in a larger system of cultural objectifications. These included: the secret ritual flutes, the female hamlet spirits, the hierarchical relations between older and younger homoerotic partners, and the later hierarchical relations between men and women. Out of this security circle protected by ritual secrecy in the men's house, a new kind of pleasure arose. It was not sufficient to generate sexual excitement within itself, but it certainly created a fetishism of desiring and admiring idealized objects of desire in their purest "male" qualities (see Read 1965: 152ff.). The initiation of boys—that is, the reproduction of secret masculinity—is iconic of these gender politics, which threaten but also reaffirm this instability.

Boys' resistance to the men's society expressed some small amount of agency or power. Sambia boys resisted initiation a lot more than one would have imagined (Herdt 1987a), particularly the younger 7- and 8-year-olds, who seemed too small, timid, and bereft of comfort to be resocialized and then indoctrinated into the harsh reality of the men's house ritual secrecy. The resistance of these little boys who were the proxy of their mothers, both in resisting and in being dominated, was timely, since they knew that by age 10 they had to go into the men's house.

The initiates were the substitutes for and symbolic icons of Woman, that is, their mothers, and they were objectified first as outsiders lumped with the women's world, as we saw in Chapter 4. Only through the harsh means of ritual ordeals, including scraping the skin and bleeding the nose, among other efforts to "defeminize" the boy's body, was the maleness enhanced sufficiently that the men could reclaim or, better yet, advance a new claim that they had "given birth" to the agentic boy. First-stage initiates are viewed as symbolically equivalent to the menarchial females in their late teens, in the secret ontology of men. We may see in this symbolic association the necessary symbolic transformation of the pre-pubertal boy-initiate into a sexual object of the post-pubertal male youth. Additionally it serves as the basis for the embodiment of the intense secret ideal that males "menstruate" through the nose to attain "pure" masculine vitality, physical growth, prowess, and, later after marriage, the continued well-being and preservation of health in spite of proximity to women, menstrual blood, and coitus (Herdt 1982). Nose-bleeding rites must therefore commence the purifications of first initiation, preceding insemination; and then they must continue throughout the male life cycle, even in old age, ceasing only at senescence. While it is viewed as dangerous and also exciting for that reason, bloodletting is critical to the production of secret masculinity for the Sambia. Only after blood is let can the "birth" of the phallus occur, electing the boy to manhood, an irreducible intentional reality of secret masculinity. Both of these physical steps, elements critical to the dietetics of Sambia practice, help to essentialize the boy as a sexual object.

The symbolism of the secret male initiation ceremonies was intended to merge the desires and developmental subjectivity of the growing boy with the larger project of maintaining the warrior population of these villages. At the early developmental stage of the pre-pubertal boy, for example, the flute and penis ritual (which introduced the boys to homoerotic practices [Herdt 1981]) stressed the penis and compared it to mother's breast, thereby condensing the meanings of semen and milk. At a more sophisticated level following matura-tion, however, the flutes signified the budding erotic relation between older ado-lescent warriors and their younger partners, initiated boys, whose insemination was supposed to make them big and strong too. These pairs of pre-pubertal and post-pubertal unmarried males were referred to in secret folklore as being "mar-ried." The secret mythology of the secret ritual flutes further explains how an ancestor of the men's society was once hermaphroditic and changed into a male through ritual practice (Herdt 1981).

To increase his agency a boy must be inseminated to become like a bachelor. Sambia make it clear why they festishized the *moongenyu:* They admire his phallus and they expect he will "grow" the philli of the initiates whom he insem-inates. Sambia men imagine that the glans penis grows in a last surge of ritual inseminations near the third-stage initiation, representing a final growth of manly phallus, signifying potency. This image is frozen in the developmental subjectivity of the male. The growth of the penis, in the men's ritual pedagogy and practice, suggests the notion that the inseminations result in an elongation of the phallus as a "pure product" of semen. The sense of this "growth" is for-ever constitutive of the man's sense of virility and body image as he approaches sexual relations with boys and then later contemplates the dangers of sex with women. This sense of timelessness pervades the formation of male subject/object desires and relationships in the lifelong practice of ritual secrecy.

*   *   *

In Sambia politics, the division between what is "good for society" (that is, the village) and what is "good for the men's clubhouse" was totally blurred, ten-uous, and often disputed—even in the internal discourse of the men's clubhouse. The homosociality of the men's house created a kind of pleasure with power and domination, in part real and responsive to the horrors of war, in another part an imaginary game, a boy's game, of "king on the mountain" with a morally supe-rior attitude toward women and children. Social inequality was created out of this structural situation, and it did much harm and caused much social suffering among the people until pacification ended warfare and the initiation system geared to it. The men saw themselves as the guardians of moral virtue, ritual orthodoxy, and preservation of the social order. They never completely trusted their own sons in the transmission of power and certainly regarded women as a necessary evil in society. Locked into such a worldview, the men themselves suf-fered as well, for their ability to trust and find purpose in life beyond war was very, very limited until recently. In the final chapter we will see how life radi-cally changed to allow a new image of social life.

7/Sexuality and Revolutionary Change

A sexual revolution has overtaken the Sambia. In the past decade or so, they have undergone huge life-changing, culture-breaking, and culture-making alterations in their sexuality—greater than anything we have experienced in our own civilization in such a short period of time—and much greater than the so-called sexual revolution of the 1960s in the United States. To go from absolute gender segregation and arranged marriages, with universal ritual initiation that controlled sexual and gender development and imposed the radical practice of boy-insemination, to abandoning initiation, seeing adolescent boys and girls kiss and hold hands in public, arranging their own marriages, and building square houses with one bed for the newlyweds, as the Sambia have done, is revolutionary.

Perhaps the same degree of dramatic transformation has occurred throughout New Guinea societies, Melanesia, and indeed the Pacific Islands as a whole over the past several generations (Herdt and Leavitt 1998). Certainly the legacy of Margaret Mead (1928, 1935), who worked in Samoa, and then in Melanesian societies, culminating in her remarkable account of change entitled *New Lives for Old* (1956), shows how some cultural things can change and others stay the same. Such discussions anticipated current debates about sexuality, globalization, and the role of the media in the Pacific Islands (Foster 2002; Knauft 1999).

When a culture changes, many but not all of its meanings and practices undergo transformation. Yet this does not necessarily mean that the sexual culture changes as much or as significantly. The United States went through a sexual revolution in the l960s, which was freeing and introduced new ideas and practices, but women continued to be the primary caretakers of children, they continued to earn less in the work place than men (Hochschild 2003), abortion remained highly contested as a reproductive right, sexual education actually has declined since that time, and its curriculum makes *pleasure* a forbidden term (Irvine 2002).

Societies that experience political revolution, such as Mexico and Russia, in the early part of the 20th century; China and Israel in the mid-20th century; followed by Cuba, Iran, and then the collapse of the Soviet Union in the late 1980s, can dramatically change sexual norms and the expectations of marriage and sexual partners. Even when a society undergoes a cultural revolution, such as Spain experienced after the death of its long-time dictator Franco or South Africa experienced after the collapse of apartheid and the election of Nelson Mandela as president of a new republic, sexuality may change dramatically. Indeed, South Africa even became the first society to write into its constitution protection of sexual orientation. Through revolution, race, and other social factors get turned around, and new standards and expectations emerge for sexual development and gender performances—what I have termed the discontinuity in cultural development of societies going through emergent periods of change (Herdt 1990).

But having acknowledged all of that, I can testify that for the Sambia, at least, sexuality has changed in revolutionary and not just evolutionary ways. Looking back over the past 30 years, I also appreciate more than ever the amazing traditions I was eyewitness to and which were passing before me. The Sambia faced a struggle for modernity as fundamentalist Christian missionaries encroached upon their ritual system, attacking the practice of initiation, polygyny, the eating of possum meat, dancing, smoking, and chewing betel nut. They were faced with the creation of a new order of sexuality and gender. Clearly, my Sambia informants and friends were in the throes of revolutionary change due to the forces of post-colonial development and globalization at the time of my arrival in the mid-1970s. This change was embodied, as young Sambia men and women abandoned their Sambia names and took Christian names, such as "Danny," that were a repudiation of the names of their fathers and ancestors— indeed a rejection of the meaning of being a Sambia ritual citizen, as I have recounted in my travels among the Yagwoia people, missionized a generation before the Sambia (Herdt 2003: Chapter 3).

We Americans are not immune, of course, to the twists and turns of social change in sexuality. The United States has undergone two large transformative sexual revolutions: the first in the 1920s, the age of the Flappers, during the time of the creation of the high school as a large public institution that provided for sexual and gender experimentation, mass marketing of beauty products for sex appeal, the opening of large dance halls, and the circulation of radical ideas about gender equality, women's rights, the introduction of contraceptives, and "free love," accompanied by the growth of an underground homosexual movement popping up in places as distant as Chicago and Harlem in New York (Chauncey 1994; D'Emilio and Freedman 1988; Herdt and Boxer 1993: Chapter 2); and the second in the 1960s, occurring in a social context of huge new identity movements, black power, student strikes, the second-wave feminist movement, the peace and freedom/antiwar movement, and of course the nascent gay and lesbian identity movement. The invention of the Pill created a new tension between recreational sex and procreation (Laumann, Gagnon, Michael, and Michaels 1994). Women's sexual freedom was unparallel in western civilization.

Popular and widespread experimentation with recreational drugs, including psychedelics, was part of a larger counter-cultural movement that, for a brief time—particularly in California as I remember it in the later 1960s—produced a revolutionary but fleeting change, followed by a backlash that we are still working through (Irvine 2002; Levine, Nardi, and Gagnon 1997).

At the beginning of my fieldwork observations during the mid 1970s, who can forget that America was suffering the effects of these social movements and the "defeat" of the Vietnam War? It was a time of such strange and shifting sands; for example, in 1973 the landmark decision of the Supreme Court of the United States, *Rowe vs. Wade,* made abortion rights legal for women in the United States for the first time; and the American Psychiatric Association officially removed homosexuality as a "disease," instead labeling it an alternative sexual style; the United States and its great nemesis, the Soviet Union—still the other great superpower—made a space connection; Deep Throat and the illegal break-in and cover-up of Watergate forced Nixon out and Ford in; the greatest economic recession since World War II occurred after an Arab oil embargo; and Papua New Guinea, coasting along on a wave of Australian political change and the death of colonialism, gained independence in 1975.

It was in that year (1975–76) that the Sambia performed their 23rd initiatory cycle of the 20th century—the rituals you have read and studied in the preceding chapters. Ritual, the omnibus Sambia mechanism for growth, maturation, gender, and sexual regulation, was under enormous pressure from the missionaries, government, and from larger economic changes, including migration. Right before my eyes the rituals were deteriorating, enhancing the existing internal resistance you have read about, deepened by the increasing effort of young

Figure 7.1 Haus lotu—local church, Sambia Valley, 1993

women and men to go to school while the ranks of the secret society were being depleted by young men who traveled to coastal towns and plantations for work and adventure and a new kind of life, just as men have done always throughout history. This incredible tradition of Sambia secret initiation is now gone, replaced by still-emerging and sometimes contradictory norms and customs of sexuality, gender, and social life to be studied in this chapter.

You might reasonably ask of me, "But didn't you see these changes coming about?" You make these seem so obvious, like they were all around. Why are you so surprised? All are excellent questions and good for us to reflect upon in the study of culture, human development, psychology, sociology, gender, and sexuality. My immediate reaction is that I never expected such radical change to occur so quickly, and I certainly did not predict such revolutionary change in sexuality and gender among the Sambia, still so isolated from the outside world. Time has proved me to be shortsighted—perhaps like many of us who live in the communities we would seek to understand. What happened along the way? How did Sambia develop "luv" marriage? That is the story with which I would like to conclude this case study.

POST-COLONIAL CHANGE

Papua New Guinea independence in 1975 brought increasing social and economic development to the country and immediate changes to Sambia society. A new political leadership and a new currency were introduced to the Sambia, and new access to schools and medical care was promised. People began to shift the government presence and influence around the district capital. A system of independent village councils, constituted of locally elected representatives, served as the primary link between local communities and the national and district governments. Agricultural development began to increase and coffee plantations began to spring up. Migration to the towns became easier than ever, and labor recruiters were actually encouraged to visit remote areas for cheap labor recruits; they favored the Sambia, who had a reputation for hard work and loyalty. The elders were unable to regulate sexuality and gender—much to their chagrin—and increasingly, they were involved in an intergenerational struggle that the missionaries seized upon to drive a wedge between individuals, families, and clans.

Missionary activity increased to eventually become the driving social force in Sambia community development, having an economic edge. Lutherans and Seventh-Day Adventists were active very early on, with a lumber mill and, later, trade stores. But it is the Seventh-Day Church, renowned in New Guinea for its "fish and rice" message of western food for Christian church worship that ultimately won ordinary Sambia over to its faith. Today, most Sambia consider themselves to be Seventh-Day Adventists and practice their liturgical ceremonies. The Seventh-Day Adventists established an extensive network of evangelists who, together with their families, lived and worked in villages throughout the district.

These evangelists were, in their own right, a remarkable force for change in sexuality and gender—offering new role models and sometimes a form of casual sexual relationships between men and women utterly unknown to the Sambia before. Meanwhile, the same missionaries preached against ritual initiation and the "heathen" ways of ritual. Their message of fire and brimstone directly attacked the elders, such as Kanteilo, who was shamed on many occasions for his outspoken support of initiation. The shamans who performed the rituals and healing rites were attacked more viciously as "witch doctors" and "devil helpers." Shamans such as Kaiyunango and Sakulambei were actually ridiculed and became extremely reluctant to perform healing ceremonies. Missionaries introduced Levitican dietary restrictions, dramatically altering the indigenous diet, so hunting largely stopped and the trade stores flourished. But since people lacked cash money, they were inevitably forced to market crops and sell produce. Thus the coffee tree plantation was born among the Sambia. You will see how much pride Danny has in his coffee trees in the CD-ROM accompanying this case study.

Local people were being educated at Lutheran mission schools, so the Lutherans sought to convert and "civilize" these local populations. Government schools followed. The platform of the school was also used for aggressive attacks on customs such as male initiation, polygyny, and shamanism, which successively undermined confidence in traditional systems of belief, a pattern well-known from elsewhere in New Guinea (reviewed in Herdt 2003; Whitehouse 1995). Material display of goods in trade stores undermined the local economy and, likewise, encouraged coffee plantations. There is little doubt that the sense of material display undermined the traditional masculinity that figured so prominently between the Sambia and their neighbors. Masculinity could no longer be achieved through the production of local goods. Concomitantly, femininity got a boost from schooling, which became a new resource for the achievement of status.

The new masculinity, which could only be produced through the accumulation of western goods, has lead to out-migration and coastal work, creating upheavals in traditional social hierarchies. Sambia men began leaving the village areas in the late 1960s, and the level of out-migration of male laborers continued apace into the mid 1980s. Under the colonial administrator's Highland Labor Scheme, men were recruited for two-year contracts to work on coastal cocoa, copra, and rubber plantations. The scheme was discontinued in 1974, but many men continue to seek work on coastal plantations. The early cohorts who left the Sambia were the first to see the wider country and to report back the stories of life outside. Some of these men (perhaps a large number of them) never returned to their villages. They chose to work and live out their lives in the coastal towns. Some of these men—and a few women, such as Penjukwi (see Chapter 3)—have secured marriages and are rearing their children in these distant towns. Gender roles are now an issue of transition, betwixt and between tradition and citizenship in the town.

Schools were introduced into the Sambia Valley in the 1970s, and rather quickly the schools began to displace initiation as a primary means for gaining access to valued positions within the expanding society. Moreover, girls aspired to attend school, and the use of schooling dovetailed with missionization to increase women's power. Children were also taught to speak and write in pidgin, and to perform simple math problems. Although the schools were initially well received by both government employees and local villagers, disillusionment with the schools increased as residents came to expect concrete results in terms of jobs or further schooling. Many felt that the schools prepared the students only for menial jobs as laborers or clerks. At best, the schools were regarded as training grounds for native evangelists (Godelier 1982).

The earliest school had to be closed because of a sexual scandal—more what we might today call a moral panic. Young people attending the school, boys and girls, were placed in classrooms together, with boys on one side of the aisle, and girls on the other. This was the first time in Sambia society that the genders were mixed in an intimate space prior to marriage. The results were perhaps predictable. The students began to flirt and engage in romantic private rendezvous, and a couple of youths were reported to have been found having vaginal sex. Word spread like wildfire, and the missionaries had to close the school down. However, the news of unprecedented gender mixing and new possible sexual relationships was launched into the small valley of the Sambia.

Nevertheless, the impact of the schools was huge and unstoppable. First, children who attended the schools came from all tribes in the Mountain Patrol Post area, thus disrupting traditional enmity and creating the possibility of sexual mixing between tribes. Second, the schools admitted girls as well as boys, allowing them access to the same knowledge and forcing them to mix in (albeit on different sides of) the same classroom. Thus norms governing sexual segregation and men's privileged access to valued knowledge were violated and ultimately could not be repaired. Third, missionaries were openly critical of and aggressively attacked ritual beliefs and customs. Children attending the schools were forbidden to participate in initiation rites or to observe traditional sex avoidance rules. Those who were shy around the opposite sex could be shamed, for example, into being more aggressive or "Western-like" in cross-sex interactions. Although these practices antagonized many local residents, the school received initial support and approval from mission converts. It seems clear that all of these patterns reinforced internal resistance to ritual initiation norms and opened the way for a much broader form of social challenge that would displace ritual as the structure of authority.

As we have seen, Sambia boys' resistance to initiation was always present, but it now capitalized upon mission and school experience. Sambia boys, such as Moondi, had traditionally resisted initiation rituals out of fear. The presence of schools and missions thus exacerbated this resistance. As Moondi has described this so vividly, he feared that initiation would "change" or "freeze" his thinking, disabling him from going to school, getting an education, or succeeding in the coastal towns. In short, the rituals would ruin his chance to become the "new man," with a new kind of modernized masculinity. Many boys who followed him have experienced a similar existential dilemma. We might call this the questioning of manhood in transition; a social panic that was a crisis of masculinity among the Sambia during the transition into modernity.

Within a five-year period, one-third of the students at the local school were girls. Today the numbers of the students by gender are closer to being equal than ever before. Both mission and government schools have contributed to changes in traditional socialization practices. Because of these constraints, many parents reject schooling for their children. Much of the evidence, however, suggests that parents do value schooling as alternative socialization, particularly for the boys. With the cessation of warfare, and out-migration of adolescent and adult males for work on coastal plantations, male initiation rites have been successfully undermined. Ceremonies that once took months to perform have been reduced to a few short weeks or abandoned altogether. As initiation rites have been increasingly undermined, parents have come to view schooling as a desirable alternative to traditional masculinity.

Nevertheless, the cultural idea remained: schooling is for boys. Because the girls' labor in their mothers' gardens is extremely important to the survival of the family (and the status of the mother as a good provider of food), it is difficult to understand why any family would endure the expense of sending a daughter to school. Despite the girls' own assertions that they go to school if they want to, it appears that school attendance is driven by two major factors: proximity to a school; and proximity to an airstrip that presumably gives the girls (and their parents) greater contact with the outside world, thereby driving the need and the desire to communicate with others in the manner taught in school. Economics influence school attendance. Girls living farthest from the school, along the airstrip, also have a high rate of school attendance, suggesting social and cultural, as well as pragmatic, forces at work. Observed departure from traditional behaviors also followed this same pattern of village residence, indicating a strong, reciprocal link between education and the influence of the outside world (Stolpe 2003).

As social change sped up, the men's secret society began to lose control of the women and children, and the intergenerational transmission of knowledge in Sambia society. The processes of change impacted quickly and strongly on the performance of ritual initiation. Within a decade—roughly 1970 to 1980—the great system of collective initiations known as the *mokeiyu* was curtailed. The boys were no longer routinely initiated into the men's house. Indeed, the boys by 1979 refused to live in the men's house, in spite of the fierce punishments from their elders. Even many women did not approve of the boys' resistance to male initiation customs, as this had assured the reproduction of gender relations, hunting, and marriage arrangements of before. The end of age-structured homoerotic relations was also at hand, since the out-migration of young bachelors and married men created an imbalance in the men's house. There no longer was a cohort of older males to socially monitor the young boys and serve as their inseminators. The end of warfare also meant that the threat of violence was over, and the social inequalities sustained by them began to change. A new social order was rising.

During the period of rapid change in the late 1970s and early to mid 1980s, the elders finally decided they could no longer trust the boys not to reveal the secrets of the men's society, and the ritual of boy-inseminating was suspended. However, other aspects of the ritual teachings were continued. For example, the nose-bleeding rituals still constituted important ritual purification. The boys were still taught the importance of bleeding at the time of initiation to strengthen them and remove their mother's pollution from their bodies. Also, they were being prepared for the time when they were adults and should bleed themselves as protection during their wives' menstrual periods. However, so much conflict emerged during this period that some men decided that they would not initiate their sons into the men's secret society. Instead, they felt that they would send their sons to the local school, to aim toward future jobs as well as to avoid the risk of having their ritual secrets revealed and thus destroyed. Weiyu, Tali, and the other men I know closely from my village all thought like this and made decisions accordingly. While they disparaged the mission and loathed the loss of the ritual system, they are pragmatists. The handwriting was on the wall, in their view: Schooling was the royal road to the future for their children.

The younger Sambia males, the ones who formerly were sexually objectified and perhaps the most socially oppressed, as suggested in Chapter 6, were meanwhile becoming adamantly opposed to the old ritual beliefs. They were provoked in part by the missionaries. Not all of the boys were like this. Some were merely disinterested; others, such as Danny, would have undergone the ritual but lacked a father and the opportunity to do so. The initiates who were also attending school openly discussed the decline or collapse of traditional customs. A new means of achieving masculinity outside of the traditional village system of warfare was unfolding and was increasingly positive. The more they had experienced social change and the longer they had attended school, the more aggressive they became in referring to custom as "the old ways" or the "pagan" ways, or they would use the disparaging pidgin term *kanaka*, in the English sense of a country bumpkin, yokel, or hick, who is not worldly wise. Today, they articulate a distinction between the "bad" parts of the traditional initiation ceremonies, those that have been eliminated; and the "good" parts, those that have remained.

These changes are explored directly in the CD-ROM. There you will find that gender change is prominent, while people's ideas of sexuality are exploding in a revolutionary way. It is clear that Sambia looking back in the film now view the domination of women as more problematic than they did a generation ago. Women reject oral sex with their husbands. They never would have dared to voice such a view in public until this revolution started. Years ago similar changes were anticipated among the neighboring Baruya people in the film *Toward Baruya Manhood,* which also suggests a more complex picture of the realities of gender domination.

Around this time, stereotyped sexual stories (Plummer 1995) about how men could be masculine and sexual in new ways began to circulate, reaching their peak in the mid-1990s. The new modernizing tradition of masculinity represents two different scenes in which these stories are being played out—in the village and out in the coastal towns. The men who go to the towns see this as an alternative to ritual initiation; as a means of testing themselves and their manhood to the ordeals and dangers once faced in the traditions of the men's house. Of course, they are doing this without the social support of their age-mates or without the collective strategy of secrecy vis-à-vis their enemies and women. The attraction of fast food, alcohol, sex with prostitutes, western goods, and other elements of "modernity" poses a great temptation to these budding young men. When they come home to the village, they love to boast of their conquests and their survival of the ordeals—proof of their new masculinity.

The men who went away to the towns left a kind of vacuum in the villages, necessitating a renegotiation of social structures. Some men have said: "If these men go away and their wives go to other men, that's their problem! Why can't we men who stay in the village marry all of them? It is more for us! Perhaps as many of three or four wives?" However, other men warned: "Oh, the women are many here and the men are few; you don't want them to overwhelm you, gobble you up, do you? That's what can result in the loss of all of your semen and strength." Thus the absence of the men and the availability of their women has intruded a new problem into the social definition of masculinity: Should a man attempt to steal other men's wives to fulfill the ideals of traditional masculinity as in the past? The whole attitude has changed against this old-fashioned ethic. In either case, the new proportion of women to men was one of the components of social uncertainty.

Women did not seem to mind their husbands going away and leaving them, possibly because some of the women had their own means, such as gardens and cash crops, while other more modernist women had designs on going to school and did not want to marry. Others were no doubt simply relieved to have one less mouth to feed and perhaps to have a reprieve from frequent beatings by their husbands. Still others had joined the Seventh-Day Adventist Church and had decided to leave or eliminate their more "traditional," or pagan, husbands. The women's pretense for power was gaining so much that some men even gasped, "What if the women achieve political office?" This would be the final blow to masculinity.

Increasingly, men who remained in the villages, especially the men who were perceived as being *wogaanyu*, or weak and cowardly, but other men too, felt that they had lost control over their wives and were no longer masculine men. As one man remarked, "Women don't follow orders very well anymore. And some men don't know how to order them. Those men are *wogaanyu*. At that time they were afraid of their food being poisoned by their wives. Some of the women only know the old ways, but others are changing." The same man continued, "The younger women, and some of the older ones too, they only want men with money. They 'rubbish' the 'poor men.' In the old days, women wanted men who could hunt possum and bring home a lot of meat for the women and children. Women would spit on a man who couldn't hunt or bag game. They say that the women want men who have money and will buy them tinned fish and rice from the trade stores. Today, a man without money is weak, unmanly, because he cannot give rice and fish . . . money is possum to them . . . women swallow their spit when thinking about money." Clearly, out-migration of men is one of the components of the cultural destabilization of gender, and it has paved the way for a new tradition of sexual love.

"LUV" MARRIAGE—THE SEXUAL REVOLUTION

Beginning in the 1990s a new form of social sexuality took shape: "luv" marriage, in which a man and a woman could chose each other out of "liking"— romantic love. Premarital sexual relations were implied in this revolutionary form of intimacy—unheard of for the Sambia. Kissing, holding hands in public, and even sleeping in the same bed—truly revolutionary ideas for the Sambia—spread among young people. Rumors spread that young men such as Danny were building square houses with tin roofs with a bedroom and one bed for husband and wife—all revolutionary ideas to the Sambia. This change forms the final part of the story of transformation.

The gender role change described through schools, missions, and out-migration has had a leveling effect upon males and females in Sambia society. Although the effect of these changes on the everyday lives of women and girls has been less dramatic, the stories of exotic places and novel conquests, as well as the material artifacts brought back, have left their marks. Young women such as Penjukwi have their own stories to tell of romantic interest in men who were not marked for their marriage—and as this was in the 1980s, she clearly was anticipating the sweeping changes of "luv" marriage.

A new discourse among many young Sambia women has taken form in public and private places regarding traditional beliefs and their domestic practices and roles. Women's lives are busy with the hard work of gardening and child care. It is difficult for most Sambia women to shy away from the responsibility of gardening because they and their families will go hungry if not enough food is harvested throughout the year.

However, child bearing and child rearing have become one domain in which women can assert some new power. Many young women today do not wish to have more than two children, despite the tremendous social, political, and economic benefit of large broods. With infanticide now forbidden by the government and boys and girls equally valued, family planning is open to influence from government health clinics, nurses, and media messages. Previously, as we have seen, the Sambia emphasized semen beliefs and their role in the creation of the fetus, without knowledge of conception as such. With a Western understanding of human reproduction supplied by means of pamphlets distributed by the missionaries, the young women have eschewed traditional reproductive teachings and are now better able to control their pregnancies. Although monthly birth control shots are now available at the health clinic (up to a six-hour walk for many of the women in at the upper end of the Sambia valley), abstinence is by far the preferred method. The combination of abstinence discourse and Christian church attendance are new ways in which women's independence from traditional marriage and sexuality is prominent. Abstinence is also a means of exerting some control over the marital relationship, as well as a means for expressing dislike for a spouse whom they were not able to choose. Never mind that "luv" marriages remain rare—they are the wave of the future, as young people take their place in a society that is undergoing a sexual revolution.

"Luv" marriage as an ideal has captured the attention of many young people in Sambia society (Stolpe 2003). It is what we might call the new social imaginary of local culture. The traditional marriage system of contracted marriages, especially bride-wealth, which is most common today, is now contrasted with a new concept, marriage for "luv." In a larger sense, the desire for the independence and freedom (sexual agency) implied in a "luv" marriage signals a significant departure from the traditional formula. Gender roles in this model become more equal; the partners more companions. Indeed the language of the discourse of "luv" is covered by the linguistic term *laik,* the pidgin word meaning "like" or "want to." To what extent it is appropriate for all individuals, especially women, to act upon their *laik*—that is at the heart of much current debate among the Sambia. You can hear young women on the CD-ROM discuss their desires for this new kind of marriage.

Generally, young people embrace the perceived enhanced freedoms of the "outside" world by renouncing traditional teachings—*laik* has become metonymic for this enlarged sense of social freedom. It reminds us of the myriad stories of young men who have returned from the coast to talk about an unrestricted world of tastes and desires, including fast food and fast sex. The story of abstinence for women also belongs to this cultural revolution. Repudiating cultural mandates that required women to successively birth and mother many children is a powerful (albeit risky) way for young women—a claim to a new agentic power. It seems likely that here, as elsewhere, the young women who attend school will have fewer children in their lifetimes than the women who do not. The reasons for this phenomenon are poorly understood (Bledsoe and Cohen 1993), although here it seems that one source of power, many children, is perhaps being supplanted by another, education, while simultaneously displaying newly appropriated power.

The desire for fewer children is driven by practical reasons as well. Despite the many perceived benefits of Christian conversion, the Levitican dietary restrictions imposed by the Seventh-Day Adventists place an even greater burden of food production on the women. This is a double-edged sword; women gain indirect social power through appeal to mission church communities, but they reap a burden of greater economic support for their families under the new regime. Until the conversions, the Sambia diet was comprised of food gathered from the surrounding forest, food produced in the women's gardens, and food hunted by the men, as well as pigs slaughtered for ritual and celebratory occasions. The missionaries adjudicated total restrictions against eating animals with cloven hooves, animals that perch, and benthic fish. Almost all of the animals hunted by the Sambia men (as well as the domesticated pigs) fell into one of these categories. Not only has the nutrition of the Sambia suffered in terms of the elimination of virtually all sources of animal protein in an already protein-deficient diet but the proportion of food provided by gardening and gathering also increased significantly. Now women are practically the sole providers of food for their families, further emasculating the Sambia men, for whom hunting was formerly such an important social and political activity. This increased responsibility also confers a slight increase in social power on the women, but in a zero-sum game: the women have gained while the men have waned. Ironically, with this increased responsibility, the addition of each child becomes greater, a real burden. "Children are work, work, work," the young women frequently lament—two are plenty.

These dreams are seldom realized as the women, at gonadal puberty, are still required to fulfill their social obligations of marriage and reproduction. The newly realized monetary benefit of daughters in terms of bride wealth paid in Kina has reconfirmed the importance of women as commodities. Once paid in pigs, other foodstuffs, and weapons, monetary bride wealth (in the amount of

$400 kina for a woman from within the valley, more for an exogenous woman) now constitutes a primary source of family income, and daughters are often talked about in terms of their cash worth. (Danny speaks on the CD-ROM of his payment—$700 kina in 1993.) One man in the valley whose wife gave birth to their fifth daughter was constantly teased that he was now the wealthiest man in the valley—his assets amounted to $2000 kina. Fear of the loss of the anticipated bride-wealth payments is one reason why girls are not often educated beyond grade school. The only woman in the Sambia valley who had attended high school was "sold" by her parents before completion because they feared losing their bride-wealth payment if she did not return to the valley. Thus, the introduction of cash into the valley has eradicated certain traditional ways of womanhood while simultaneously strengthening others.

Coffee has opened a new economic chapter for the Sambia, and its production during the past decade has further destabilized sexuality and gender. Coffee production presented the Sambia with a dilemma: Garden work was women's work; money and extracultural interests were the men's province. Coffee was both. Now the genders compete for competence and money through coffee production. We must not forget that sexual relations between husband and wife typically occurred in private in their gardens. How has this impacted their sexual relations? We still do not know the answer to that question. But on the gender side, another question has opened up: How should the labor of coffee be divided between the sexes? A similar dilemma was faced more than a century earlier with the introduction of agricultural tools in Africa. Gardening had been the domain of women; tools had been the domain of men. The resolution resulted in the shift of agricultural labor from women to men (Comaroff and Comaroff 1997). Sambia have blurred gender distinctions, and men and women generally work together in their gardens today. This may be the first time in Sambia history that gender cooperation has been attempted. Is it also being attempted in sexual relations?

Coffee income has both direct and indirect effects on the lives of the women. With monies, food can be purchased, and this decreases the stress of daily harvesting in the gardens and the very real fear of disease destroying entire gardens, resulting in starvation. These purchased goods, primarily rice, tin fish, and Maggie Noodles, also increase the dietetic variation of the family diet. Thus families with more money who can purchase more food will have healthier diets. The healthier diet increases the woman's fecundability as well as fertility and, no doubt, reduces the likelihood of infant and child morbidity and mortality. The greater survivability of each child born makes the woman's agency in reducing her number of pregnancies more acceptable. In all of these changes we see how consumerism is a kind of citizenship, even at the level of buying noodles and all the way up to the use of telephones and automobiles, suggesting how Sambia are part of "western" life ways in a material nation linked to the global consumer marketplace (Foster 2002).

Today Sambia girls express new aspirations, which complement the ideas of "luv" marriage. With decreased pressure on gardening and with the profits from the coffee gardens, more girls are able to attend school, often filling girls with expectations of lives different from their mothers'. Many of these girls express

Figure 7.2 Kanteilo, showing off! Gil Herdt's house 1993

a desire to change the trajectory of their lives—to "do anything but work in the gardens," as one educated young woman in the CD-ROM laments. A young boy also aspires to attend school, get a job in a town, and leave behind the ways of the elders, including the ritual ordeals that are such an incredible part of the heritage of the Sambia. Their collective aspirations are limited by the realities of globalization, the forces already hinted at: coffee production and consumption, schools that produce workers without jobs, and missions that demand support in prayer and money. All of this is part and parcel of the social changes that have revolutionized Sambia sexuality.

Throughout New Guinea the process of change that has followed pacification and colonialism has brought about a growing recognition of the rights of women in traditional cultures. The Sambia are no different. The end of the men's secret societies is part of this process, whereby the conditional masculinity of entrance into male initiation was purchased in part by the subordination and social suppression of women and initiated boys. More recently the import of fundamentalist Christianity into Melanesian cultures has come at the price of new restrictions and limitations on the full personhood and citizenship of women, at least in some cases. However, the expansion of coffee and cash crops and the opportunities of increased transportation have opened new vistas for younger Sambia, especially women, who aspire to be educated and affirmed in the 21st century and desire to be more equal to their brothers, fathers, sons, and husbands. The next leap for the Sambia will come when "luv" marriage achieves the status of being the norm, old traditions giving way to companionate sexual and gender intimacy increasingly noticed in Papua New Guinea and long ago embraced as part of modernity. It is an image both desired and dreaded by the Sambia.

Glossary

aamooluku: war leader; the highest ideal of masculine achievement.

age-mate: a person initiated into an age-set with a group of others similarly aged.

attraction: the experience of being emotionally, socially, or sexually interested in another person.

bisexuality: expressed sexual behavior with people of both genders, although not necessarily equally or at the same point in time.

composite hamlet: a village formed from the union of two previously separate hamlets of the same phratry.

confederacy, danceground: political alignment between different villages who initiate their sons together and intermarry; identified with a ritual danceground. Confederacies are usually composed of same-phratry villages, but those of the Sambia Valley are interphratry in makeup.

danceground: *see* Confederacy.

enculturation: the transmission of cultural knowledge, rules, and attitudes across generations.

erotic: that which stimulates sexual desire and behavior.

ethos: the culturally patterned form of emotional expressions characteristic of a group.

gender: cultural behaviors, skills, ideas, and feelings associated with "masculinity" and "femininity."

gender identity: the sense of belonging to the male or female sex, and of being masculine or feminine.

gender roles: typical behavioral patterns expected of men or women in various status positions (for example, "elder," "shaman," "man," "woman," and so on).

gender signs: symbolic emblems or tokens of one's gender status in culture (for example, noseplugs, mustaches).

great clan: the widest form of patrilineal affiliation between people descended from common fictitious ancestors. The great clan is composed of two or more component clans, which usually reside together but who may have dispersed clan segments elsewhere.

hamlet: a village community defined by Sambia as a mutually supporting extended-family residential unit. *See also* Composite hamlet.

havalt-nunta: the principle of sameness or likeness between age-mates or others who are culturally identified as belonging to one category.

homosexuality: sexual attraction to people of the same gender, composed of: homosexual identity—an identification with habitualized same-gender roles and sexual activities, and homo-erotic behavior—and sexual relations based upon attraction to the same gender.

jerungdu: the principle of male strength, virility, and manliness associated with semen and warrior prowess in Sambia culture.

marriage, forms of: infant-betrothal (delayed exchange) marriage is assignment at birth of a girl to a boy of another clan for future marriage as adults; sister-exchange (direct exchange) marriage occurs when two adult males agree to exchange their sisters to each other for marriage.

magical age of 10: the onset of attraction, emotional and sexual, leading to adolescent sexuality and adult social and sexual roles.

patriclan: people tied by bonds of demonstrable patrilineal descent from a common real ancestor. These people recognize common rights and duties as a corporate group in marriage, land tenure, ritual, and village defense.

patrilineal: a kinship descent principle linking people, especially men, by descent from common male ancestors, real or fictitious.

patrilocal: a principle of residence that requires or encourages people, especially men, to set up residences as adults in the same place or village as their fathers.

phallic: symbols, rituals, or cults modeled on the penis or related to maleness.

phratry: a kin grouping recognized by Sambia as the widest related set of people linked by blood relation to fictitious ancestors, by common geographic origins in myth, and by ritual customs practiced in common and demarcators of ethnic distinctiveness.

resocialization, radical: discontinuity with and unlearning of early training, and the use of ritual ordeals (that is, brainwashing techniques) to modify boys' behaviors and gender identities to conform with adult standards.

secret society: ritual and political organization requiring initiation for membership and adequate cultural knowledge.

sex: refers to biological attributes associated with being either male or female in a particular sexual culture.

sexual behavior: any sexual activity understood as being sexual in a particular society.

sexual culture: the formation of a social and poltical group around a set of shared sexual meanings and practices.

sexual identity: the social and sexual identification of a person with a particular sexual role or sexual culture.

sexual life way: the development of self around a particular set of cultural expectations about sexuality and their meanings for individual conduct.

sexual objectification: the stylized social and conventional treatment of a gender or person as an object of desire, often reciprocated by that person accepting the position of being a sexual object.

sexual orientation: habitualized and enduring preference for a particular gender or type of sexual practice.

shaman (*kwooluku*): religious healer and ritual specialist able to engage in "magical flight" and control trance and spirit familiars for the good of society.

socialization: the teaching of social roles and performative skills necessary for social behavior.

socialization group, primary: early caretakers, especially the family, who teach language and early skills.

socialization group, secondary: later role training, associated with initiation and resocialization, for behavior in wider social institutions beyond the family.

spirit familiars (*numelyu*): "magical" counterparts of one's soul substance that aid health, longevity, and, in shamans, trance and healing ceremonies.

subtribe: *see* Phratry.

symbolic learning: understanding that stems from exposure to rituals and symbols and that occurs at conscious and unconscious levels.

transitional object: a symbolic process involving attachment to a person or a thing (for example, a doll) halfway between a loved person and the self; associated with the development of independence in the person.

tribe: a social grouping identified by common language, cultural traditions, and some sense of a recognized territory defended against outside groups.

warfare, Sambia forms of: bow-fighting—intratribal feuding between villages that uses bows and arrows, with more deadly technology forbidden; war-raiding—intertribal stealthful raids launched against outside groups to destroy and loot; all forms of technology are used here.

wogaanyu: the principle of weakness and unmasculineness (as opposed to *jerungdu*) in Sambia culture.

worlds (men's and women's): men's and women's "worlds" and their forms of sex-distinctive worldviews.

worldview: shared understandings, beliefs, and orientations about the world, including notions of space, time, and the person's place and spirituality in the cosmos.

wusaatu: rubbish man; the lowest form of masculinity.

Bibliography

Adkins-Regan, S. 1984. Sex hormones and sexual orientation in animals. *Psychobiology* 16: 335–347.

Bailey, J. M., & Oberschneider, M. 1997. Sexual orientation professional dance. *Archives of Sexual Behavior* 26: 433–444.

Bech, H. 1997. *When Men Meet: Homosexuality and Modernity.* Chicago: University of Chicago Press.

Bell, A., & Weinberg, M. 1978. *Homosexualities.* New York: Simon and Schuster.

Bell, A. P., Weinberg, M. S., & Hammersmith, S. 1981. *Sexual Preference.* Bloomington: Indiana University Press.

Bem, D. 1996. Exotic becomes erotic: A developmental theory of sexual orientation. *Psychological Review* 103: 320–335.

Bledsoe, C., & Cohen, B. (Eds.) 1993. *Social Dynamics of Adolescent Fertility in Sub-Saharan Africa.* Washington DC. National Academy Press.

Bonnemere, P. 2004. *Women as Unseen Characters.* Philadelphia: University of Pennsylvania Press.

Boswell, J. 1980. *Christianity, Social Tolerance, and Homosexuality.* Chicago: University of Chicago Press.

Bowra, C. M. 1957. *The Greek Experience.* London: Methuen.

Brookfield, H. 1964. The ecology of Highlands settlement: Some suggestions. *American Anthropologist* 6(Part 2): 20–38.

Brookfield, H., & Hart, D. 1971. *Melanesia: A Geographic Interpretation of an Island World.* London: Methuen.

Brown, P. 1978. *Highland Peoples of New Guinea.* New York: Cambridge University Press.

Byne, W., & Parsons, B. 1993. Human sexual orientation: The biologic theories reappraised. *Archives of General Psychiatry* 50: 228–239.

Carrier, J. 1980. Homosexual behavior in cross-cultural perspective. In J. Marmor (Ed.), *Homosexual Behavior: A Modern. Reappraisal* (pp. 100–122). New York: Basic Books.

Chauncey, G. 1994. *Gay New York.* New York: Basic Books.

Comaroff, J. L., & Comaroff, J. 1997. *Of Revelation and Revolution.* Chicago: University of Chicago Press.

Connell, J., & Dowsett, G. (Eds.) 1993. *Rethinking Sex: Social Theory and Sexuality.* Philadelphia: Temple University Press.

D'Emilio, J. and E. Freedman.1988. *Intimate Matters: A History of Sexuality in America.* New York: Harper and Rowe.

Dover, K. J. 1978. *Greek Homosexuality.* Cambridge, MA: Harvard University Press.

Duggin, L. 2003. *The Twilight of Equality.* Boston: Beacon.

Dundes, A. 1976. A psychoanalytic study of the bull-roarer. *Man* 11: 120–138.

Evans-Pritchard, E. E. 1970. Sexual inversion among the Azande. *American Anthropologist* 72: 1428–1434.

———. 1971. *The Azande.* Oxford: Claveudor.

Ford, D. S., & Beach, F. 1951. *Patterns of Sexual Behavior.* New York: Harper and Bros.

Foster, R. 2002. *Materializing the Nation: Commodities, Consumption, and Media in Papua New Guinea.* Bloomington: Indiana University Press.

Foucault, M. 1986. *The Uses of Pleasure* (Trans. R. Hurley). New York: Viking.

Freeman, D. 1983. *Margaret Mead and Samoa.* Cambridge, MA: Harvard University Press.

Freud, S. 1935. Letter to an American mother. In R. Bayer, *Homosexuality and American Psychiatry* (1987, p. 27). Princeton, NJ: Princeton University Press.

———. 1962 [1905]. *Three Essays on the Theory of Sexuality* (Trans. J. Strachey). New York: Norton.

Gagnon, J. 1990. The explicit and implicit use of the scripting perspective in sex research. *Annual Review of Sex Research* 1: 1–44.

———. 2004. *An Interpretation of Desire.* Chicago: University of Chicago Press.

Gewertz, D., & Errington, F. 1999. *Emerging Class in Papua New Guinea.* New York: Cambridge University Press.

Gillison, G. 1993. *Between Culture and Fantasy: A New Guinea Highlands Mythology.* Chicago: University of Chicago Press.

Godelier, M. 1969. Land tenure among the Baruya of New Guinea. *Journal of the Papua New Guinea Society* 3: 17–23.

———. 1982. Social hierarchies among the Baruya of New Guinea. In A. Strathern (ed.), *Inequality in New Guinea* (pp. 3–34). New York: Cambridge.

———. 1986. *The Production of Great Men.* Cambridge: Cambridge University Press.

———. 1989. Betrayal: The case of the New Guinea Baruya. *Oceania* 59(3): 165–180.

Gorman, Michael R. 1994. Male homosexual desire: Neurological investigations and scientific bias. *Perspectives in Biology and Medicine* 38: 61–81.

Green, R. 1987. *The Sissy Boy Syndrome and the Development of Homosexuality.* New Haven, CT: Yale University Press.

Greenberg, D. 1986. *The Construction of Homosexuality.* Chicago: University of Chicago Press.

———. 1995. The pleasures of homosexuality. In P. Abramson & S. Pinkerton (Eds.), *Sexual Nature, Sexual Culture* (pp. 223–256). Chicago: University of Chicago Press.

Greenberg, D. F., & Bystryn, M. H. 1982. Christian intolerance of homosexuality. *American Journal of Sociology,* 88: 515–548.

Halperin, D. 1990. *One Hundred Years of Homosexuality.* New York: Routledge.

———. 2002 *How to Do the History of Homosexuality.* Chicago: University of Chicago Press.

Hamer, D. H., Hu, S., Magnuson, V. L,. Hu, N., & Pattutucci, A. M. L. 1993. Linkage between DNA markers on the X chromosome and male sexual orientation. *Science* 261: 321–327.

Harris, M. 1981. *America Now: The Anthropology of a Changing Culture.* New York: Simon and Schuster.

Heider, K. G. 1979. *Grand Valley Dani: Peaceful Warriors.* New York: Holt, Rinehart and Winston.

Herdt, G. 1977. The shaman's "calling" among the Sambia of New Guinea. *Journal de la Societe des Oceanistes* 56–57: 153–167.

———. 1981. *Guardians of the Flutes: Idioms of Masculinity.* New York: McGraw-Hill.

———. 1982. Editor's preface. In G. H. Herdt (Ed.), *Rituals of Manhood* (pp. ix–xxvi). Berkeley: University of California Press.

———. 1984. (Ed.). *Ritualized Homosexuality in Melanesia.* Berkeley: University of California Press.

———. 1987a. *The Sambia: Ritual and Gender in New Guinea.* New York: Holt, Rinehart and Winston.

———. 1987b. Transitional objects in Sambia initiation rites. *Ethos* 15: 40–57.

———. 1989. Father presence and masculine development: The case of paternal deprivation and ritual homosexuality reconsidered. *Ethos* 18: 326–370.

———. 1990. Developmental continuity as a dimension of sexual orientation across cultures. In D. McWhirter, J. Reinisch, & S. Sanders (Eds.), *Homosexuality and Heterosexuality: The Kinsey Scale and Current Research* (pp. 208–238). New York: Oxford University Press.

———. 1991a. Representations of homosexuality in traditional societies: An essay on cultural ontology and historical comparison, Part I. *Journal of the History of Sexuality* 1(1): 481–504.

———. 1991b. Representations of homosexuality in traditional societies: An essay on cultural ontology and historical comparison, Part II. *Journal of the History of Sexuality* 2(2): 603–632.

———. 1992. Sexual repression, social control, and gender hierarchy in Sambia culture. In B. Miller (ed.), *Gender Hierarchies* (pp. 121–135). New York: Cambridge University Press.

———. 1993. Introduction. In G. Herdt (ed.), *Ritualized Homosexuality in Melanesia* (pp. vii–xliv). Berkeley: University of California.

———. 1997. *Same Sex, Different Cultures: Perspectives on Gay and Lesbian Lives*. New York: Westview Press.

———. 1999. *Sambia Sexual Culture: Essays from the Field*. Chicago: University of Chicago Press.

———. 2003. *Secrecy and Cultural Reality*. Ann Arbor: University of Michigan Press.

Herdt, G., & Boxer, A. 1993. *Children of Horizons*. Boston: Beacon Press.

———. 1995. Toward a theory of bisexuality. In R. Parker & J. Gagnon (Eds.), *Concerning Sexuality: Approaches to Sex Research in a Postmodern World* (pp. 69–84). New York: Routledge.

Herdt, G., & Koff, B. 2000. *Something to Tell You*. New York: Columbia University Press.

Herdt, G., & Leavitt, S. C. (Eds.) 1998. *Adolescence in the Pacific Island Societies*. Pittsburgh, PA: University of Pittsburgh Press.

Herdt, G., & McClintock, M. (Eds.) 2000. Special issue on the development of sexual attraction. *Archives of Sexual Behavior* 29(6).

Herdt, G., & Stoller, R. J. 1985. Sakulambei—A hermaphrodite's secret: An example of clinical ethnography. *The Psychoanalytic Study of Society* 11: 115–156.

———. 1990 *Intimate Communications: Erotics and the Study of Culture*. New York: Columbia University Press.

Herdt, G., & Stolpe, B. 2006. Sambia sexuality, gender and social change. In J. Stockard & G. Spindler (Eds.), *Cultures through Case Studies: Continuity, Change, and Challenge* (in press). New York: Thompson.

Herman, D. 1997. *The Antigay Agenda: Orthodox Vision and the Christian Right*. Chicago: University of Chicago Press.

Hochschild, A. 2003. *The Second Shift*. New York: Penguin.

Hoffman, R. J. 1984. Vices, gods, and virtues: Cosmology as a mediating factor in attitudes toward male homosexuality. *Journal of Homosexuality* 9: 27–44.

Ihara, S. 1972. *Comrade Loves of the Samurai* (Trans. R. Shively). Rutland, VT: Charles E. Tuttle.

Irvine, J. 2002. *Talk about Sex*. Berkeley: University of California Press.

Kinsey, A., Pomeroy, W. B., & Martin, C. E. 1948. *Sexual Behavior in the Human Male*. Philadelphia: W. Saunders.

Knauft, B. 1999. *From Primitive to Postcolonial in Melanesia and Anthropology*. Ann Arbor: Michigan University Press.

Koch, K. F. 1974. *War and Peace in Jalemo*. Cambridge, MA: Harvard University Press.

Langness, L. L. 1967. Sexual antagonism in the New Guinea Highlands: A Bena Bena example. *Oceania* 37: 161–177.

———. 1972. Political organization. In *Encyclopedia of Papua New Guinea* (pp. 922–935). Melbourne: Melbourne University Press.

Laumann, E., Gagnon, J.H., Michael, R.T., & Michaels, S. 1994. *The Social Organization of Sexuality: Sexual Practices in the United States*. Chicago: University of Chicago Press.

Lawrence, P. 1966. The Garia of the Madang district. *Anthropological Forum* 1: 371–392.

Levine, M., Nardi, P. M., & Gagnon, J. H. (Eds.) 1997. *In Changing Times: Gay Men and Lesbians Encounter HIV/AIDS*. Chicago: University of Chicago Press.

Levy, R. I. 1984. The emotion in comparative perspective. In K. R. Scherer & P. Ekman (Eds.), *Approaches to Emotion* (pp. 397–412). Hillsdale, NJ: Erlbaum.

Lewin, E., & Leap, W. 1996. *Out in the Field*. Urbana: University of Illinois Press.

Lidz, T. 1976. *The Person*. New York: Basic Books.

Lindenbaum, S. 1979. *Kuru Sorcery*. Palo Alto, CA: Mayfield Publishing Co.

Lloyd, G. E. R. 1979. *Science, Folklore, and Ideology*. New York: Cambridge University Press.

Luria, Z. 1979. Psychosocial determinants of gender identity, role and orientation. In H. A. Katchadourian (Ed.), *Human Sexuality: A Comparative and*

Developmental Perspective (pp. 163–193). Berkeley: University of California Press.

Malcolm, L. A. 1968. Determination of the growth curve of the Kukukuku people of New Guinea from dental eruption in children and adult height. *Arch. and Physical Anthropology in Oceania* 4: 72–78.

Masters, W. H., & Johnson, V. E. 1966. *Human Sexual Response*. Boston: Little, Brown.

McClintock, M., & Herdt, G. 1996. Rethinking puberty: The development of sexual attraction. *Current Directions in Psychological Science* 5: 178–183.

Mead, M. 1928. *Coming of Age in Samoa*. New York: William Morrow.

———. 1935. *Sex and Temperament*. New York: William Morrow.

———. 1949. *Male and Female*. New York: Dutton.

———. 1956. *New Lives for Old*. New York: William Morrow.

———. 1961. Cultural determinants of sexual behavior. In W. C. Young (Ed.), *Sex and Internal Secretions* (pp. 1433–1479). Baltimore, MD: Williams and Williams.

Meggitt, M. 1974. "*Pigs* are our hearts!" The Te exchange cycle among the Mae Enga of New Guinea. *Oceania* 44: 165–203.

———. 1977. *Blood is Their Argument*. Palo Alto, CA: Mayfield.

Meyer-Bahlburg, H. 1984. Psychoendocrine research on sexual orientation. Current status and future options. *Progress in Brain Research* 61: 375–398.

———. 1997. The role of prenatal estrogens in sexual orientation. In L. Ellis & L. Ebertz (Eds.), *Sexual Orientation: Toward Biological Understanding* (pp. 41–51). Westport, CT: Praeger.

Minturn, L., et al. 1969. Cultural patterning of sexual beliefs and behavior. *Ethnology* 8: 301–317.

Money, J. 1987. Sin, sickness, or society? *American Psychologist* 42: 384–399.

Money, J., & Ehrhardt, A. 1972. *Man and Woman, Boy and Girl*. Baltimore, MD: Johns Hopkins University Press.

Murphy, T. 1992. Redirecting sexual orientation: Techniques and justifications. *Journal of Sex Research* 29: 501–523.

Murphy, Y., & Murphy, R. 1974. *Women of the Forest*. New York: Columbia University Press.

Pattatucci, A., & Hamer, D. 1995. Developmental and familiarity of sexual orientation in females. *Behavior Genetics* 25: 407–420.

Paul, J. 1985. Bisexuality: Reassessing our paradigms of sexuality. *Journal of Homosexuality* 11: 21–34.

Piaget, J. 1971. Structuralism. Trans. C. Maschler. New York: Harper Torchbooks.

Plummer, K. 1995. *Telling Sexual Stories*. New York: Routledge.

Read, K. E. 1954. Cultures of the Central Highlands, New Guinea. *Southwestern Journal of Anthropology* 10: 1–43.

———. 1955. Morality and the concept of person among the Gahuku-Gama, Eastern Highlands, New Guinea. *Oceania* 25(4): 233–282.

———. 1965. *The High Valley*. New York: Scribner's.

Rocke. 1996. *Forbidden Friendship*. New York: Oxford University Press.

Roheim, G. 1932. Psycho-analysis of primitive cultural types. *International Journal of Psycho-Analysis* 13: 1–224.

Rosaldo, M. Z. 1974. Women, culture, and society: A theoretical overview. In M. Z. Rosaldo & L. Lamphere (Eds.), *Woman, Culture, and Society* (pp. 17–42). Stanford, CA: Stanford University Press.

Schieffelin, E. L. 1976. *The Sorrow of the Lonely and the Burning of the Dancers*. New York: St. Martin's Press.

Schwartz, T. 1973. Cult and context: The paranoid ethos in Melanesia. *Ethos* 1: 153–174.

Serpenti, L. M. 1965. *Cultivators in the Swamps: Social Structure and Horticulture in a New Guinea Society*. Assen: Van Gorcum.

Shweder, R. A. 1989. Cultural psychology— What is it? In J. W. Stigler et al. (Eds.), *Cultural Psychology: Essays on Comparative Human Development* (pp. 1–43). New York: Cambridge University Press.

Sillitoe, P. 1998. *Melanesia: Culture and Tradition*. New York: Cambridge University Press.

Spindler, G., & Spindler, L. 1982. Do anthropologists need learning theory?

Anthropology and Education Quarterly 13: 109–124.

Spiro, M. E. 1979. Whatever happened to the id? *American Anthropologist* 81: 5–13.

———. 1982. *Oedipus in the Trobriands.* Chicago: University of Chicago Press.

Stoller, R. J. 1979. *Sexual Excitement.* New York: Random House.

Stoller, R. J., & Herdt, G. 1982. The development of masculinity: A cross-cultural contribution. *Journal of the American Psychoanalytic Association* 30: 29–59.

———. 1985. Theories of origins of male homosexuality: A cross-cultural look. *Archives of General Psychiatry* 42(4): 399–404.

———. 1990. *Intimate Communications: Erotics and the Study of Culture.* New York: Columbia University Press.

Stolpe, B. 2003. *Cultural Endocrinology: Menarche, Modernity, and the Transformative Power of Social Reconfigurations.* Doctoral dissertation, University of Chicago.

Storms, M. 1981. A theory of erotic orientation development. *Psychological Review* 88: 340–353.

Strathern, A. J. 1972. *One Father, One Blood.* Canberra. Australia: A.N.U. Press.

———. 1979 The self in decoration. *Oceania* 49: 224–257.

Teunis, N., & Herdt, G. (Eds.) 2006. *Sexual Inequalities and Social Justice.* Berkeley: University of California Press.

Trumbach, R. 1998. *Sex and the Gender Revolution: Heterosexuality and the Third Gender in Enlightenment London.* Chicago: University of Chicago Press.

Turner, V. W. 1964. Symbols in Ndembu ritual. In M. Gluckman (Ed.), *Closed Systems and Open Minds* (pp. 20–51). Chicago: Aldine.

———. 1967. Betwixt and between: The liminal period in Rites de Passage. In V. Turner, *The Forest of Symbols* (pp. 93–111). Ithaca, NY: Cornell University Press.

———. 1971. *The Ritual Process.* Chicago: Aldine.

———. 1978. Encounter with Freud: The making of a comparative symbologist. In G. D. Spindler (Ed.), *The Making of Psychological Anthropology* (pp. 58–583). Berkeley: University of California Press.

Tuzin, D. F. 1980. *The Voice of the Tamaran.* Berkeley: University of California Press.

———. 1997. *The Cassowary's Revenge: Women and the Death of Masculinity in a New Guinea Society.* Chicago: University of Chicago Press.

Van Baal, J. 1966. *Dema.* The Hague: Martinus Nijhoff.

Van Gennep, A. 1909. *Les Rites de Passage.* Paris: E. Nourry.

Vance, C. S. 1991. Anthropology rediscovers sexuality: A theoretical comment. *Social Science and Medicine* 33: 875–884.

Westermarck, E. 1917. *The Origin and Development of the Moral Ideas* (Vol. 2., 2nd ed.). London: Macmillan.

Whitehouse, H. 1995. *Inside the Cult: Religious Innovation and Transmission in Papua New Guinea.* Clarendon: Oxford.

Williams, C. 1998. *The Greeks and Sexuality.* New York: Oxford University Press.

Williams, F. E. 1936. *Papuans of the Trans-Fly.* Oxford: Oxford University Press.

Index